A New Illustrated History of
WORLD WAR II
RARE AND UNSEEN PHOTOGRAPHS 1939–1945

A New Illustrated History of
WORLD WAR II
RARE AND UNSEEN PHOTOGRAPHS 1939–1945

D&C

David and Charles

Project editor and texts
Flavio Fiorani

Copy editor
David Scaffei

Graphic design
Daniele Forconi

Page layout
Giovanni Bartoli

Maps and tables
Sergio Biagi Comunicazione Grafica

Translation
Jeremy Carden (NTL, Florence)

A DAVID & CHARLES BOOK
David & Charles is a subsidiary of F+W (UK) Ltd.,
an F+W Publications Inc. company

First published in the UK in 2005
Originally published in Italy in 2000 © Giunti Editore S.p.A., Florence–Milan
Original Title: Storia Illustrata della Seconda Guerra Mondiale
Copyright © 2000 Giunti Editore S.p.A. Florence–Milan

Distributed in North America
by F+W Publications, Inc.
4700 East Galbraith Road
Cincinnati, OH 45236
1-800-289-0963

A catalogue record for this book is available from the British Library.

ISBN 0 7153 2102 1 paperback

Printed in Italy by Giunti Industrie Grafiche S.p.A., Prato
for David & Charles
Brunel House   Newton Abbot   Devon

Visit our website at www.davidandcharles.co.uk

David & Charles books are available from all good bookshops;
alternatively you can contact our Orderline on (0)1626 334555 or write to us at
FREEPOST EX2 110, David & Charles Direct, Newton Abbot, TQ12 4ZZ
(no stamp required UK mainland).

Contents

Japan on the retreat 217

From Yalta to Hiroshima 241

The legacy of the conflict 265

The impossible peace

The world in which we live today is the direct consequence of the outcome of World War II. Fought on an almost worldwide scale, this catastrophe of the contemporary age led to appalling human and material destruction, involved civilians and armed forces to an extent previously unknown, devastated economies and societies, and was characterized by extraordinary technological developments used for the destructive purposes of the belligerent states. It was a conflict that revealed the total nature of modern warfare; this could even be seen in the fact that, as the victors demanded, the losers surrendered unconditionally.

The causes of the war were rooted in the peace settlement worked out at the end of World War I, which had devastated Europe 30 years previously. While the 1914–18 war can justifiably be defined as a 'European war', the same cannot be said for the conflict that pitted the Allied and Axis powers against *(p.10)* **Young Spanish refugee in Barcelona.** *The plight of the losers in a celebrated photo by Robert Capa.*

(p.11) **Military parade in Paris to celebrate victory in World War I.**

The Pillars of Society and Hell. *Paintings by George Grosz and George Leroux.*

each other between 1939 and 1945. The 'European phase' of the war that broke out on 1 September 1939, when the Germans invaded Poland, effectively ended with the capitulation of France in June 1940.

From then on emerging factors would shift the war's centre of gravity, opening new theatres in Africa and Asia and transforming the conflict into the most catastrophic event in human history. It ended with over 51 million dead and the appearance on the world scene of a weapon – the atomic bomb, dropped by the Americans on Japan – that would condition the world order in the second half of the century. While World War I had been fought to reorder the balance of power between the major European nations (France, Great Britain, Germany and the Austro-Hungarian empire), what was at stake in World War II was world supremacy. The alliance between the victorious nations and the geopolitical system that was established after 1945 resulted in the predominance of two superpowers, the United States and the Soviet Union, which shaped world destinies until the fall of the Berlin Wall in 1989 and the disintegration of the Soviet system.

THE CONDITIONS OF THE VICTORS

The underlying cause of the conflict lay in the precarious equilibrium that had arisen from the peace conference of Versailles in 1919, which did not produce a stable, lasting order. The 'peace of the victors' (Great Britain, France, United States and Italy) rested on the predominance they exercised over the losers. Germany, the most powerful of the defeated nations, had to accept territorial losses both on its western border (restitution of Alsace-Lorraine to France and the occupation of the Saar) and to the east (Poznan, part of East Prussia and Silesia became part of Poland). The Rhineland was demilitarized; Danzig

THE LEAGUE OF NATIONS

The League of Nations was founded in 1919 during the Versailles conference with the aim of helping to build peace and a new international order. The organization was the result of a tangle of American, British and French interests, and it was the linchpin of the 'new diplomacy' inspired by US President Woodrow Wilson. Based in Geneva, the league had an assembly, comprising all the member states, a council and a permanent secretariat. The five permanent council members were the United States, Great Britain, France, Italy and Japan; a further four temporary members were elected by the assembly every three years. Its work was blocked from the outset by the refusal of the US Senate to ratify the Treaty of Versailles. Furthermore, the League of Nations only agreed later (1926) to include Germany and set up a kind of 'quarantine' around Soviet Russia. The organization had a few successes, especially when Aristide Briand was the French Foreign Minister (1925–32), but also many failures. It did not have the armed forces to achieve its goals and on many issues was incapable of reaching practical decisions. Virtually reduced to a diplomatic forum and unable to come to significant decisions, it proved ineffective in halting the drift towards war. It was dissolved in April 1946 and was replaced by the United Nations.

ARMISTICE DAY.
Parisians celebrate victory in World War I, waving the flags of the Allied powers.

became a free city and its hinterland was given to Poland. Germany had to hand over its navy to the British and, in accordance with a new principle that made Germany responsible for the conflict, it was forced to pay enormous reparations to the Allied powers. Germany was humiliated, and left in a political situation prone to extremism. The conditions imposed by the victors did not prevent the economic and military rebirth of a country that wanted a leading role in European affairs.

THE GEOGRAPHY OF EUROPE

Austria had been reduced to a mere territory inhabited by German-speaking populations, and Hungary also lost territory (Transylvania) to Romania. From the ruins of the former Austro-Hungarian empire there arose a new 'Kingdom of Serbs, Croats and Slovenes' (Yugoslavia), which

was racked by dangerous ethnic and national tensions, and Czechoslovakia (the most economically developed of the new East European states), which was characterized by conflict between the Bohemian majority on the one hand, and the Slovaks, in the eastern region, and the German-speaking minority in the Sudetenland on the other. In eastern Europe, Poland found itself in the weak position of being a buffer state between Germany and the Soviet Union. Italy obtained Trieste, Istria, Trentino, Alto Adige and some of the Dalmatian islands from the former Austro-Hungarian empire. After the success of the Bolsheviks in the 1917 October Revolution in Russia, the Soviet Union saw its territories reduced in favour of Poland and three new Baltic republics (Latvia, Lithuania and Estonia). The victorious powers adopted a 'quarantine policy' towards the Communist state in order to isolate it from the rest of Europe.

FOOLING THE ENEMY.
A French inflatable tank being positioned in the countryside. Franco-German relations remained tense after the Treaty of Versailles.

WOODROW WILSON.
In this satirical cartoon the American president, proclaiming his famous 'Fourteen Points' for peaceful international relations, is depicted with the stern appearance of a preacher.

The isolation of the Soviet Union, German resentment of the victors and Italian discontent about their meagre territorial gains were some of the factors that would lead to the gradual crumbling of the geopolitical order resulting from an unbalanced peace settlement. Burdened by crippling debts that hindered its economic recovery, Germany drifted towards the instability that distinguished the fragile democracy of the Weimar Republic. The new East European states would not be capable of curbing the expansionist designs of Germany and the Soviet Union. The goal of peaceful agreement was pursued by the League of Nations, a permanent assembly of states that, according to the US President Woodrow Wilson, the man who conceived it, was to preserve the peace and settle disputes by negotiation rather than by war. However, the work of the League was

HYPERINFLATION IN GERMANY.
German children play with kites made from banknotes. Inflation was the death blow for the fragile equilibrium of the Weimar Republic. In 1923 the dollar was worth a record 4 billion marks.

undermined by the non-participation of the United States (where an isolationist mood prevailed), the Soviet Union (excluded from the peace agreements and considered an extraneous entity by liberal democratic European states) and, until 1926, Germany.

THE CHALLENGE OF ECONOMIC REVIVAL

The attempt to normalize political and trade relations between Germany and the other European nations initially bore fruit with the Locarno Agreement in 1925 and, three years later, with the Briand–Kellogg Pact, which banned the use of arms to settle controversies between states. It then ran up against the intransigence of France, which tried to block Germany's economic and military revival. Conceived by France as an anti-German measure, the geopolitical order of

(Left:) **FASCIST PROPAGANDA.**

(Far left:) **PROTEST DEMONSTRATION IN BERLIN.** *The heavy unemployment suffered by German society after World War I generated a widespread sense of insecurity and discredited democratic institutions.*

the Danube and Balkan regions was precarious and in the second half of the 1930s these areas became the focus of Nazi German aspirations and European diplomatic initiatives. In Italy, resentment concerning the limited territorial gains following victory in 1918 was fed by the rhetoric of the Fascist regime, whose chief targets were the Treaty of Versailles and the non-dynamic foreign policy of liberal *Italietta* ('little Italy'). The 'Versailles system' clashed with the aspirations of the 'proletarian nation' to assume a role befitting its demographic (but not economic) size, and the Fascists fuelled hostility towards Anglo-French hegemony over the League of Nations and the countries that Fascist propaganda defined as Western 'plutocracies'.

Building a peaceful, stable international order also meant facing the challenge of bringing about economic and industrial revival and an upturn in trade. Industrial production in the major European countries was burdened by the enormous debts that France and Great Britain had incurred with the United States to pay for the war.

The situation was made even more precarious by the financial tangle preventing the economic recovery of the two major European powers, which were convinced that they could rely on the payment of German war reparations. International collaboration and a joint commitment to finding agreements capable of stimulating economic recovery and unblocking the circuit of international payments injected short-term impetus into the European economies. For instance, there was the 1924 Dawes Plan, whereby Wall Street banks granted credit to Germany in order to stabilize the mark and enable the partial payment of the reparations, and the 1929 Young Plan, which involved a further

ROMAN SALUTE. *Adult and child perform one of the characteristic rituals of the new Italian regime, which arose out of the crisis in the liberal system. The reactionary nature of the regime was confirmed by laws abolishing civil rights and legal checks.*

BANKNOTE FOR 50 MILLION MARKS.
In 1923 this banknote was worth just 5 dollars.

reduction of reparations. However, the initiative of the American financial world was accompanied by Washington's disengagement from Europe and its unwillingness to act as a guarantor of the continent's political and military equilibrium.

THE RISE OF NAZISM

The economic crisis of 1929–33 marked a watershed between the precarious stability that followed World War I and the beginning of the path towards fresh conflict. The Wall Street Crash led to a plunge in world trade and mass unemployment (2 million in Great Britain, 6 million in Germany, 15 million in the United States). The currency crisis that forced many countries to adopt protectionist and restrictive measures reinforced existing world divisions. The gold standard, which had been fixed in

1925 in order to guarantee the convertibility of currencies and the flow of capital required for economic growth and the development of world trade, was abandoned by Germany, Japan and Great Britain. The economic depression undermined the legitimacy of international free trade capitalism, and measures had to be taken to sustain employment and production. The protectionist closure of economies stirred nationalist sentiment and the recession provoked a lack of trust in democracy.

With the collapse of the international economic system and the political and ideological gulf between the democracies and the European fascist regimes, a crucial turning point was the rise to power of Adolf Hitler's

ADOLF HITLER ON THE PODIUM.
The rise of Nazism was accompanied by daily acts of violence by the National Socialist Party's paramilitary groups, which used terror tactics against political adversaries.

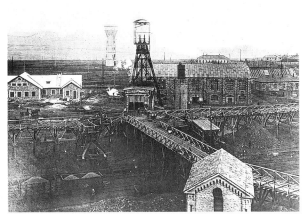

(Left:) **HANDS OFF THE RUHR!**
In 1923 France occupied the rich border region between the two countries.

(Far left:) **COAL MINE IN RUSSIA.**
The Soviet Union initiated an accelerated process of industrialization under strict state control.

(Below:) **WORKERS PROTEST IN PARIS.**

National Socialist Party in 1933. The pressure exerted by the German Reich in central Europe worsened international relations, and the degeneration of liberal democracy and capitalism was yet another blow to the pacifist values of Woodrow Wilson's internationalism, the precarious balance of power sanctioned by the treaties of 1919, and a crumbling world order.

TENSIONS IN EUROPE

The paradox of the situation in Europe is that the 'chains of Versailles' triggered a confrontation that was an opportunity for the 'revisionist' powers (Germany, Soviet Union, Italy) to increase their political clout and room for manoeuvre, and which led the victors to take measures to reinforce their military security (the building of the Maginot Line on the eastern border of France), or to acquiesce, as the British did, to Nazi requests to revise the treaties in order to ensure a more stable equilibrium of forces.

The relative isolation of the Soviet Union also had a bearing on the European situation. Intent on building 'socialism in one country', Stalin's Russia subordinated its international strategy to the defence of its European geopolitical position, even when it was faced by Japanese expansionism in Manchuria and northern China. The attempt to break 'encirclement' by the 'imperialist' powers resulted in a series of pacts of non-belligerence with nearby eastern European countries, the aim being to delay the establishment of an anti-Soviet block. However, the Kremlin's calculation that British hostility

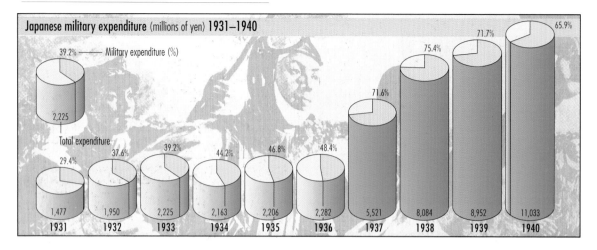

Japanese military expenditure (millions of yen) 1931–1940

39.2% — Military expenditure (%)

2,225

Total expenditure

29.4%	37.6%	39.2%	44.2%	46.8%	48.4%	71.6%	75.4%	71.7%	65.9%
1,477	1,950	2,225	2,163	2,206	2,282	5,521	8,084	8,952	11,033
1931	1932	1933	1934	1935	1936	1937	1938	1939	1940

towards Russia would be redirected towards Nazi Germany proved unfounded.

JAPANESE AGGRESSION IN ASIA

In addition to the political and diplomatic tension between France and Great Britain on the one hand and Germany, Italy and the Soviet Union on the other, new crisis hot spots developed elsewhere in the world. The United States abandoned its policy of economic intervention in Europe, leaving it up to France and to Great Britain to maintain stability there, and its international strategy proved unable to curb the aggressive policy of Japan in the Far East.

Hard hit by the economic crisis of 1929, Japan opted for a sharp turnabout in its foreign policy, shifting the main focus of its trade towards the Asian markets, which were considered a vital space for the creation of a 'co-prosperity sphere' in which Japan aspired to extend its influence. Having absorbed Korea and reduced it to the status of a colony, in 1931 Japan took possession of Manchuria and set up the puppet state of Manchukuo. It ignored the outcry from the League of Nations and left that international body in 1933.

In 1936, after signing an anti-Comintern pact with Nazi Germany (for anti-communist and anti-Soviet purposes), the bellicose and imperial radicalization of Japan led to the military conquest of a broad swathe of territory in eastern China, including Peking, Shanghai, Canton and Nanjing. Tokyo's policy of foreign expansion was supported by unbridled nationalism at home; civil power was increasingly subordinated to the armed forces; and the state, following the model of European fascist regimes, imposed a strong corporative imprint on economic and social life. Japan became a strategic player in the Pacific and its

THE SINO-JAPANESE WAR

After the aggression that had led to the setting up of the puppet state of Manchukuo in 1932, the Japanese government increased its military contingent in China. In September 1937, 150,000 troops, divided into two army groups, invaded the south of the country. Here they encountered resistance from Kuomintang nationalists led by

Chiang Kai-shek and from the communists under Mao Zedong. By the end of this phase of operations, Japan had seized much of northern China, the valleys of the Yellow River (Huang He) and the Yang-tze, the main ports and a large proportion of the country's railway network. After suffering considerable losses, the Japanese occupied first Shanghai and then Nanjing, where they were responsible for looting, destruction and also the massacre of some 250,000 people. Negotiations with the nationalists failed

and the Japanese government gave a general mobilization order to continue the war. However, they were incapable of breaking Chinese resistance, which later led to the communists and nationalists forming a united front that lasted, with various ups and downs, until 1945. Japan made the error of underestimating the scale of the conflict, which ended up being fought on a front extending some 3,000km. Western protests were to no avail and the United States maintained an isolationist policy.

(Left:) **JOACHIM VON RIBBENTROP.**

(Far left:) **THE DEVASTATIONS OF THE WAR IN CHINA.**

(Below:) **MEMBERS OF THE RED CROSS AMIDST THE RUINS OF A CHINESE CITY.**
Japan wanted to make East Asia a strategic and economic space free from interference by the Western powers.
Photo by Robert Capa.

aggression was welcomed by Germany (especially the Foreign Minister, Joachim von Ribbentrop, who conceived the notion of a 'world political triangle consisting of Germany, Italy and Tokyo'), which also wanted to undermine British imperialism.

THE FAILURE OF DIPLOMACY

Reactions to the disintegration of the postwar order were hesitant. Faced with the dual threat of Nazi Germany to the west and Japan to the east, the Soviet Union adopted a new diplomatic approach. It sought to avoid war by stipulating pacts of non-aggression with nearby countries in eastern Europe and with France, and also by joining the League of Nations in 1934. Germany had abandoned the League the year before and had started to rearm. This was the principal instrument of a radical subversion of the Versailles settlement and the European order, and was part of a racial ideology of which the core was a radical anti-Semitism.

Hitler's long-term strategy was directed against the Soviet Union (conquest of 'living space to the east'), Great Britain (which he hoped would become a subordinate partner to German dominance in Europe) and the United States, seen as the last and most tenacious adversary in Germany's struggle for 'world supremacy'. The strategic decision of the Third Reich to give priority to the militarization of the economy and society had repercussions both at home and abroad. Between 1936 and 1939 the

(Right:) **HITLER AS GULLIVER.**
The giant surrounded by Lilliputian European politicians.

(Far right:) **STAMP COMMEMORATING THE ANSCHLUSS.**

(Below left:) **WOMAN FROM THE SUDETENLAND GREETS THE ARRIVAL OF THE GERMANS.**

(Below right:) **NAZI TROOPS IN PRAGUE.**

path to the re-establishment of the great German Reich involved several stages, starting with the satisfaction of German territorial claims and culminating with the attack on Poland. In March 1936 German troops occupied the Rhineland; in March 1938 the *Anschluss* (annexation) of Austria sanctioned German control of southern and south-eastern Europe, while the occupation and breaking up of Czechoslovakia (on the pretext of satisfying the claims of the German minority in the Sudetenland) led to the retreat of France and Great Britain from central and eastern Europe.

THE LIMITS OF APPEASEMENT

If in retrospect Japanese expansionism in Asia and Germany's aggressive policy in Europe seem to be steps in an inexorable march towards the abyss of war, this was not how it was perceived at the time by those in Great Britain, France and the United States who believed that there was still scope for negotiation in order to ward off the danger of a new conflict. After the Munich Agreement (September 1938) the British and French were convinced they had put a brake on Hitler's revanchism by conceding German-speaking territories around the Reich, such as the Sudetenland. The policy of appeasement adopted by the Western democracies (the leading exponent of

THE SPANISH CIVIL WAR

After centuries of being on the fringes of European affairs, Spain became the centre of world attention in the mid-1930s. On 17 July 1936, Spanish military forces based in Morocco and led by General Francisco Franco revolted against the legitimate Popular Front Republican Government in Madrid, formed by a coalition of democratic parties that had won elections the previous February. This insurgency marked the start of a civil war that lasted three years, caused great loss of life, and devastated the country. Spain was split into two: the Nationalists controlled the regions of Navarre, western Aragon, Castile, León, Galicia and Andalusia, while the Republicans held Catalonia, the Basque Provinces, eastern Aragon, Asturias and the capital, Madrid.

The government forces were undermined by bitter disagreements (especially between the anarchists and the communists), which were detrimental to its military effectiveness and political cohesion. By contrast the rebel Nationalists were kept firmly united by a 'crusading' spirit in defence of Catholicism and hostility towards democracy and the programme

of social reforms initiated by the Popular Front. Despite being defeated at the gates of Madrid and in the Battle of Guadalajara in 1937, the Nationalists launched a further offensive, aided by massive foreign aid in the form of troops (the Italian expeditionary force was thousands strong) and arms (from Germany). Germany sent an air corps, the Condor legion, which bombed cities controlled by the Republicans. When the two sides met in the Battle of Ebro at the end of September 1938, the outcome of the war was still uncertain.

To a great extent Spain's destiny was played out at the Munich Conference, where both sides pressed their cases with those discussing the future of Czechoslovakia. With no external aid save from the Soviet Union and from the volunteers of the International Brigade, and isolated by the hypocritical British and French policy of non-intervention, the Republicans were ultimately doomed. When Franco's troops conquered Catalonia in February 1939, the fate of the Republic was sealed and over 400,000 refugees crossed the border into France. On 1 April, Franco announced the surrender of the enemy, marking the start of a dictatorship that lasted until the General's death in 1975. The final death toll was horrifying: a million dead, besides thousands of Republicans who were shot in the following years. The Spanish Civil War was the first armed confrontation between the three great twentieth-century ideologies of liberal democracy, fascism and communism, and, with its international consequences, anticipated in some respects the sides that were to form in World War II.

(Above:) Demonstration in support of the Spanish Republicans. (Left:) Farm workers on a collectivized property.

(Right:) **NEVILLE CHAMBERLAIN.**
The champion of appease-ment tried to halt the slide towards war.

(Far right:) **IT IS PEACE FOR OUR TIME.**
English newspaper head-line with the declaration of the British Prime Minister after the signing of the Munich Agreement.

(Below left:)
UNEMPLOYMENT IN FRANCE.

which was the British Prime Minister, Neville Chamber-lain) was confounded by the German occupation of Prague in March 1939. It now appeared evident that Ger-many's quest for continental domination did not exclude recourse to war. Moreover, the alliance between Fascism and Nazism had undermined the peace treaties of 1919, what with Italian aggression in Abyssinia (1935–39); the Spanish Civil War (1936–39), which was a kind of 'dress rehearsal' for the conflict during which Germany and Italy supplied Franco's rebels with arms and troops; and the offensive nature of the 'Pact of Steel' (May 1939) made by the two dictatorships, whereby Berlin recognized the expansionist goals of fascism in the Mediterranean, while at the same time obtaining free rein for its plans to con-quer the East.

The international balance of power was extremely frag-ile, and the defence of collective security clashed with the deep-rooted ideological hostility between communism and capitalism. The reciprocal distrust between the West-ern democracies and Russia reinforced Stalin's conviction that the only feasible strategy to counter the establishment of an 'imperialist' anti-Soviet front aimed at extending its control over large areas of eastern Europe was to come to an agreement with Germany. Signed in the summer of 1939, this agreement offered Russia some security, though only temporarily .

GERMAN EXPANSION IN THE LEAD-UP TO THE WAR

- Frontier in 1935
- Annexation of the Saar by plebiscite (1935)
- Occupation of the Memel district (1939)
- Annexation of the Sudetenland (1938)
- Annexation (*Anschluss*) of Austria (1938)
- Protectorate of Bohemia and Moravia 1939

(Left:) **MUSSOLINI, THE FIRST MARSHAL OF THE EMPIRE.**

(Far left:) **HAILE SELASSIE AT THE DEATHBED OF THE LEAGUE OF NATIONS.** *In the cartoon, the Negus waits in vain for help from the moribund international organization.*

THE WAR IN ABYSSINIA

Desired by Mussolini notwithstanding the wariness of Italy's King Vittorio Emanuele III and the upper hierarchies of the armed forces, the Abyssinian campaign revealed an aggressive potential in Italian foreign policy that until then had appeared to be restricted to the Fascist regime's propagandistic rhetoric.

The last independent African state and a member of the League of Nations, Abyssinia was ruled by its emperor, Haile Selassie. Counting on the tacit consent of France and Great Britain, Mussolini had a dual purpose for his African venture: to provide the large Italian population with territory to settle in; and to cut a bold figure on the international scene. On 3 October 1935, Italian troops crossed the frontiers of the country without declaring war. The Italians fielded about half a million men, commanded by General Pietro Badoglio. The campaign ended with entry into Addis Ababa in May 1936. Air raids and the use of poison gas against villages and the helpless population testified to the ruthlessness of the military operations, which marked the peak of popularity

for Fascism at home. Mussolini proclaimed the return of the empire to the 'fated hills of Rome' and King Vittorio Emanuele took the title of Emperor of Abyssinia. This further aggressive challenge to the Versailles settlement accentuated the crisis of Western diplomacy, led to the diplomatic isolation of Italy, and brought the Fascist regime even closer to Nazi Germany.

Advertisement for a light bulb using the regime's imperialist rhetoric. (Left:) Salute by Italian troops in the African campaign.

The outbreak of conflict

The Czechoslovakia crisis culminated in the seizure of Prague and the setting up of the protectorates of Bohemia and Moravia. With this act, Germany crossed ethnic boundaries for the first time. The Third Reich now turned its attention to the city of Danzig and the 'Polish Corridor' separating East Prussia from Germany, as part of a design to 'extend its living space eastwards'. Germany's quest to achieve military supremacy over its potential adversaries and its policy of massive rearmament was a race against time.

Hitler wanted to cross the 'narrow corridor' as soon as possible, thus paving the way for the realization of the Thousand-Year Reich. On the military strategic level he wanted to surprise his adversaries with *Blitzkriegs* ('lightning wars') in order to eliminate their military potential before completion of their own rearmament, which began later. To this end he regarded *(p. 24)* **Hitler depicted as a medieval paladin.**

(p. 25) **The Reichstag acclaims the Führer.**

(Right:) **Anyone who buys from a Jew is a traitor of the people.** *German beer mat.*

(Far right:) **The world in the grip of the 'Tripartite Pact'.**

it as essential to fight just one enemy at a time, in order to avoid the dual-front situation in which Germany had found itself during the 1914–18 war.

The principles of collective security and the European balance of power crumbled in the face of a series of aggressive acts by the totalitarian regimes and the inability of the Western democracies to halt German designs.

The Reich's expansionist ambitions in the Danube region were supported by German industry's interest in gaining control of raw materials in the area. The quest for continental economic supremacy was part of the more global project for political and racial domination outlined by the Führer even before he came to power. In his speech to the Reichstag on 30 January 1939, Hitler threatened 'international financial Jewry in or outside Europe' (the latter was directed at the United States under Roosevelt): if this Jewish group were to push people towards world war it would end, he claimed, not with the 'Bolshevization of the world and thus a victory of Jewry, but the annihilation of the Jewish race'.

ITALY AND GERMANY

The anti-Comintern pact signed with Japan did not result in a genuine alliance. The real fruit of incessant German diplomatic initiatives was the 'Pact of Steel' signed with Italy on 22 May 1939. Under Mussolini, who was acclaimed at home as the 'saviour of peace' after the Munich Conference, Italy confirmed its totalitarian vocation by siding with Hitler. The fundamental tenets of the Fascist state, as well as some political calculation on Mussolini's part, led Italy to choose a side that was war-oriented.

With German connivance, Italy attacked Albania in April 1939 to signal that it was preparing its war machine

GERMAN AIRCRAFT MANUFACTURING PLANT. *The German rearmament programme concentrated particularly on air power. The lethal effectiveness of the German war machine was based on perfect coordination between land and air operations. On the eve of war, Goering's Luftwaffe had a formidable offensive capacity.*

DORNIER.
*This twin-engine recon-
naissance bomber was
one of the most efficient
and versatile aircraft in
the Luftwaffe.*

THE PACT OF STEEL

On 22 May 1939, Italy and Germany formed a military alliance that the Italian Foreign Minister did not hesitate to describe as 'pure dynamite'. The pact was viewed as a deterrent that would sweep away the laxity of the Western democracies, scornfully defined by Fascist propaganda as 'plutocratic, Masonic and Jewish'. The pact included a clause stating that if one of the two signatories became involved in a conflict (either offensive or defensive), the other one would take the same side. Reaffirming 'the close bonds of friendship and solidarity between Fascist Italy and National Socialist Germany', the 'Pact of Steel' stated that if 'the common interests of the two Contracting Parties were to be put in danger by international events of whatever nature, they [the parties] shall without delay enter into consultation on the measures to be adopted to safeguard these interests. In the event of the safety or other vital interests of one of the Contracting Parties being threatened by an outside danger, the other Contracting Party shall give the menaced Party its full political and diplomatic support for the purpose of eliminating this threat. If in spite of the desires and hopes of the two Contracting Parties, it were to happen that one of them were to become involved in complications of war with one or more Powers, the other Contracting Party shall immediately come to its aid as ally and shall support it with all its military forces on land, on the seas, and in the air.'

(Above:) Italian and German officials signing the 'Pact of Steel'. (Below:) Ribbentrop, Ciano and Hitler salute the crowd at the end of the ceremony.

(Right:) **GERMAN DESIGNS ON POLAND.** In this satirical French cartoon, a Polish soldier blocks the entrance to the 'Corridor' between East Prussia and Germany.

(Far right:) **THE HYENAS HITLER AND MUSSOLINI.** The British sit watching on a tree branch.

and was determined to play a role as a 'great power'. The Duce's decisions, however, were the result of an assessment of events that was contradictory, to say the least. Having thrown in his lot with Germany, he believed it would be possible to keep worsening international tensions within diplomatic channels, and that he would be able to mediate in order to delay direct involvement in a war that was now viewed as inevitable.

GREAT BRITAIN AND POLAND

Chamberlain's policy of appeasement was based on the acceptance of German requests in the hope of creating a new European order that would replace the one established at Versailles. This would involve cooperation between the four great powers (Great Britain, France, Germany and Italy) but the exclusion of the Soviet Union. London had

begun a rearmament programme and was preparing for the eventuality of war. The nation's strategy was based on protecting the seas, above all the Atlantic routes, and its air and sea forces were being reorganized accordingly. To counteract German expansionism, in March 1939 Great Britain gave guarantees for the independence and sovereignty of Poland, which would mean war in the event of a German attack.

The deep-rooted hostility between the British and the Russians resulted in further isolation of the Soviet Union. By binding its fortunes to the security of Poland, Britain's intention was to discourage a military alliance between Germany, Italy and Japan (the three powers with aggressive intentions in Europe, the Mediterranean and East Asia), which would threaten Britain's world position. In

BRITISH INFANTRY ON EXERCISES WITH A MARK VI TRACKED VEHICLE. At the outbreak of the war, British armoured vehicles were greatly inferior to those of their adversary.

CORDELL HULL.
The US Secretary of State was a strong advocate of taking a firm line against Japan's expansionist goals in Asia.

the event of a war, it also wanted to ensure that such a conflict remained within the confines of Europe.

THE ATTITUDE OF THE UNITED STATES

The crisis in Europe was made even more intractable by the hands-off approach adopted by America, and the absence of a concerted response exacerbated the degeneration of international order. Washington's position swung between warnings of the need to combat Hitler's open aggression in Europe and appeals for peace. In this, Roosevelt's government paid a high price for giving priority to internal economic recovery, although this on its own would create the resources required to be

authoritative in foreign policy affairs at a later date.

While the United States responded weakly to the threat to world peace until 1938, in the following year Roosevelt put pressure on Congress to abrogate laws governing American neutrality (passed during the Abyssinian war to ensure that the nation did not slide into war, as had happened in 1914–17) and to offer concrete support to France and Great Britain.

The American administration tried to avoid the risk of the country being embroiled in a war and pushed for maintaining a status quo. However, not only in Europe but also in the Far East, this had already been irreversibly undermined by German

NEVILLE CHAMBERLAIN AND HIS CABINET IN 1939.
Standing behind the Prime Minister is Winston Churchill, who would succeed Chamberlain as head of government on 1 May 1940.

GERMAN REARMAMENT

After coming to power, Hitler tried to promote the recovery and development of German industry in the framework of a general militarization of society. From 1936 onwards, when a four-year economic plan was passed, the fundamental objective pursued by the Nazi regime was preparing for war. For Hitler the mobilization of German society had to be total, in order to achieve objectives with 'National Socialist energy and vigour'. The Wehrmacht had to become an unrivalled war machine, to be used as an instrument to conquer 'living space' (*Lebensraum*) for the German people. The key points of the plan were protectionism, a policy of economic independence and control of the labour market. There was an increase in state control of the economy and the launching of a major reorganization that involved not only production but also political and administrative bodies. Significantly, the task of managing the four-year plan was placed in the hands of Hermann Goering, a party official and the man who set up the Gestapo, the secret police. Invested with extensive powers that exceeded those of ministers with posts relating to the economy, Goering succeeded in building a vast personal economic empire.

The regime propaganda talked of a radical transformation of the economy in corporative and National Socialist terms, but in reality the large private industrial groups were able to maintain their dominant position and also to interfere in public sector affairs. Existing monopolies were further reinforced and not one of the large enterprises was nationalized. Results were not slow in coming. Thanks to the policy of rearmament and public works, in 1938/39 the entire labour force of the country was in employment. Fundamental impetus for the economic recovery came from state commissions, which particularly favoured chemical and heavy industry. The production of iron ore rose from 443,000 tonnes in 1932 to 3,928,000t

in 1939; synthetic rubber from 1,000t (1936) to 22,000t (1939); and aviation fuel from 43,000t (1936) to 302,000t (1939).

The rearmaments programme focused particularly on sectors regarded as crucial for facing the country's main enemy, Great Britain. This explains the marked increase in air strength (Junker-88 bombers in particular) and the navy. For Hitler, it was essential that the programme be activated quickly so that the start of the war could be brought forward. This would enable Germany to exploit the advantage it had over its adversaries, which, in response to the German threat, had also begun to rearm.

In 1939, 22 per cent of industrial employees were working directly for the Wehrmacht and many others were in areas relating to war production. In 1936/37, military spending amounted to more than a third of the state's budget; by 1938/39 it had reached 58 per cent. Calculated in relation to national income, war spending amounted to 32 per cent in 1939. In no other country in the modern age has such a massive proportion of resources been devoted to armaments.

By the summer of 1939 Germany possessed modern weaponry and could mobilize the majority of its armed forces, about four and a half million men, within 12 hours. The core of the land forces consisted of six armoured, four mechanized, four light armoured, 86 infantry and three mountain divisions. The navy possessed two battleships, three light battleships, one heavy cruiser and six light cruisers, 21 destroyers, 12 torpedo boats and 57 submarines (but the programme of naval construction was due to be completed in 1944). The Luftwaffe, commanded by Goering, comprised 302 *Staffeln* (12-plane squadrons), with 2,370 crews and 2,564 operational aircraft (bombers, dive bombers and fighters), plus a crack parachute corps. Aircraft production rose from 1,968 in 1934 to 5,112 in 1936 and 8,295 in 1939.

Submarines in a German naval base at the beginning of 1939.

(Left:) **THE THREAT FROM THE RISING SUN.**
Rampant Japanese militarism in an American cartoon from the end of the 1930s.

(Below:) **THE POPULAR FRONT CELEBRATES 14 JULY.**
The government led by the socialist Léon Blum made France a standard-bearer of anti-Fascism, but did not offer an alternative to British appeasement and fell in April 1938.

and Japanese aggression. Washington's foreign policy was conducted in a climate of increasing aversion at home to anti-democratic ideologies and European and Japanese totalitarianism. From a global perspective of American 'national security', the threat was regarded as geopolitical as well as ideological; the tangle of political, economic, military and ideological factors making up the world crisis not only had repercussions for the security of the United States but also created the possibility that German and Japanese aggression might result in the closure of both European and Chinese markets to American products.

Until the summer of 1939, the perception of the looming dangers facing the world did not induce Roosevelt to change policy. His warning to Stalin that German supremacy in Europe would also pose a threat to Soviet security went unheeded.

WHY DIE FOR DANZIG?

France, the country that had suffered most during the Great War, clung to the conviction that the only effective antidote to the threat of conflict was tenacious defence of the Versailles settlement. The nation had adopted a stance of 'passive' defence (exemplified by the construction of the Maginot Line) that, until then, had amounted to accepting Hitler's moves with clenched teeth, even though they were openly hostile to France, with the breaking of peace treaties, remilitarization of the Rhineland and rebuilding of the German air force. Overinfluenced by British appeasement, France did all it could to avoid war, and the uncertainty displayed by the Prime Minister Edouard Daladier, even after the breaking of the alliance with Czechoslovakia at the Munich Conference, reflected the deeply divided state of public opinion.

'Why die for Danzig?' This blunt question, in strident

(Right:) **TWO GREEDY SNAKES.**
On the bellies of Hitler and Stalin are the names of the prey they have just ingested.

(Far right:) **MARRIAGE OF STALIN AND HITLER.**

(Below:) **RUSSIAN POWER STATION AND TEXTILE MILL.**

WONDER HOW LONG THE HONEYMOON WILL LAST?

contrast to the mood in 1914, reflected France's loss of credibility as a world power. But possible war scenarios were being considered, at least by the French Chiefs of Staff. The British were asked to provide a land force in the event of a German attack on the Low Countries. Pressure was exerted on Poland to persuade it to consent to German demands, thereby saving Paris from the embarrassment of having to abandon an ally once again, as it had with Czechoslovakia. It is difficult to establish to what degree the governments that led their countries into war in September 1939 enjoyed the population's support.

Almost everywhere the entry into war failed to raise the enthusiasm it had in 1914; the memory of that bloodbath in Europe was still very much alive and everyone was convinced that it would be a defensive war – paradoxically the defence of what little was left of the balance of power established at Versailles.

THE NAZI–SOVIET PACT

The fact that Britain and France yielded over Czechoslovakia was confirmation, in Stalin's eyes, that the capitalist democracies were allowing Germany a free hand in the east partly for anti-Soviet reasons. As a consequence he adopted a pragmatic attitude that did not rule out overlooking the incompatibility of dealing with the European fascist nations. While his calculation that an overturning of the balance of powers in Europe might lead to a war between the 'imperialist' powers proved mistaken, there

(Left:) **DESTROYED RUSSIAN ARMOURED CAR.** *In the early stages of the attack on Finland, the Soviets suffered heavy casualties and transport losses.*

(Below right:) **BOMB DAMAGE IN HELSINKI.** *Finland was part of the Tsarist Empire in the nineteenth century, but gained independence during the Civil War in Russia.*

powers, but Britain and France had already declared war.

Based on the principle of passive defence, the Allied strategy relied on French and British military strength growing over time and on undermining German strength through an economic embargo and aerial bombardment. The prospect of becoming bogged down in an exhausting static war in France (as had happened in 1914–18), combined with a shortage of military supplies that would have made it difficult to sustain a long war, led Hitler to his decision to launch an attack on France. The date fixed for this was 12 November 1939, but it was put off for as many as 29 times before the fateful attack finally started on 10 May 1940.

THE RUSSIAN INVASION OF FINLAND

After stationing its troops in the Baltic states following the German victory in Poland, the Soviet Union availed itself

of the secret clause in its pact with Germany to extend the sphere of Soviet influence. Stalin's objective was Finland, which had been part of Russian territory until 1917 and which had won independence at the beginning of the 1920s, fighting against the Bolsheviks when Russia was in the throes of a civil war.

On 30 November 1939, faced with the Finnish government's refusal to cede a strip of territory in the isthmus of Karelia and to allow the Soviets to install naval bases there, Stalin gave the order to attack the eastern frontier of Finland. The Finns were heavily outnumbered: they had an army of 150,000 poorly equipped soldiers, while the

POLAND AND THE BALTIC REPUBLICS IN 1940

— 1939 frontier

▨ Territory annexed by Germany

▦ German 'General Government'

▨ Territory annexed by Russia

Tallin
ESTONIA to USSR in 1940
Göteborg
SWEDEN
Riga
LATVIA to USSR in 1940
Memel
LITHUANIA to USSR in 1940
Copenhagen
Königsberg
Danzig
East Prussia
Kaunas Vilnius
Minsk
to Lithuania in 1939
Berlin
Elbe
Oder
Poznan Warsaw
Vistula
GERMANY P O L A N D
U S S R
Rhine
Prague
Krakow Lublin
to USSR in 1940
Kiev
Dnieper
Danube
CZECHOSLOVAKIA
Vienna
Munich
Bessarabia
Dniester

W E A P O N S

 TANKS

Tanks had first been used by the British during the Great War, but had proved slow and unreliable, besides being vulnerable to artillery. In the following years all the major powers worked to develop improved models, and on the eve of World War II they were all ready to be used in battle. Tanks were a particularly important part of the German battle strategy, based as it was on a war of movement. They no longer simply provided support for infantry troops but were used to cut through the enemy's defences, and were capable of long-range operations. The use of tanks played a determining role in the *Blitzkrieg* in Poland, in France and on the Russian front. The new models dominated the major battles fought on open terrain, both in western Europe and in the Balkans, in the icy terrain and steppes of the eastern front and in the North African desert.

The German Panzer divisions were equipped for all phases of the war on land. The medium-sized PzKw (Panzerkamfwagen) III and IV proved effective at the beginning of the war, but subsequently, in the face of the superiority of the Soviet T-34 and KV, two heavier models were produced: the

Panther and the Tiger. The former, used from 1943 onwards, was one of the best tanks in the war; it emulated the T-34, weighed as much as 45t, had a 600 horsepower engine and was fast (46km/hour). It had a long cruising range (200km), formidable 120mm armour plating and a powerful 75mm cannon. The Tiger was preferred for defensive action; when it first came out, during the final stages of the campaign in North Africa, it surprised the Allies because shells bounced off its armour without inflicting damage. The German tank-building effort was intense: 2,200 were produced in 1940, 22,100 in 1944 and more than 57,000 in the conflict as a whole.

The British army was completely mechanized but its tanks were initially not as advanced as the German ones. The British only managed to redress the balance with the help of American technology. The best-known British model was the Churchill (1942), a 40t vehicle with 150mm frontal armour. It was suited to all kinds of terrain and was designed to breach any kind of defensive line.

The Russians had a formidable tank, possibly the best there was: the T-34. Produced from 1939 onwards, it had excellent all-round performance; it was of medium size

(26t) and powerful (500 horsepower), with enormous range (450km) and speed (53km/hour), and exceptional manoeuvrability. It was unbeatable on muddy, snowy and icy ground and was decisive at Stalingrad in the winter of 1942/43. In addition to the massive and extremely powerful KW 85, in 1944 the Soviet Union started producing, in response to the Tiger and Panther, the enormous 51t Josif Stalin (JS), which had frontal armour 210mm thick and a formidable, high-speed 122mm gun. Following a massive effort, the Russians managed to establish their primacy in this field, replacing their heavy losses. From 1942 annual tank production topped 24,000 and total production in the war was over 105,000.

The top US model was the M-4, called the Sherman by the British. Designed to counteract the 'lightning war' of the Germans and produced from 1942 onwards, it lived up to expectations. Though inferior to the heaviest German tanks, the American models were favoured by air support and exceptional logistics. The 400 Shermans supplied to the British 8th Army were decisive in defeating the Germans at El Alamein in the autumn of 1943. They also played a prominent role in the attack on Germany following the invasion of Normandy. The exceptional industrial war machine of the Americans was such that over 88,000 tanks were produced from 1941 to 1945, almost 30,000 of which were built in 1943 alone.

(Above:) Panzer Tiger. (Left:) British MK IV.

(Left:) **RUSSIAN CARTOON ABOUT THE WAR AGAINST FINLAND.**

(Below right:) **FINNISH SOLDIER EQUIPPED WITH A RIFLE WITH TELESCOPIC SIGHTS.** *Trained in winter warfare, the Finnish infantry put up stubborn resistance to the Russians.*

Russians fielded 45 divisions totalling 800,000 men, 1,500 tanks and about 1,000 aircraft. However, the tenacious resistance of the Finns, commanded by Field Marshal Carl Gustav Mannerheim, extended a war that Stalin had imagined would be brief. The snow-covered territory of Finland turned into a trap for the poorly trained invaders, who even had to deal with a counter-attack in Karelia.

The Soviets did not manage to breach the Finnish defensive line until February 1940. A peace agreement was signed on 12 March, whereby the Soviet Union obtained what it had requested prior to a conflict that had made the Finns heroes in the eyes of Western public opinion. The Russians lost 200,000 men in the war (mainly due to the cold) and the Finns 25,000.

In November of the previous year the Soviet Union had been expelled from the League of Nations, which in truth was by then nothing more than an empty shell. The Soviet

victory came shortly before French and British plans to send an expeditionary force and military aid to Finland had materialized.

The end of hostilities in northern Europe did not conclude Allied military involvement in the region. Norway was viewed as a key country, because occupation by Allied troops would seriously prejudice the vitally important flow of Swedish steel to the German war economy.

THE RUSSIAN ATTACK ON FINLAND

→ Russian attacks
→ Finnish counterattacks

Petsamo
Nautsi
Murmansk
14TH ARMY
Kemijarvi
Kandalakša
Luleå
Suomussalmi
9TH ARMY
Oulu
USSR
Kuoma
Trondheim
Umeå
Vaasa
Ilomäntsi
8TH ARMY
Sortavala
Tampere
Viipuri
13TH ARMY
Helsinki
7TH ARMY
Leningrad
Oslo
Stockholm
Tallinno
Kristiansand
ESTONIA

NORWAY
SWEDEN
Gulf of Bothnia
FINLAND

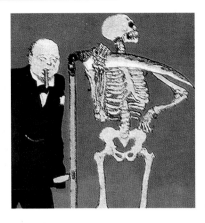

CHURCHILL AND DEATH.
German satirical cartoon.

THE TIME FACTOR

There were various reasons for the military stalemate, with the exception of the Soviet attack on Finland. The Allied High Commands examined the possibility of opening new theatres of war on the edge of Europe, and of bombing Russian oil wells in the Caucasus in order to interrupt supplies to Germany. The possibility that the Soviet Union might enter the war on Germany's side was also considered.

Hitler was not looking for an extensive war in the west at all; his plan was to deal with France as soon as possible, negotiate peace with the British and then launch an attack on Russia. For different reasons the 'time factor' was the key criterion adopted in political and military planning on both sides. Mindful of the enormous human and material losses on the French front in the Great War, the German High Command tried to prevent

Hitler from taking the plunge. They were also well aware that Russian and American neutrality could not last in the long term.

Time was important for the Allies as well. The mobilization of troops and economic resources had begun. They were counting on the erroneous supposition that the German economy was close to collapse and that the holding of defensive positions and a naval embargo would suffice to persuade Germany not to press any attack westwards.

A plan of defence was drawn up and the British Expeditionary Force (BEF) was sent to France. In their assessment of France's defensive capacity, the Allies made a glaring and historic error. Informal contacts with leading members of the Reich (in particular with Hermann Goering, the second most important figure in the

GENERAL MOBILIZATION.
After the German invasion of Poland, the French government ordered the mobilization of all able-bodied males. The French army and British divisions took up positions on the German and Belgian borders, respectively.

(Left:) **'Wanted!'**
American newspaper
headline.

(Far left:) **Hermann**
Goering.
Before the outbreak of the
war, the Commander-in-
Chief of the Luftwaffe was
the owner of an economic
empire based on mining
and synthetic materials.

regime) to sound out the possibility of an agreement to ward off further conflict bore no fruit whatsoever.

THE PHONEY WAR

The strange stalemate on land (the German submarine fleet was already active in the North Sea) in the winter of 1939 was effectively described by the French expression *drôle de guerre* ('strange war') and was known in the Anglo-Saxon world as the phoney war. The Germans call it the *Sitzkrieg* – the 'sitting war'. Counting on the invulnerability of the Maginot Line, which stretched from the Swiss border along the French–German frontier as far as Belgium, France stuck to a defensive strategy that rendered it immobile. The various plans drawn up by the French High Command fatally underestimated the principles of the German *Blitzkrieg* in Poland: that static firepower is less important than speed backed by the formidable punch of combined tank and air attack. The French also counted on Germany respecting the inviolability of the frontiers of Belgium, Holland and Luxemburg. The notion that the German thrust might come from this direction was not taken into consideration.

An armoured attack through the Ardennes forests and across the rain-soaked plains north of the Maginot Line was also opposed by the German High Command. Some German generals, however, believed that the optimum move, given more favourable weather conditions, was a thrust aimed at dividing the enemy forces along the line of the Somme. This was the plan drawn up by Erich von Manstein (the so-called 'sickle cut'), which gambled everything on the prediction that the Anglo-French troops would push forward in Belgium, thereby allowing the German forces to move round them by going through the Ardennes.

Underground tunnel
in the Maginot Line.
There was fierce dispute
about the usefulness of
the key component of the
French defences.
However, the success of
the German attack was
due not so much to
France's defensive strategy
as to the Allied plans for
attack, which played into
German hands.
By pushing into Belgium,
the French army exposed
its rear to a circling
manoeuvre by the more
mobile German forces.

The capitulation of France

In the first half of the year 1940, Scandinavia became the new theatre of military operations in Europe. In just the same way as the Allies needed to cut the line of supply of Swedish iron ore and bauxite to Germany, so also was it vitally important to the latter to gain strategic control of the North Sea. With a view to waging a naval war against Great Britain, Admiral Erich Raeder drew up plans for the German Navy to seize naval bases in northern Norway, and this Scandinavian country was quickly incorporated into the great German Reich.

The strategic advantage that was obtained by Germany when Finland surrendered following the Soviet Union's invasion also prevented the Allies from sending a military force that would take control of the railway line which crossed northern Norway and Sweden.

(p.48) **SOLDIERS OF THE GERMAN REICH ON THE CHAMPS-ÉLYSÉES.**

(p.49) **AIR RAID ON LONDON.**

(Right:) **NAZI PROPAGANDA IN DENMARK AND NORWAY.**

(Below:) **GERMAN AIRMEN IN NORWAY.**

THE OCCUPATION OF DENMARK AND NORWAY

The invasion of Denmark began on 9 April 1940. Completely unprepared for war, and with Germany threatening to bomb Copenhagen, Denmark surrendered immediately and was occupied in just one day. It would remain as a German protectorate for the duration of the conflict. With this move Germany gained control of the Skagerrak.

Operations in Norway were more difficult. Supported by the intervention of the Allies in the centre and north of the country, the Norwegians put up stubborn resistance that prolonged the war there until the middle of May. With the backing of raids by the Luftwaffe, German troops landed in the main ports, where they established solid bridgeheads. The British were driven back by German forces moving north from Oslo and were forced to evacuate their contingent from Namsos on 3 May.

The German Navy suffered a serious setback in two battles at Narvik (10–13 April), where the British Home Fleet sank ten German destroyers. The Norwegians, British and French held Narvik until 8 June, but abandoned it when the Allied front in France collapsed. Sweden opted to remain neutral; this was to the advantage of Germany, which obtained geostrategic control over an area of northern Europe that was of vital importance for naval operations in the Atlantic (partially offset by the British occupation of the Faroe Islands and Iceland).

The German U-boat fleet threatened Britain's supply lines. The government of Oslo went into exile in London and the Civil Commissariat

LET US GO FORWARD TOGETHER.
After his appointment as Prime Minister, Churchill appealed to the British fighting spirit.

L E A D E R S

![Winston Churchill silhouette logo]

WINSTON CHURCHILL

One of the most prominent figures in 20th century British history, Winston Churchill (1874–1965) had a long political, journalistic and military career to his name before he was appointed Prime Minister in 1940. He served as a cavalry officer in India and Sudan; he was elected as a Conservative MP in 1900 but joined the Liberal Party in 1904. He was a member of various governments, held the post of First Lord of the Admiralty (1911) and was a minister again after World War I. He was in favour of military intervention against Bolshevik Russia. Having left the Liberal Party and joined the Conservatives in 1922, Churchill was sympathetic to Italian fascism. In the 1930s he remained politically isolated for a long time, a period in which he was not sparing in his criticism of Chamberlain's policy of appeasement. At the beginning of the war he was once again Lord of the Admiralty, and then headed the coalition government – a Conservative majority that was supported by the Liberals and the Labour Party – until the war was over. He remained in office until the General Election in July 1945, which was won by the Labour Party. He was Prime Minister again between 1951 and 1955, and in 1953 was awarded the Nobel Prize for Literature for his historical works. In a celebrated speech in the House of Commons on 13 May 1940, three days after the German attack on France, Churchill responded to those who still believed in the possibility of a negotiated peace with Hitler: 'I have nothing to offer but blood, toil, tears and sweat . . . .You ask, what is our policy? I can say: It is to wage war, by sea, land and air, with all our might and with all the strength that God can give us...You ask, what is our aim? I can answer in one word: It is victory, victory at all costs, victory in spite of all terror, victory, however long and hard the road may be.'

(Above:) One of the many German caricatures of Churchill. (Left:) The English statesman with his customary cigar.

WEAPONS

THE MAGINOT LINE

Between 1930 and 1937, the French built a grandiose system of fortifications along their eastern frontier. These defences were known as the Maginot Line, after André Maginot, the Minister of War from 1929 to 1931, whose idea it was. Planned during the 1920s, the Line was based on military thinking deriving from the 1914–18 war and failed to take account of more recent advances in military technology. In particular it was designed for the waging of a static, defensive war and did not consider the crucial importance of fast-moving mechanized units.

In 1934 a young officer named Charles De Gaulle saw the potential of a war of movement and denounced the building of the Line as a colossal error; in his view, efforts should focus on building up armoured units supported by air power, which was precisely the strategy adopted to such great effect by the Germans. The British Army's General Fuller described the Maginot Line as 'the tombstone of France'.

The construction of the fortifications required an enormous amount of work and massive financial resources. Once it was completed, the defensive line stretched for about 400km along the French–German frontier (from the Swiss border to Montmédy on the border of Luxembourg), protecting important industrial and mining regions. The final result was an enormous underground city made from concrete and steel. A system of tunnels, elevators, ventilation units and railway tracks enabled communication between sleeping quarters, hospitals, canteens, arsenals and stores for food and water. At some points there were as many as six underground levels. It also included power generation plants, telephone and telegraph switchboards, and equipment for monitoring the atmospheric pressure in order to provide protection from possible gas attacks. At ground level there was a chain of gun emplacements equipped with modern artillery pointing in the direction of the eastern frontier.

The French public was under the illusion that the Maginot Line was an absolute guarantee of safety. On the eve of battle great faith was still placed in the solidity of the defences in Belgium, which were considered to be a kind of extension of the Maginot Line. The French High Command also counted on the numerical strength of their army and the quality of their artillery, which appeared overall to be superior to that of the Germans. Right until the end, the French military leaders stuck to a strategy that proved disastrous. In instructions to his officers, General Huntzinger, commander of the French Second Army in the Sedan sector, confirmed that the priority was to ensure that the Line was not breached or turned. Consequently, much of the total strength of the army was deployed behind the Line, depriving more at-risk sectors of valuable forces, where the numerical inferiority of the French facilitated the German advance. This is how the Germans managed to confound French illusions, skirting round the Maginot Line at Sedan and opening up a route towards Paris. Paradoxically, when the armistice was signed on 22 June 1940, the fortifications of the Maginot Line were still intact.

(Left:) **GERMAN MINESWEEPERS IN THE NORTH SEA.**

(Below:) **PANZERS INVADE BELGIUM.**

of the Reich was put in its place. Two years later local Nazi leader, Vidkun Quisling, was put at the head of a puppet government.

THE COLLAPSE OF BELGIUM AND HOLLAND

During a debate in the British House of Commons about the outcome of the Norwegian campaign, it was acknowledged that Chamberlain's policy of appeasement had been a tragic failure and that a new political leader was needed to guide the nation in its battle for survival. The Prime Minister resigned following a vote of no confidence in the House of Commons. On the afternoon of 10 May 1940 another Conservative, Winston Churchill, was appointed Prime Minister. That morning the German army had invaded Belgium and Holland, bringing the 'phoney war' to

an end and beginning Hitler's great offensive, which would lead, in the space of just six weeks, to the defeat of the Allied forces and the capitulation of France.

The war in the West began with the landing of German airborne units in Holland and Belgium. On 11 May, German paratroopers captured the fort of Eben-Emael, the linchpin of the Belgian defences and considered until then to be impregnable. In the meantime armoured divisions forced a way through the Ardennes in the south. On 12 May the Germans reached the Meuse, and by the time the Allied troops met up with the Belgian forces it was too late: Liège had fallen, the country was no longer defendable and the Franco-British front line was at risk of being cut off by the German pincer movement. Holland also quickly collapsed, and Queen Wilhelmina and the Dutch Government left for Great

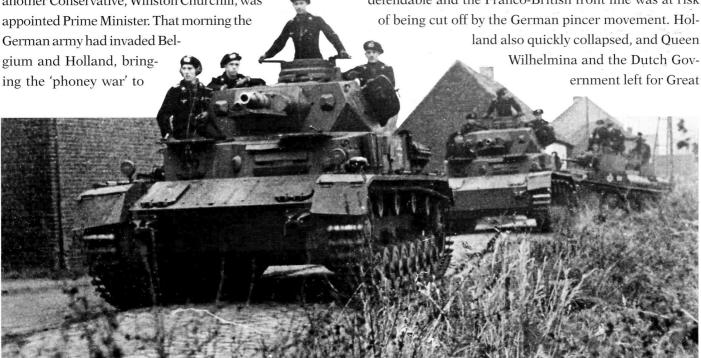

B A T T L E S

OPERATION 'SICKLE CUT'

Operation *Sichelschnitt* ('sickle cut') was a reworking of the plan devised by General Alfred von Schlieffen for the 1914–18 war, when the Kaiser's army was to have gone through Belgium and rapidly annihilated the French army with a pincer movement.

The 1939 plan assigned specific orders to three German army groups. Army Group B (29 infantry divisions, three of which were armoured and two mechanized, under the command of General Fedor von Bock) was instructed to attack Belgium and northern Holland, drawing the Franco-British forces eastwards and then turning them from the north. Army Group C (19 infantry divisions, commanded by General Wilhelm Ritter von Leeb) had the task of breaching the Maginot Line. Gerd von Rundstedt's Army Group A (45 infantry divisions, seven of which were armoured and three mechanized) had the most difficult task: on a front extending from Aquisgrana to Treviri it had to advance in the centre through the Ardennes, cross the Meuse between Sedan and Dinant and then continue along the Somme as far as the Channel coast. The commander-in-chief of the German forces was Field Marshal Walther von Brauchitsch.

There were three armies on the other side of the frontiers: the Dutch (eight divisions) and Belgian (18 divisions) armies, which faced German Army Group A, and the Anglo-French forces deployed as follows: the French 7th Army from the North Sea to Bailleul, the nine divisions of the British Expeditionary Force (BEF) from Bailleul to

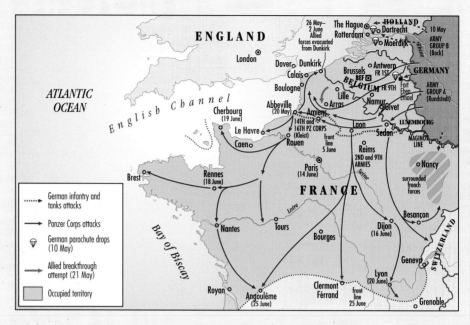

Maulde, the French 1st Army Group (22 divisions) from Maulde to the end of the Maginot Line and the French 2nd and 3rd Army Groups (respectively, 35 and 14 divisions) along the Maginot Line as far as the Swiss border. The commander-in-chief of the Allied forces was General Maurice Gamelin.

The Allies fielded 2,900,000 men and the Germans 2,750,000. As for weapons, the Allies had 2,574 tanks and 2,128 planes, comprising 1,648 French (219 bombers, 946 fighters and 483 reconnaissance planes) and 480 British aircraft. The Germans could count on 2,600 tanks and 3,227 planes.

The German command structure was organized hierarchically. At the top was Hitler himself (*Oberkommando der Wehrmacht*, OKW, namely the Supreme Commander), then there was the Army Chief of Staff (*Oberkommando des Heeres*, OKH) and then the commanders of each army group. The commander of the Luftwaffe (*Oberkommando der Luftwaffe*, OKL) coordinated air operations

with the land forces. This command structure operated very efficiently in the field.

By contrast, the Allied command structure was much less efficient. It was headed by the French Commander-in-Chief (Maurice Gamelin) but was exercised through a commander of land forces (Joseph Doumenc) and then a commander of the north-east sector (Joseph Georges), under whom there was both the French army groups and the BEF, whose commander, Viscount John Gort, responded operationally to Georges but politically to the British government. The Royal Air Force (RAF) in France answered to Gort, but also, in the case of the Advanced Air Striking Force (AASF), to Bomber Command in England.

The invasion of France was preceded by a series of successes on the left flank of the Anglo-French lines: German airborne operations in Belgium and Holland managed to distract the Allies' attention from the main thrust of the German attack through the Ardennes.

(Left:) **HITLER WILL SEND NO WARNING.** *British poster warning of the danger of gas attacks.*

(Far left:) **EVACUATION.** *In view of the expected German air raids, one of the measures taken by the British government after the war broke out was to evacuate children from London.*

Britain. Rotterdam fell on 14 May, after German air raids had caused 1,000 civilian casualties. With lightning speed, Heinz Guderian (the commander of the German armoured forces, which in just two days had reached the banks of the Meuse) thrust forward into southern Belgium and Luxembourg, meeting only weak resistance. Seven German armoured divisions (1,800 tanks) from Army Group A made a mockery of the laborious Allied plans. Gamelin's strategy for defending Belgium crumbled before the rapidity of the German forces, which advanced an average of 50km each day. The main thrust of the German offensive was through the forest of the Ardennes and via the city of Sedan. On 23 May the French 1st Army, the

Belgian army and the British Expeditionary Force (BEF) became separated from the bulk of the French army and were trapped between the German Army Groups A and B. The Allies retreated to the port of Dunkirk. The German's 'sickle cut' had achieved its first objective.

THE FRENCH DÉBÂCLE

To the south, the Wehrmacht occupied positions on the French border. Efficient coordination of air and land operations and the strength of the armoured divisions were accompanied by the extraordinary speed with which the Germans operated in the field. The Panzer divisions (mainly consisting of tanks, infantry and motorized artillery) outmatched the French forces; the latter, though they were not numerically inferior, were hopelessly scattered and consisted of slow infantry divisions. Gamelin's cumbersome army moved

FRENCH TEARS. *The German invasion, and the lightning speed of the military campaign, shocked the French, but there was considerable ambivalence in French society about Nazi Germany.*

BRITAIN'S APPETITE.
In this German cartoon, the English lion is waiting to profit from the defeat of the French cockerel (which is impaled on a sword) by taking over the French colonies.

at a speed that was still dictated by the pace of marching troops and horses. Although the Germans were vulnerable to a French counter-attack, the latter were never in the right place at the right time.

France was in a state of shock. On 20 May 1940, General Maxime Weygand took over as joint commander. The British troops left Arras. French counter-attacks against the enemy's bridgeheads were completely ineffective and the German offensive capacity remained virtually intact. The Allied command did not have the means to launch a joint attack against the wedge of German armour, which had already penetrated into French territory. As in Poland, the Reich gave a further demonstration of the formidable impact of the *Blitzkrieg*.

HITLER IN PARIS.
Early on the morning of 23 June 1940, the Führer made a brief trip to the French capital. German propaganda acclaimed him as the 'greatest field commander of all time'. From that moment on, his military directives were almost never questioned by the German High Command.

THE DUNKIRK POCKET

The evacuation of the British Expeditionary Force took place between 26 May and 4 June. Exceeding even the most optimistic estimates, 340,000 British and French soldiers were rescued by an armada of destroyers, fishing boats, leisure craft and river ferries that arrived from the English coast. Although Goering's Luftwaffe carried out repeated attacks during the operation and the BEF had to abandon all of its tanks, artillery and vehicles on the beach, the evacuation of over 300,000 men from the beach of Dunkirk was celebrated in Great Britain as a memorable enterprise. About 150,000 French soldiers were taken prisoner; and in a country that was on its knees, there was inevitably bitter resentment towards the British. The

(Left:) **SIGNING THE SURRENDER.** *The front page of an American weekly newspaper features a photo of French generals climbing into the railway carriage to sign the official surrender document.*

(Far left:) **FRENCH EXODUS.** *Civilians fleeing from the German advance.*

110,000 French soldiers that were rescued were re-embarked for the ports of Brittany, where they joined the remainder of the forces still opposing the German advance.

THE AGONY OF A GREAT POWER

With just 50 divisions, many of which had very low morale, in opposition to 95 German divisions (including ten armoured divisions), Weygand organized a last line of defence on the Somme, but the Germans breached it between 5 and 9 June. French resistance was crippled by the three thrusts of the German attack: one went through Normandy towards Brittany; another moved through Champagne and got round behind the Maginot Line; and the third advanced south to Lyon. On 10 June, German armoured and mechanized units crossed the Seine and two days later the French government declared Paris an open city in order to prevent it being destroyed. On 14

June, while the Germans swept towards central France, the troops of the Reich paraded along the Champs-Élysées and soldiers in Wehrmacht uniforms thronged the capital's boulevard cafés.

The weeks in which France collapsed were also marked by the death throes of the Anglo-French alliance. Views about how to conduct operations diverged as sharply as those regarding what position to adopt in the immediate future. Churchill's attempt to convince the French Prime Minister, Paul Reynaud, to resist on the basis of a 'Franco-British Union' (which basically involved fusion of the two states) ran up against French pride. Reynaud resigned and was succeeded by Marshal Henri-Philippe Pétain, the hero of Verdun in World War I, who, fearful of a sudden attack from the left wing, asked Hitler for an armistice.

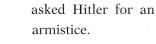

THE HUMILIATION OF COMPIÈGNE. *The Germans made the French generals sign the surrender terms in the same railway carriage in which Kaiser Wilhelm's generals had signed the armistice on 11 November 1918. Hitler and his generals await the arrival of the envoys of a humiliated France.*

LOOK OUT, CHILDREN!
A Local Defence Volunteer warns a London child not to do anything in the bombed area. Varied forms of communication were used to give instructions to the civilian population.

LEAVE THIS TO US
SONNY — <u>YOU</u> OUGHT
TO BE OUT OF LONDON

MINISTRY OF HEALTH EVACUATION SCHEME

BATTLES

CODENAME 'SEA LION'

On 16 July 1940, Hitler issued Directive no. 16 regarding plans for the invasion of England, which was to take place in mid-September. The original plan was that the first wave of attack should consist of 13 infantry divisions, to be followed by six Panzer and three mechanized divisions, and then a further 17 infantry divisions. The German High Command estimated that by the third day of the invasion 260,000 men would have landed on English soil. The Luftwaffe had the task of off-setting German naval inferiority and of

ENEMY INVASION.
WHAT YOU MUST DO.

Remain at work: when unable to do so and you have no invasion duty
CONTACT YOUR LOCAL WARDEN.
He will arrange for you to help the City to carry on.
If you are in Civil Defence, that is your job.
If you have no invasion duty, stand firm.
Do not leave your district; do not block the roads.
Do not listen to rumours; only obey orders given by the military, police, Civil Defence personnel or Ministry of Information.
Be on your guard against Fifth Columnists.
Apply to your local Warden for more detailed instructions.
Keep by you a 48 hours' supply of food and water.

Issued by the Birmingham Invasion Committee.

supporting the land forces. The plan suffered continual modification and postponement, and the landing zone was restricted to a 75-mile (121km) stretch on the English Channel between Folkstone and Brighton.

As of September the British were in a position to deploy 27 infantry divisions, of which only four were fully equipped. There was a lack of field, machine and anti-tank guns. Just two armoured divisions and two armoured brigades were to have 600 tanks, clear evidence of an inflexible command structure that was ill prepared for various eventualities. The defence of British soil relied on the Home Guard, consisting of some 500,000 uniformed volunteers equipped with antiquated American rifles. The premise of the entire operation, that the Luftwaffe would be able to cripple the RAF and gain control of the skies over the Channel, was confounded by the outcome of the Battle of Britain.

(Above:) Instructions to the population about what to do in the event of an invasion, and the badge of the Civil Defence Corps. (Left:) Soldiers are given a warm cup of tea after exercises in the English countryside.

(Left:) **INFANTRYMEN OF THE TRIPARTITE PACT.**
Illustrated Italian postcard featuring three child infantrymen – Italian, German and Japanese – marching over their British peers.

(Below:) **ARE THE GERMANS COMING?**
A common sight: an air-raid warden on lookout duty on the rooftop of a London house.

THE HUMILIATION OF COMPIÈGNE

On 22 June 1940, in the same railway carriage that had been used for signing the surrender of Germany at the end of World War I, France accepted the harsh armistice conditions that were imposed by the enemy: three-fifths of the nation's territory was occupied by the Germans; the army was reduced to 100,000 men; the cost of the occupation (which was calculated according to an exorbitant rate of exchange between the two currencies) was to be paid in entirety by the French; the colonial empire remained under the control of the French government (which had to establish its capital in Vichy); the Navy was demilitarized; and finally prisoners of war were to remain in German hands. For the French, the figures of the 'lightning war' were a

humiliation: their final losses were 120,000, as compared with 27,000 on the German side.

ITALY'S ENTRY INTO THE WAR

On 10 June, Mussolini had declared war on France and Great Britain, hoping to win a military victory against an exhausted nation and obtain significant territorial gains at the negotiating table. During the night, Italian planes bombed the British naval base in Malta. With ammunition reserves sufficient for barely two months and with just 19 battle-ready divisions, Italy was dragged into a conflict in accordance with a logic that matched the regime's policy of aggression. The Fascist leaders

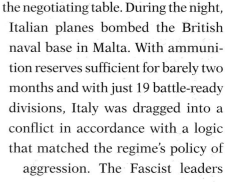

BATTLES

THE BATTLE OF BRITAIN

In 1940/41 the German Luftwaffe had various combat aircraft. The *Junkers Ju 87* 'Stuka' (an abbreviation for *Stukageshwader*) was a formidable dive-bomber for ground attack, equipped with a 500kg bomb load. Devastatingly effective in Poland and France, it had a maximum speed of 383km/hour and a cruising range of 788km. The *Junkers Ju 88*, a twin-engine bomber, night fighter and reconnaissance plane, formed the backbone of the Luftwaffe. Capable of a maximum speed of 626km/hour, it had a cruising range of 2,250km. The single-engine *Messerschmitt Bf-109* (BF stands for the name of the construction plant, Bayerische Flugzeugwerke; technical manager was an engineer named Willy Messerschmitt) was the fastest German fighter. Manoeuvrable and well armed, it had a maximum speed of 550km/hour and a cruising range of 660km. This craft was flanked by the twin-engine *Messerschmitt Bf-110* fighter, subsequently used as a reconnaissance plane and fighter-bomber, which had a maximum speed of 540km/hour and a cruising range of 1,125km.

The *Heinkel He-111* was a medium-sized twin-engine bomber that was effective for daytime missions; it had a maximum speed of 405km/hour and a cruising range of 2,060km. Finally, there was the *Dornier Do-17*, which had a top speed of 410km/hour and a cruising range of 1,160km and was known for its qualities as a combat aircraft.

The Royal Air Force fielded the *Spitfire*, the best British fighter of World War II, with a maximum speed of 602km/hour and a cruising range of 750km. Designed by Reginald Mitchell, it was the only Allied plane to remain in production throughout the war, further proof of its extraordinary qualities. There were 40 versions in all, and total production was 20,000. Initially used for defensive purposes, later on in the war it was used on all the fronts of the European theatre of war. Besides the Spitfire, there was the *Hawker Hurricane Mk 1*, with a top speed of 545km/hour and a cruising range of 740km. In 1940 Britain was producing some 500 aircraft a month (this was a mixture of Spitfires and Hurricanes), while the Germans could only manage 140 Me-109 and 90 Me-110 aircraft. At the beginning of the Battle of Britain, the Luftwaffe was superior to the RAF in the air, with 1,000 planes (Do-17s, He-111s and Ju-88s) plus 300 Ju-87 dive-bombers. However, this capacity was not deployed according to a coordinated and prolonged strategic plan. Between July and October 1940 the RAF lost over 700 planes, the Luftwaffe more than 2,400. At the height of the Battle of Britain the RAF had at least 600 planes available for missions (though there was a shortage of pilots). The performance of the British fighters was on a par with that of the Germans in terms of speed and armaments. The bombers of the Luftwaffe had a limited range of action, and the reduced cruising range of the German fighters (they could cross the English Channel in a few minutes but had to take off from France and Holland) was such that they could not escort the bombers for very long.

(Above:) A German fighter deployed in the Battle of Britain, and a British Spitfire.

Map labels:
Edinburgh
Glasgow
British fighter bases
German fighter bases
German bomber bases
FIGHTER GROUP 13
Newcastle
Liverpool
FIGHTER GROUP 12
LUFTFLOTTE 5 (from Norway and Denmark)
Nottingham
Derby
Coventry
FIGHTER GROUP 11
Filton
Bristol
FIGHTER GROUP 10
London
Rochester
Ramsgate
Dover
Portsmouth
Brighton
Folkestone
Calais
Wissant
Boulogne
Cherbourg
LUFTFLOTTE 2
LUFTFLOTTE 3

'BRITAIN SHALL NOT BURN' AND 'BOMBS ON COVENTRY'.
On 15 November 1940 the Midlands city of Coventry suffered terrible bombing. A third of the city's houses were destroyed and 600 people killed in what was one of the worst air raids ever suffered by the British. The word 'Coventrize' became a synonym for the flattening of a city in a single raid.

were under the illusion that the war would be brief and that Italy was capable of waging a 'parallel' but completely independent war to that of Germany. Italy occupied some 50km of French border territory beyond the Alps.

Stunned by a defeat that was as unexpected as it was humiliating, France ceased to be a great power. German supremacy stretched from the Vistula to the Atlantic, from the North Cape to the Alps. In the House of Commons, Churchill declared: 'The Battle of France is over. I expect that the Battle of Britain is about to begin.'

THE BLITZ

If the humiliation of the Allies in France was the consequence of strategic errors, the Battle of Britain marked an epochal change in how war was waged. The massive use of air power subverted the dictates of conventional land-based military operations. Goering's objective was to destroy the enemy's air force in order to pave the way for the planned invasion of Britain. German plans also envisaged strategic bombing (a full-blown instrument of mass destruction) and fighter support for the armoured and infantry forces that were to operate on British territory. The Battle of Britain began on 13 August 1940, and in the following four weeks the blue skies of the English summer were the scene of bloody aerial combat. Night and day, waves of German bombers escorted by fighters targeted cities, air bases, radar stations, military factories and barracks.

The heavy losses suffered by the Germans on 15 September, the day that saw the largest of all the bomber formations heading for the English capital, forced Hitler to shelve his plans for invasion. As of October the tally of aircraft losses was in Britain's favour: 832 planes lost, compared with 668 fighters and about 600 bombers on the

LONDON BRIDGE AND THE SMOKE OF FIRES.
The British air-raid defences, which included 1,500 barrage balloons, 2,000 anti-aircraft guns and 2,500 pilots of highly manoeuvrable Spitfires and Hurricanes, staved off the brunt of the German bomber formations, which were made up of formidable but sluggish Heinkels, Dorniers and Junkers.

ATTACKING STUKAS.
A variant on Chinese draughts devised to amuse German children.

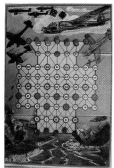

German side. This heavy imbalance frustrated Goering's plans: the Luftwaffe had not proved to be strategically decisive, and British factories were able to replace the lost planes. The Blitz, as the peak of the German bombing offensive was called by the British, was followed by bombing raids on London and other major British cities until July 1941. However, the aim of crippling the British defences and weakening the morale of the nation so as to obtain a separate peace – which Hitler continued to hope for in order to avert the entry of the United States into the war – was thwarted by British supremacy in the air.

BRITAIN STANDS ALONE

Following the collapse of France, and with the United States still neutral albeit generous in its aid, Great Britain was the target of German air raids. Between September and December 1940, London was bombed for 86 nights in succession. It also suffered from the constant sinking of ships in the Allied convoys by German U-boats, and had to deal with the intermittent supply of raw materials for its industries and of food for the population. The second winter of the war was particularly hard for Great Britain, which had to face Hitler's military power on its own.

Supported by growing American assistance, the nation remained determined to continue the war. Although the first phase of Hitler's *Blitzkrieg* had produced sensational successes on land, the Battle of Britain had scuppered Hitler's plans for a separate peace with London.

The threat of invasion having subsided, the British now had to deal with the all-out submarine campaign that Germany was about to

WEAPONS

 RADAR

British Fighter Command had a warning and monitoring system enabling it to intercept incoming enemy planes. The network of 50 radar stations established along the English coast before the outbreak of the war proved to be a formidable technological benefit and provided the Allies with a decisive advantage during the Battle of Britain and throughout the war. Invented by Robert Watson-Watt of the National Physical Laboratory, radar (an acronym for 'radio detecting and ranging') is a device that emits pulse-modulated electromagnetic waves, with which the position of an object in space can be determined. The waves reflected by the object form a sequence that allows for the calculation of the direction, distance, speed and altitude of a plane.

L E A D E R S

HENRI-PHILIPPE PÉTAIN

In 1914, Colonel Pétain was already reaching retirement age (he had been born in 1856) and was known chiefly for the fact that he taught at the École de Guerre at Saint-Cyr. During World War I he had been a firm supporter of a static defensive war. Promoted to the rank of general, he had been the architect of the defence of Verdun and became a national hero. He was appointed commander-in-chief in May 1917 and reorganized the army for the victorious 1918 offensive. The prestige of this elderly war hero remained intact throughout the 1930s. On 18 May 1940 he became Vice-Premier in Paul Reynaud's government, but he soon clashed with Reynaud, who was against surrendering to the Germans. Charged with forming a new government, on 16 June 1940 Pétain asked the Germans for an armistice. The National Assembly granted him full powers, paving the way for the collaborationist Vichy regime. On 20 August 1944, Pétain was removed from Vichy by the Germans and transferred to Sigmaringen. He returned to France on 24 April 1945, as soon as the Germans had been defeated, to face trial for treason. Before shutting himself off in total silence, he declared: 'The French people will not forget. They know that I defended them as I did at Verdun.'

Pétain was sentenced to death, declared a national disgrace and had his assets confiscated. In view of his age, the sentence was commuted to life imprisonment, the order being signed by his former pupil, General de Gaulle. He died in 1951, after six years of imprisonment.

CHARLES DE GAULLE

Born in 1890, Charles de Gaulle graduated from the military college of Saint-Cyr in 1912. He fought in World War I and was seriously injured at Verdun before being taken prisoner by the Germans. After the war he studied military theory and described, in his 1934 book *The Army of the Future*, a war of movement based on modern mechanized divisions. In military circles his position remained an isolated one, and it was only when Paul Reynaud came to power in March 1940 that de Gaulle was given command of the 4th Armoured Division. In June 1940 he was appointed brigadier, and a few days later Under Secretary for Defence. When Pétain took over as head of the government, de Gaulle

left France for England and on 18 June 1940, speaking on BBC radio, he called upon the French people to resist. He was condemned to death in absentia by a court martial in Toulouse.

In July 1940 he founded the Comité National Français, which had a following of 45,000, participated in various campaigns and took control of French colonial territories. On 3 June 1943 he set up the Comité Français de la Libération Nationale in Algiers, which became the provisional government of France in June 1944. On 26 August 1944 he entered Paris in triumph, where he headed a provisional government formed from the various Resistance forces. He managed to establish his authority in liberated France and his position was confirmed by the constituent assembly in November 1945. In favour of a presidential system, he resigned in January 1946 as a protest against the political parties. He fiercely opposed the Fourth Republic and in 1947 he founded the right-wing Rassemblement du Peuple Français, but then retired in 1953. During the crisis in Algeria (1958), he was recalled to the government. He obtained approval for a new constitution, which gave strong powers to the Head of State, and managed to gain election as President. He dominated French politics for over a decade, before retiring in 1969, a year before his death.

Charles de Gaulle inspecting 'Free French' naval units. In his appeal to the French people after the fall of France, transmitted on Radio London, he declared: 'This war is not finished by the Battle of France. This war is a worldwide war. Whatever happens, the flame of the French resistance must not and shall not be extinguished.'

(Right:) **PÉTAIN IN VICHY.**
Pétain's regime was in many ways openly fascist, even though at the outset the elderly general's aim in collaborating with the Reich was to obtain economic benefits.

(Below:) **OCCUPIED PARIS.**

launch on the Atlantic routes in order to keep America away from Europe. The RAF and the Royal Navy had the task of waging this war of attrition with the enemy, which came to be known as the Battle of the Atlantic.

THE VICHY REGIME

With the defeat of France, the Third Republic came to an end and the nation was divided into two: in the north and west was the German occupation zone, including Paris, while to the south-west there was a limited-sovereignty French state with its capital in Vichy. The Republic of Vichy was established on 11 July 1940, with an institutional framework that concentrated executive, legislative and some judicial powers in the hands of Marshal Pétain. The Republican motto of 'Liberty, Equality, Fraternity' was replaced by 'Work, Family, Country'. The unions and political parties were disbanded, and with the drawing up of

a special 'statute for the Jews', a policy of anti-Semitic discrimination was implemented. The aim of the 'state collaboration' offered to Germany by this independent French creation was to gain recognition for France in the 'new European order' that was expected to ensue at the end of the war following the rapid victory of the Third Reich.

THE TRIPARTITE PACT

Although the Germans and Italians thought that Britain would collapse in a matter of months, diplomatic initiatives continued. On 27 September 1940, Italy, Germany and Japan signed the 'pact of the three powers', which committed each of the parties to support the other in the event of attack by a country not involved in the Sino-Japanese dispute or in the war in Europe. Japan recognized the primary role of Germany and the secondary role

Military production	1939	1940	1941	1942	1943	1944	1945	
Great Britain	7,940	15,049	20,094	23,672	26,263	26,461	12,070	Planes
	969	1,399	4,481	8,611	7,476	5,000	–	Tanks
	–	1,900	5,300	6,600	12,200	12,400	–	Artillery
	57	148	236	239	224	188	64	Surface ships
USA	5,856	12,804	26,277	47,836	85,898	96,318	49,761	Planes
	–	400	4,052	24,997	29,497	17,565	11,968	Tanks
	–	1,800	29,614	72,658	67,544	33,558	19,699	Artillery
	–	–	544	1,854	2,654	2,247	1,513	Submarines
Germany	8,295	10,247	11,776	15,409	24,807	39,807	7,540	Planes
	1,300	2,200	5,200	9,200	17,300	22,100	–	Tanks
	–	5,000	7,000	12,000	27,000	41,000	–	Artillery
	15	40	196	244	270	288	103	Submarines
Japan	4,467	4,768	3,180	6,335	13,406	21,058	8,263	Planes
	–	1,023	812	1,633	1,415	1,126	247	Tanks
	21	30	16	18	20	36	6	Submarines
USSR	10,382	10,565	15,735	25,436	34,900	40,300	20,900	Planes
	2,950	2,794	6,590	24,446	24,089	28,963	15,400	Tanks
	17,348	15,300	42,300	127,000	130,000	122,400	93,000	Artillery
	–	33	62	19	13	23	11	Submarines

(Below:) **WOMEN AT WORK.**
Women employees polish plane cockpits in a Douglas aircraft-manufacturing plant in California.

of Italy in the reorganization of Europe, where the Axis armies dominated and British power had been drastically weakened. An analogous role was attributed to Japan in East Asia. Japan's commitment to fighting the Soviet Union if the latter attacked Germany, and a similar commitment on the part of Germany in the event of an American attack on Japan, did not translate into a full-blown co-belligerence treaty. In the framework of its global strategic vision, Tokyo gained recognition for its policy in the Pacific and South-East Asia, but preserved full freedom of action and the option of attacking the United States or Russia.

AMERICA, THE 'ARSENAL OF DEMOCRACY'

Faced with the deteriorating situation in Europe, the nature of American involvement gradually changed. This was partly because the Tripartite Pact put the principle of hemispheric defence, shared both by the isolationists and those in favour of helping democracies threatened by Fascist expansionism, in even greater danger. It was also because 'Fortress America' was becoming subject to geopolitical and military encirclement that threatened Washington's global vision of its national security.

The Roosevelt administration considered the survival of Great Britain to be crucial in order to maintain equilibrium in Europe and the Pacific. Consequently, in the space of a year it introduced the draft (June 1940); ceded warships to Britain; obtained Congress approval for the 'Lend-Lease' Act, which authorized the loan of war materials; drew up war plans in which priority was given to control of the Atlantic; and then stipulated, with the signing of the Atlantic Charter (August 1941), a military alliance with the British.

Roosevelt's strategic decision to keep America out of

(Right:) **THE ENEMY IS LISTENING.**
Government poster warning the French of the danger of loose talk.

(Far right:) **UNDERWRITE THE WAR.**
The French were asked to contribute financially to the war effort.

LEADERS

FRANKLIN DELANO ROOSEVELT

The political career of Franklin Delano Roosevelt (1882–1945) began when he was elected as the Democratic Party's senator for New York in 1910. In his youth he studied in France, Germany and Great Britain. During World War I he served as Assistant Secretary to the Navy. In 1921 he was struck by polio. He was elected governor of the state of New York in 1929. He stood for the presidency in 1932 and defeated the incumbent, Herbert Hoover. With the launching of the 'New Deal', he regenerated the American economy, which had been floored by the 1929 Depression, and embarked upon a large-scale economic and social policy of state intervention, including steps to increase employment, curbs on monopolistic capital, the introduction of social security benefits, the setting up of a negotiating system for better labour relations and the increase of federal spending on public works. A tenacious supporter of Wilson's internationalism, Roosevelt steered American foreign policy away from isolationism, which was deep-rooted in many sectors of society. Before the outbreak of the war he condemned on a number of occasions the aggression of the fascist regimes. Roosevelt applied a principle that lay at the heart of all his political action: in a democratic system like that of the United States, the president can only pursue a global foreign policy with broad consensus at home. He firmly supported Great Britain in 1940 and 1941, and regarded direct US involvement in the war as an opportunity to establish America definitively as a world power. In his famous 'fireside chats' after his re-election in 1940, he announced his intention to make the United States the 'great arsenal of democracy'. In March 1941, due to his determination, Congress approved a programme to aid Great Britain, with the passing of the 'Lend-Lease' Act (later extended to Soviet Russia as well). Thanks to his good relationship with Churchill, he managed to persuade him of the necessity of an Allied landing in Normandy. Roosevelt was the president who more than any other made a lasting impact on the modern history of the United States. He died in April 1945, six months after being re-elected for the fourth time, two months after the conference at Yalta (which he attended in a poor state of health) and following an uninterrupted mandate of 12 years.

President Roosevelt at work.

(Left:) **AMERICAN BOMBS IN BRITISH PLANES.**

(Below:) **MUSSOLINI ON THE GREEK FRONT.**
The Fascist regime decided to invade Greece from Albania, but underestimated the capacity of the Greek forces to respond.

the conflict for the time being made it a kind of logistical reserve (the 'arsenal of democracy'), while its massive political and material support for the British increased the consensus of American public opinion.

'BREAKING THE KIDNEYS' OF GREECE

Following the agreement between Berlin and Rome about each nation's area of influence, Italy was keen to achieve a prestigious victory and thus decided to embark upon an independent initiative by attacking Britain's remaining ally on the European continent: Greece. With this move, Mussolini believed he could contribute to Hitler's design to squeeze Britain even further (especially if Franco's Spain and Vichy France also joined the anti-British alliance) and seriously threaten British military capacity in North Africa. The invasion of Greece, with which Mussolini sought to 'break the kidneys' of a nation that was vital to the control of the Mediterranean, was an improvised affair, based on the illusion of a brief war. On 28 October 1940, the anniversary of the march on Rome, Italian troops stationed in Albania crossed the border,

ITALY'S PATH TO WAR

The Fascist regime conducted an extensive propaganda campaign to instil in the Italian people a bellicose spirit and a strong sense of national pride, and to convince them of the need for territorial expansion at the expense of the Western 'demo-plutocratic' powers. Foreign policy moves were backed by the massive use of propaganda, the aim being to ensure that certain messages penetrated the collective imagination, thereby obtaining mass consensus for the government's strategies.

The increasingly close relations with Nazi Germany were a natural consequence of the ideological affinity between the two regimes. Italy's intervention in the war certainly did not depend simply on a personal decision by Mussolini, but was a direct consequence of the overall political stance of the regime, which was also supported by the monarchy, military chiefs and powerful sectors of Italian capitalism. However, war broke out sooner than expected. Aware of Italy's military and economic unpreparedness for war, Mussolini decided to keep out of the conflict temporarily, declaring the nation's 'non-belligerence'. This was not a declaration of neutrality, but rather a postponement of intervention alongside the German ally. After years of exalting a warrior spirit, this decision was rather a humiliation for the regime and was greeted with scorn at home. At the end of 1939 the support granted to Finland, which had been attacked by the Soviets with Hitler's agreement, was dictated also by home policy concerns.

Mindful of the tragedy of the Great War, the majority of the Italian

Mussolini's declaration of war on the front page of the Corriere della Sera.

population was opposed to entering the war and there was considerable anti-German feeling. News of the decision not to intervene was greeted with relief, and the development of events was followed with great apprehension, in the hope of avoiding the spread of the conflict and the direct involvement of Italy. Uncertainty was soon replaced by passive expectation and resignation. During the phoney war on the French–German front, the Allies tried to transform Italy's non-belligerence into neutrality but a choice of this kind, despite being favoured by certain parts of the regime, was politically impossible because it would have been a glaring contradiction of the regime's policies and propaganda. There was already a climate of war in the country: sugar and coffee were rationed, fuel supplies were increasingly hard to come by and prices were rising. Living conditions were made even tougher by a hard winter. Latent discontent began to spread, though it did not result in significant social and political protest, partly because of police control and partly due to problems within the anti-Fascist movement. A trusted party member in Milan reported that 'the state of mind of the masses is increasingly exasperated, and disgust and discontent will soon erupt if a brake is not put on impositions, expenses and above all on the policy of supporting Germany'.

With the appointment of Alessandro Pavolini as Minister of Popular Culture in October 1939, the propaganda effort was stepped up. In fact, Mussolini and the military leaders wished to extend their country's non-belligerence. Italy's attitude towards its German ally remained cautious, partly because of the anti-German position of the Foreign Minister Galeazzo Ciano, which found support in court circles and in some sectors of the military command. Mussolini, who feared the negative consequences for Italy of an all-out victory for either of the two sides, wavered and played a waiting game. A turning point came in March 1940, when Mussolini, pressed by Hitler, became convinced of the inevitability of intervention alongside Germany. In April the press received the order to 'gradually heat up the Italian population' and the Fascist squads resumed their activities. The successes of the German *Blitzkrieg* made a powerful impression on public opinion, and there was widespread indignation when Belgium and Holland fell. On 10 June 1940, while France was collapsing, Italy's intervention in the war was announced by Mussolini from the balcony of Piazza Venezia in front of a truly enormous crowd, with a celebrated speech that epitomized the imperialist rhetoric of the regime.

(Left:) **ITALIANS AND GERMANS.** *After the Italian lack of success in the Greek invasion, Hitler received Ciano at Berchtesgaden, expressing his full concern about the course of military operations in the Balkans.*

(Below:) **ITALIAN BOMBERS BEFORE TAKE-OFF.**

aiming for Macedonia and for Epirus. Two weeks later the Greek forces – 250,000 men – were already counter-attacking and the Italians found themselves bogged down in the mud and ice of the Balkan trenches. The 105,000-strong Italian force (seven infantry divisions, the 'Centauro' armoured division and the 'Julia' alpine division) suffered heavy losses and fell back, with difficulty, to Albanian territory, taking up positions in the area around Vlorë, the strategic port for the Italian expeditionary force. The Italian military disaster was compounded on 12 November by a raid on port Taranto by British torpedo bombers, which sank three Italian battleships at anchor there. Italy held its positions in Greece with difficulty, and the Royal Navy had struck a devastating blow to Mussolini's aspirations to establish himself as the gendarme of the Mediterranean and to create an empire around *mare nostrum*, or 'our sea'.

THE ISOLATION OF THE SOVIET UNION

The successes of Hitler's *Blitzkrieg* worried Stalin. The signing of the Tripartite Pact increased his fear that the benevolent stance adopted by Moscow regarding German plans to conquer Europe was no longer sufficient. The Soviet Union's 'great power' interests were directed towards controlling the straits of the Baltic Sea and Estonia, Lithuania and Latvia, which were incorporated into the Soviet Union in the summer of 1940 in accordance with the terms of a secret protocol contained

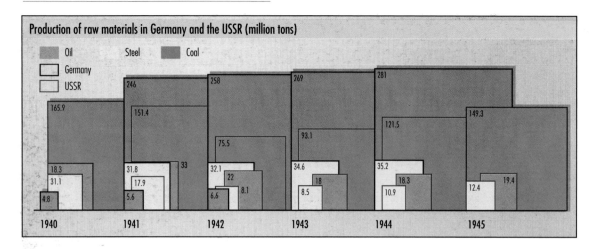

Production of raw materials in Germany and the USSR (million tons)

Oil · Steel · Coal · Germany · USSR

	1940	1941	1942	1943	1944	1945
Coal	165.9 / 31.1	246 / 151.4	258 / 75.5	269 / 93.1	281 / 121.5	281 / 149.3
Steel	18.3	31.8 / 33	32.1 / 22	34.6 / 18	35.2 / 18.3	12.4 / 19.4
Oil	4.8	17.9 / 5.6	6.6 / 8.1	8.5	10.9	

in the Nazi–Soviet pact of 1939. Hitler hoped to turn Soviet attention towards the Persian Gulf as a way of countering the British, but at meetings held in Berlin in November 1940, the Soviet Foreign Minister Molotov restated the Soviet intention to create a 'security zone' in central and south-east Europe and held to the principle that Finland was part of the 'Soviet sphere of influence'. The Red Army occupied Bessarabia and the north of Bukovina (regions of Romania). Moscow then demanded the right to 'protect' Bulgaria and wanted guarantees of passage through the Dardanelles, respect of Sweden's neutrality and recognition of its interests in Hungary, Yugoslavia and Greece.

Agreement with the Tripartite Pact powers depended on Japan giving up oil and coal resources on the Sakhalin Peninsula. Although Russia continued to supply Germany with essential raw materials, Moscow's neutrality in the 'imperialist' conflict was in a dangerous phase of stalemate. With the decapitation of the upper ranks of the Red Army after the purges of 1937/38, the Soviet Union was unprepared for a war. Evaluation of Germany's military capacity was hopelessly inaccurate and relations between Britain and Russia continued to be very tense, because Churchill rejected out of hand any possibility of including Soviet Russia in the coalition against Hitler.

(Right:) **SOVIET TRACTOR FACTORY.**
Before the outbreak of hostilities between Germany and the Soviet Union, Stalin's big production drive was undermined by the 'terror' that marked the second half of the 1930s. The repression of Russian farm workers suspected of sabotaging the regime because they were hostile to enforced collectivization led, in many areas of the country, to the flaring of nationalist sentiment in opposition to the power of Moscow.

(Far right:) **MOSCOW STREET.**

WAR ARCHIVES: THE LONDON BLITZ

The battle in the English skies began with an attack by over 2,600 German planes, which struck at airfields and inland cities. London had a population of seven million, making it the largest metropolis in the world, and it was subjected to an unending series of bombing raids. Air-raid sirens sounded day and night, explosions destroyed entire neighbourhoods and hundreds of fires devastated the city centre. The most celebrated monuments of English civilization were hard hit. The Londoners made every effort to carry on living and working normally. The total casualty figures at the end of the Blitz were 14,000 dead and 20,000 injured, but the Germans had been repulsed. In his memoirs Charles de Gaulle noted: 'If the enemy had succeeded in gaining control of the skies, it would have been the end of England. Those in the know whispered the names of politicians, bishops, writers and businessmen who would, in such an event, have come to terms with the Germans to ensure the rule of the country under their control.'

From Tobruk to the Atlantic

While Britain was still suffering heavy bombing by the German Luftwaffe, a new theatre of war opened – in Africa. Following the French surrender in July 1940, the Armée d'Afrique, stationed in Tunisia, Algeria and Morocco, was immobilized. When the French Navy refused to hand over its fleet to the British after the armistice, the latter did not hesitate to bomb their naval units (3 July 1940) at the base of Mers el-Kebir near Oran. Relations between Great Britain and the Vichy Government worsened. Italy decided to exploit the numerical superiority of its troops over what was the largest colonial empire in the world to push into British-controlled territory in Kenya and to occupy British Somaliland, which bordered the Gulf of Aden. The presence of Italian naval forces in the Mediterranean and the troops stationed in Libya and East Africa threatened the Suez Canal, the main communications route to the British *(p. 72:)* **ITALIAN PRISONERS.**

(p.73:) **BRITISH SHIP IN MALTA.**

(Right:) **AMEDEO, DUKE OF AOSTA.**
Viceroy of Abyssinia from 1937.

(Far right:) **RODOLFO GRAZIANI.**
Commander of the Italian troops in North Africa.

(Below:) **BRITISH ARTILLERY IN THE AFRICAN DESERT.**

colonies in the Far East. While military operations in North Africa were marking time, the conflict took an unexpected turn: following the Japanese attack on the American base of Pearl Harbor on 7 December 1941, the United States entered the war.

THE WAR IN THE DESERT

Between September 1940 and the first half of 1941, North Africa became a new theatre of the war on land. Superior in numbers but poorly equipped, Italian troops commanded by Marshal Rodolfo Graziani penetrated into Egypt with the ambitious objective of capturing the British base of Alexandria. The hesitant Italian advance came to a halt amidst the dunes of Sidi el-Barrani.

The geography of North Africa required new strategies, partly because of the nature of the terrain but above all due to the necessity, on both sides, for units not to be too far away from their source of supplies. In the absence of natural obstacles, infantry and artillery massed in the Libyan desert in areas protected by minefields. Venturing into the 'sea' of sand, armoured forces had great freedom of movement to carry out surprise attacks. It was a very fast-moving war, characterized by a succession of advances and retreats in a vast desert territory. Tracked vehicles were often out of service due to lack of fuel or to mechanical faults.

In December 1940 the British counter-attacked. With just 35,000 men and 275 tanks, but with an astute strategy based on speed of movement, General Richard O'Connor outflanked the enemy's line of trenches, causing an Italian retreat that finally came to a halt

THE LICTOR'S FASCES.
Fascist propaganda placed no limits on possible targets of Italian expansionism in the Mediterranean and Africa: Malta, Gibraltar, Tunis, British and French Somaliland, and Corsica.

in February 1941, 400km to the rear of their original positions. The Italians were driven westwards along the coast road, with the enemy snapping at their heels, and Cyrenaica fell into British hands. Just two divisions routed ten Italian divisions and took 130,000 prisoners.

The Italian army, which had lost 1,100 artillery guns and 390 tanks, was reduced to expeditionary corps status and had to rely on supplies that arrived occasionally from Sicily. However, neither of the two sides could boast supremacy in the Mediterranean, and the exceptional length of the front line also created major difficulties for the British Western Desert Force in North Africa, which was unable to push on as far as Tripoli. The rapid British success in North Africa was also undone by an unexpected turn in events: on 5 April 1941, Hitler ordered the invasion of Yugoslavia and Greece, obliging the British once again to concentrate their forces in Egypt.

THE DEFENCE OF THE BRITISH EMPIRE

In East Africa, following initial Italian successes, the tide turned in favour of the British. The Italian forces, under Duke Amedeo d'Aosta, also had a numerical advantage in Ethiopia, but they were isolated from home. For the British it was of vital importance to break the encirclement in a key region of the world, an economic and strategic crossroads that Berlin was putting under pressure. The French Armée du Levant, stationed in Syria and Lebanon, was potentially a powerful bridgehead for striking to the British rear in Egypt.

In January 1941, Allied forces that had arrived from India, South Africa and Kenya launched an offensive, penetrating into southern Ethiopia and Somalia. In March, after the hard-fought Battle of Harrar, the British conquered central Ethiopia and Eritrea. Addis Ababa fell on 5 April, and Emperor Haile Selassie, who had been

B A T T L E S

CAPE MATAPAN
The night of 28 March 1941 marked a turning point in the naval war in the Mediterranean. The battle fought off Cape Matapan, the southernmost point of the Peloponnese peninsula in Greece, established the Royal Navy's superiority over the Italian surface fleet. The British formation under Admiral Andrew B. Cunningham,

who commanded the British Mediterranean Fleet, first damaged the Italian battleship *Vittorio Veneto* (which managed to reach the naval base of Taranto) and shortly afterwards sank three cruisers (the *Pola*, *Zara* and *Fiume*) and two destroyers (the *Alfieri* and *Carducci*). Casualties on the Italian side, commanded by Admiral Angelo Iachino, were very high — about 2,400 men. The British picked up about 900 sailors from the sea and a further 160 men were saved by an Italian hospital ship that arrived on the scene

three days later. The battle at Cape Matapan was one of the heaviest defeats suffered by the Italian Navy. The technical and tactical superiority of the British (who also had carrier-based aircraft) was enhanced by the use of radar. From this point on, Mussolini's battleships stayed in port. Although the Italian fleet subsequently managed to get its convoys through to Tripoli, the only Italian successes at sea were the result of bold attacks by motor torpedo boats and assault craft.

(Right:) **FOREIGN LEGION.**
The élite French fighting force was divided between those who supported Vichy and those who sided with the 'Free French'.

(Below:) **SENEGALESE INFANTRY.**
When fighting broke out in Africa, the British forces were greatly inferior in numbers to the Italians and so they recruited thousands of men from Allied colonial possessions.

deposed by the Italians in 1936, returned in triumph the following month. The Red Sea was once again open for American convoys supplying the British base at Suez. The Ethiopia campaign ended in less than three months, although the last Italian contingent held out in the city of Gonder until November 1941.

THE 'FREE FRENCH' AGAINST VICHY

Not all the French had accepted the surrender of Pétain. In West Africa the soldiers of the 'Free French' Government, established at the initiative of General Charles de Gaulle, managed to gain control of a number of colonies (Cameroon, Chad, Gabon) for the anti-Nazi cause. Units of both white and black soldiers commanded by General Philippe Leclerc fought successfully alongside the British in North Africa. While the Armée

d'Afrique in Morocco, Algeria and Tunisia remained out of the war for the time being, the lot of the Armée du Levant, commanded by General Henri Dentz, was less happy. This army became the object of Axis designs after General Rashid Ali, who was openly pro-German, took power in Iraq and the Grand Mufti of Jerusalem also sided with the Axis powers. Pétain's government conceded the use of Syrian air bases to the Luftwaffe, and there was the possibility that the area would become a German outpost used to send supplies to North Africa.

De Gaulle urged the British to intervene in Syria, thereby creating the conditions for a war between Frenchmen, which led to the disintegration of the protectorate

(Left:) **BRITISH AND GERMAN BADGES.** *These include the badge of the 7th British Armoured Division (the so-called Desert Rats), which featured a jerboa, and that of the Afrika Korps.*

(Below:) **GERMAN TANKS.** *German intervention put a brake on the rapid British advance in Cyrenaica.*

conferred on Paris by the League of Nations. Operations were launched against Vichy forces in Iraq, Lebanon and northern Palestine. Units of the Foreign Legion and the 'Free French' raised the Cross of Lorraine and fought alongside British, Indian and Australian troops against the Armée du Levant (including other units of the Foreign Legion), which surrendered on 11 July 1941. The defeated Vichy soldiers who were unwilling to join the 'Free French' returned to France.

THE *AFRIKA KORPS* ENTERS THE FRAY

The landing of divisions of the German *Afrika Korps* at Tripoli in February 1941 shifted the balance of power in the field. In just three weeks the forces led by General Erwin Rommel advanced almost 1,000km, recapturing

Cyrenaica (12 April) and forcing the Allies to hole up in the fortress of Tobruk. The lightning German and Italian advance reached the frontier with Egypt. In North Africa, fighting took place along a thin but very long strip (Tripoli is 2,000km from Alexandria), which brought out all of Rommel's strategic ability and his masterly use of armour. A lack of sufficient fresh troops and supplies proved decisive: by leaving Rommel with only a very limited number of armoured units, Hitler had missed an opportunity to conquer Egypt in turn forcing the British out of the Mediterranean

COLONIAL ITALIAN TROOPS IN NORTH AFRICA.

LEADERS

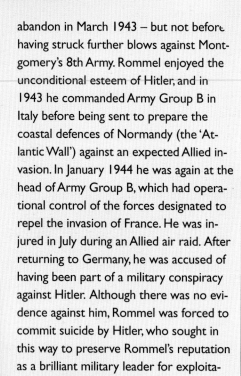

ERWIN ROMMEL

Born in 1891, Erwin Rommel served as an officer in World War I and was awarded Germany's highest military decoration. In 1937 he was put in charge of Hitler's personal security detail. Having been promoted to the rank of general, he commanded an armoured division in the French campaign in 1941. The following year he was put in command of the Afrika Korps. Nicknamed the 'Desert Fox' during the war in North Africa, Rommel was a brilliant strategist who employed armoured forces to great effect, and he used to direct operations from a captured British armoured car. After the capture of Tobruk in May 1942, he was made a field marshal. His retreat in Tunisia was a strategic masterpiece on a par with his victories in North Africa, which he was forced to abandon in March 1943 – but not before having struck further blows against Montgomery's 8th Army. Rommel enjoyed the unconditional esteem of Hitler, and in 1943 he commanded Army Group B in Italy before being sent to prepare the coastal defences of Normandy (the 'Atlantic Wall') against an expected Allied invasion. In January 1944 he was again at the head of Army Group B, which had operational control of the forces designated to repel the invasion of France. He was injured in July during an Allied air raid. After returning to Germany, he was accused of having been part of a military conspiracy against Hitler. Although there was no evidence against him, Rommel was forced to commit suicide by Hitler, who sought in this way to preserve Rommel's reputation as a brilliant military leader for exploitation by Nazi propaganda.

(Above:) The half-track from which Rommel commanded operations. (Left:) Rommel examines a map, together with General Clavi.

ITALIAN COLONIAL HELMETS.
The standard model was made from cotton-lined cork, while the helmet of the bersaglieri had a small pocket for their distinctive plume. The insignia on the front are made from pressed brass.

at a time when they were still highly vulnerable.

In order to free Tobruk, the British launched a counter-attack, denominated Operation 'Battleaxe', which aimed to breach the German–Italian lines and 'destroy' the German forces. The attack was halted by a barrage of fire from 88mm anti-aircraft guns used by Rommel as anti-tank guns and positioned in well-camouflaged trenches.

The overwhelming numerical superiority of the British forces was to no avail and they were unable to breach the mobile, flexible defence organized by the 'Desert Fox'. After this setback, Churchill replaced General Archibald Wavell with Claude Auchinleck, formerly Commander-in-Chief in India. The British only managed to break the siege of Tobruk in November 1941, and the Axis forces (which had lost 33,000 men, mostly Italians, and over 300 tanks) then withdrew to El Agheila. This was yet another partial success in this 'accordion war': the enormous distances involved left the British (who had regained the initiative) exposed, just as they had caused the stalemate after the earlier Axis victories. The British success crowned Churchill's dream to obtain a clear-cut victory in North Africa, though at a cost that was to prove very high: the heavy reinforcements sent to North Africa were at the expense of Singapore, the bastion of the British

FRENCH HEAVY MACHINE GUN.
De Gaulle wrestled many colonial possessions from the Vichy forces and Cameroon, Chad, French Congo and Gabon fell under the control of the 'Free French'. Some units commanded by generals loyal to De Gaulle fought in the North African campaign against the Axis armies.

(Right:) **AVOIDING WASTE.** *British propaganda designed to encourage the prudent use of resources.*

(Far right:) **WAR BONDS.** *The US population was invited to finance the cost of the war.*

WASTE HELPS THE ENEMY

CONSERVE MATERIAL

Don't Let That Shadow Touch Them
Buy **WAR BONDS**

LEADERS

BERNARD LAW MONTGOMERY

The battle in the African desert in October 1942 marked the rise of a new star in the firmament of Allied commanders. Born in 1887, Bernard Law Montgomery (familiarly known as 'Monty') served on the French front in World War I and in India and Palestine during the 1930s. He became a general in 1937, and in 1942 succeeded Claude Auchinleck as head of the 8th Army. His victory at El Alamein made him a popular hero and he was greatly loved by his troops. 'Monty' planned his military operations meticulously, and staunchly held the principle that battles should be won with the minimum loss of life. An energetic, brusque-mannered man and a great organizer, he seized the opportunity offered by his new command, reviving morale and galvanizing a force that had become demoralized by the course of events in North Africa. He subsequently took part in the Allied landings in Sicily and in the Italy campaign; here he was under American command and relations were often tense. In June 1944 he led the British forces in the invasion of Normandy and was involved in facing the German counter-attack in the Ardennes. During the offensive that followed the Allied landings, he often clashed with Eisenhower, whose strategy of a broad front for the final attack on Germany he did not share. His insistence on giving priority to the capture of the French city of Caen attracted considerable criticism and above all hostility from many American generals. This was accentuated when he claimed the credit for the Allies' success in blocking the German counter-attack in the Ardennes forests. Popular with the troops for his informal, direct manner, on the eve of battle he would often turn to some low-ranking soldier or other with a quip or confident prediction of victory.

He received the surrender of the enemy forces in northern Germany on 4 May 1945. In the immediate aftermath of the war he was made 1st Viscount Montgomery of Alamein and commanded the British occupation troops in Germany. He was Deputy Supreme Commander of NATO forces in Europe from 1951 to 1958. He died in 1976.

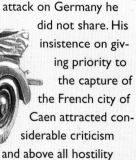

(Above:) Bernard Montgomery. (Left:) The open Humber staff car, known as the 'Old Faithful', in which Montgomery generally moved around.

(Left:) **BRITISH INTERNMENT CAMP IN NORTH AFRICA.**

(Below:) **BRITISH PRISONERS.**
One of the features of the desert campaign was the large number of prisoners taken on both sides. The speed of military operations often left entire units cut off.

Empire in the Far East. Britain and its Prime Minister would pay heavily for this decision when, shortly afterwards, Japan launched its offensive to conquer Asia.

THE BRITISH 8TH ARMY FIGHTS BACK

At the beginning of 1942 the situation in North Africa was that the British and Axis forces were facing each other along the border of Cyrenaica; in other words, they were where they had been a year before. In June, Rommel anticipated an enemy offensive and advanced 500km, forcing the British into a hasty retreat. Two Italian Army Groups and the *Afrika Korps* won a crushing victory at Tobruk, taking 26,000 prisoners and forcing the British

to retreat once again to Egypt. The stalemate in the desert war continued to worry Churchill, but things changed with the reorganization of the 8th Army, which was placed under the command of General Bernard Montgomery. It was re-equipped with vehicles and new weapons, and morale improved. By August the British had military superiority (11 divisions, four of which were armoured, against ten Axis divisions). At the end of the month Rommel opted for another sudden surprise attack and launched a thrust against the southern flank of the British defensive line. His armoured columns were met by a massive barrage of

(Right:) **CAMOUFLAGE NETS.**
British gun batteries camouflaged against attack by the 'Hun'.

(Far right:) **CAPTURED *AFRIKA KORPS* SOLDIERS IN THE MIDDLE OF THE DESERT.**

BATTLES

EL ALAMEIN

Between 23 October and 4 November 1942 the fiercest of all the battles fought in the North African desert took place at El Alamein, a village about 80km west of Alexandria. Although Churchill had been pressing for rapid action, Montgomery only launched the attack when he was sure he could obtain a crushing victory. The reasons for Churchill's insistence were both strategic and political: the British Prime Minister wanted the offensive to start before the Allied landings in North Africa (Operation 'Torch'), set for early November. Success against Rommel would have encouraged the French in North Africa to greet the Allies with favour and would have dissuaded the Spanish dictator, Franco, from allowing German troops into Spanish Morocco and Spain. The attack commenced when Montgomery had a clear-cut numerical and qualitative advantage. British air superiority served to hinder Axis troop movements and disrupt supply lines. The latter suffered from a shortage of fuel, which limited the range of

SECOND BATTLE OF EL ALAMEIN (Oct.–Nov. 1942)

Ghazal
Sidi Abdel Rahman
MEDITERRANEAN SEA

4 November
1st, 7th and 10th armoured divisions pass through breach

El Alamein
XXX CORPS
X CORPS
XII CORPS

Axis armoured corps

Axis minefields

Axis infantry

8th Army minefields

8th Army attacks

Main Afrika Korps movements

action of the Panzerarmee and forced it to disperse its mobile units. The British fixed the attack to coincide with a full moon, which enabled them to attack at

night and open passages through the minefields for their tanks. When the offensive commenced, Rommel was convalescing in Austria. He rushed back, arriving on the scene two days later to find that the Axis troops had lost half of their tanks. The disparity in forces was also enormous: at the start of the massive barrage of shelling (the prelude to the British infantry attack), the British had 200,000 troops compared with 105,000 Germans and Italians. They also had the edge in terms of weapons: over 1,000 tanks (including new 40t Churchills and American Shermans, which could knock out German anti-tank guns from a long range) as opposed to 540 on the Axis side; 1,000 artillery guns against 480; 530 aircraft against 350; and 1,400 anti-tank guns against 744. About 20,000 Italians and 10,000 Germans were taken prisoner. Of the 5,000 parachutists of the Italian Folgore division, fewer than 300 returned to Italy. If Stalingrad was to prove the turning point of the conflict in Europe, El Alamein was the turning point for the war in North Africa.

The American-made M3 Grant, used by the British in the battle.

IN MEMORY OF A BRITISH OFFICER. *In the Libyan desert, a German soldier buries an enemy officer.*

fire and they had to fall back. They also had fuel reserves for just one day. The *Afrika Korps* was forced to return to its original positions, where it dug in to wait for the next enemy attack.

On the night of 23 October, a day before the full moon, the British 8th Army launched a fresh offensive with infantry and artillery. Instead of trying to push the enemy back to its strongholds, the objective was to destroy methodically the enemy's capacity for offensive action. At the beginning of the battle there was a clear disparity in forces: the British had 1,450 tanks compared with 540 on the German–Italian side, few of which had weapons comparable to those of the British. British air superiority was even greater: 96 squadrons against 350 planes.

Furthermore, less than half the supplies expected by Rommel reached their destination, because Axis transport ships were targeted by the RAF in the Mediterranean. Montgomery used the tactical advantage offered by his superiority in tank forces to land some decisive punches on the enemy, which was subjected to massive British artillery fire.

After a series of offensive thrusts carried out by his tank units, Montgomery managed to breach the enemy lines at the link between the Italian army and the Afrika Korps. Heavily outnumbered, further resistance around El Alamein was futile and the surviving units had no choice but to withdraw precipitously towards the Tunisian frontier.

ERWIN ROMMEL. *Although suffering from bad health, the 'Desert Fox' managed to keep Montgomery's 8th Army in check even while retreating towards Tunisia. The crushing numerical superiority of the Allies would ultimately frustrate the brilliant plans of one of Germany's sharpest strategists.*

(Right:) **BOGGED DOWN IN THE MUD.** *German motorbikes and horsedrawn vehicles find the going rough in the Balkans.*

(Below:) **FORMATION OF STUKA BOMBERS.**

THE GERMAN INVASION OF THE BALKANS

The desperate situation of the Italian troops in Albania at the beginning of 1941 had forced Hitler to put back the date of his invasion of the Soviet Union. Having secured the support of Romania, Hungary and Bulgaria (the latter joined the Tripartite Pact on 1 March 1941), Germany could also count on the benevolent neutrality of Yugoslavia to extend its sphere of influence in the Balkans, a valuable premise for the opening of the Russian campaign. However, on 27 March 1941 a military coup in Yugoslavia overturned the Regent, Prince Paul, who, after having passionately attempted a diplomatic balancing act in order to keep his country out of the war, had joined the Tripartite Pact a few days previously.

Hitler's decision to invade Yugoslavia – in order to gain complete control of the Balkans, help his ally out of a jam and keep the British out of Greece – resulted in a surprise attack on 6 April, when Axis forces invaded the country. The 12th Army under Field Marshal Wilhelm List proceeded from Bulgarian territory in the direction of Belgrade, while the 2nd Army under General Weichs crossed the Yugoslav border from the north.

The Hungarian 3rd Army intervened from Hungary, while the Italian 1st Army commanded by General Vittorio Ambrosio was deployed along the north-east frontier. At dawn on 6 April the Luftwaffe bombed Belgrade, even though it had been declared an open city. In just two weeks the Yugoslav resistance was crushed and the country was carved up; a German protectorate was set up in Serbia and Slovenia, Macedonia was ceded to Bulgaria and an Italian-controlled Fascist state was established in Croatia. List's 12th Army pushed into Greece from Bulgaria and

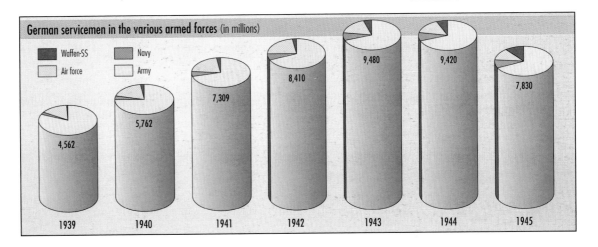

German servicemen in the various armed forces (in millions)

- Waffen-SS
- Air force
- Navy
- Army

4,562 — 1939
5,762 — 1940
7,309 — 1941
8,410 — 1942
9,480 — 1943
9,420 — 1944
7,830 — 1945

B A T T L E S

THE AIRBORNE ASSAULT ON CRETE

The *Sprung nach Kreta*, or invasion of Crete, was the brainchild of General Kurt Student, a veteran of the air force in World War I. It was the first major German airborne operation in World War II. The objective was to consolidate the conquests of the Axis forces in the Balkans, which had culminated in the capture of Athens on 27 April 1941. On 20 May, the appearance of German paratroopers in the skies above the island caught the British garrison (and two Greek divisions) under General Bernard Freyberg by surprise. The success of this new version of the *Blitzkrieg* – the British considered that Crete impossible to take without having control of the sea – was due to a combination of two elements: aerial bombing of the airfields followed by the arrival of paratroopers.

Although Freyberg had been informed about the German operation and had requested reinforcements, his superiors refused any help whatsoever so as not to compromise the secrecy of Ultra, the code being used to decrypt the messages exchanged by the Germans while planning the final details of the attack. Freyberg only had six tanks, and the handful of planes at his disposal was unable to intercept the airborne troops arriving in gliders and transport planes. After ten days, during which the Luftwaffe controlled the skies, thwarting any possibility of intervention by the Royal Navy (which lost three cruisers and six destroyers), and notwithstanding heavy German losses, Student secured victory. The Maleme and Retimo airfields on the north of the island soon fell into German hands. The British suffered about 3,000 dead and injured, while 18,000 soldiers were evacuated. In the process, a significant amount of British shipping was destroyed by the German air force and about 12,000 soldiers were taken prisoner. The capture of Crete was a brilliant success for the Germans, giving them a presence in a zone that was strategically vital for the British Mediterranean Fleet, which thereby lost its control of the Aegean.

The capture of the island, which was achieved entirely from the air, was one of the most audacious military enterprises in the entire conflict. However, the high number of German casualties (about 4,000 dead and a similar number of wounded) discouraged the Germans from conducting similar airborne operations in enemy territory. Soon afterwards a Greek partisan resistance movement, aided by some British survivors, became active. The Germans abandoned the island in 1944.

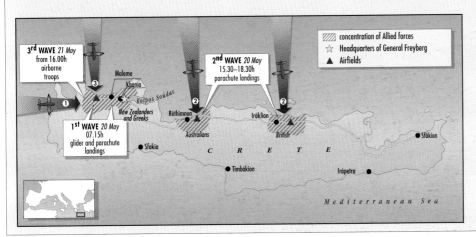

3rd WAVE 21 May from 16.00h airborne troops

2nd WAVE 20 May 15.30–18.30h parachute landings

1st WAVE 20 May 07.15h glider and parachute landings

///// concentration of Allied forces
☆ Headquarters of General Freyberg
▲ Airfields

Maleme
Khania
Kolpos Soúdas
New Zealanders and Greeks
Réthimnon
Iráklion
Australians
British
Sfákion
Sfakia
C R E T E
Timbákion
Irápetra

Mediterranean Sea

(Right:) **THE CLAWS OF THE AXIS.**
Canadian poster inviting mothers to protect their children by buying war bonds.

(Below:) **A GERMAN SOLDIER THROWING A HAND GRENADE.**

quickly reached Salonika, cutting off a large Greek force stationed in Thrace. The superior Axis forces had the better of the Greek troops, who were aided by four British divisions. Advancing towards the west coast of Greece, the German army cut off the Greek divisions in Albania. With a series of rapid manoeuvres, the Germans outflanked the British defensive line and resistance soon collapsed. The British therefore had no option but to evacuate to Crete from Piraeus and the Peloponnese.

While the outcome of the war in North Africa was still uncertain, the Balkan campaign was yet another demonstration of the effectiveness of the *Blitzkrieg*. Nazi Germany was thus able to extend its control of continental Europe and acquire a massive source of foodstuffs and also raw materials for the Reich.

THE 'LEND-LEASE' ACT

At the end of 1940 Britain's need for war supplies, combined with the serious state of its finances, transformed its relationship with the United States into a full-blown economic and military alliance. After Roosevelt was re-elected for the third consecutive time in November 1940, the policy of American aid obtained legal sanction in the form of the 'Lend-Lease' Act, approved by Congress on

WEAPONS

THE *BISMARCK*

The *Bismarck* was the pride of German military shipbuilding. This colossal 51,000t battleship had eight 380mm and nineteen 152mm guns and a top speed of 20 knots.

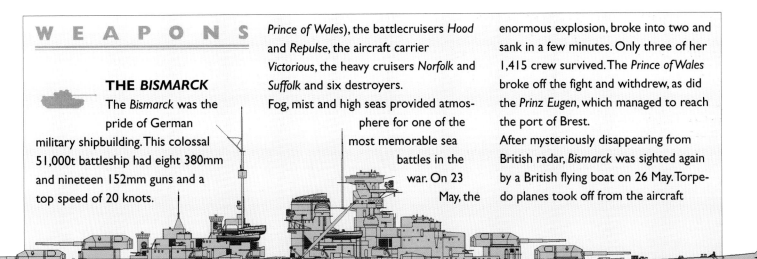

Prince of Wales), the battlecruisers *Hood* and *Repulse*, the aircraft carrier *Victorious*, the heavy cruisers *Norfolk* and *Suffolk* and six destroyers.

Fog, mist and high seas provided atmosphere for one of the most memorable sea battles in the war. On 23 May, the two German ships were sighted by the cruiser *Suffolk*. The next day the *Bismarck* and *Prinz Eugen* opened fire on the *Prince of Wales* and the *Hood*, which had moved in and engaged battle. A 380mm shell from the *Bismarck* made a direct hit on the *Hood*, which, following an enormous explosion, broke into two and sank in a few minutes. Only three of her 1,415 crew survived. The *Prince of Wales* broke off the fight and withdrew, as did the *Prinz Eugen*, which managed to reach the port of Brest.

After mysteriously disappearing from British radar, *Bismarck* was sighted again by a British flying boat on 26 May. Torpedo planes took off from the aircraft

Commanded by Capt. Ernst Lindemann, it left its base at Gdynia in the Baltic on 18 May 1941 and headed into the North Atlantic together with the heavy cruiser *Prinz Eugen* (18,000t) under Captain Brinkmann. Their mission was to prey on Allied convoys and create a serious threat for them. The ships were under the overall command of Admiral Günther Lütjens. Alerted by intelligence despatches, the British stepped up aerial reconnaissance in the North Sea and the Home Fleet mobilized its full forces. On 21 May, the German ships were spotted by British reconnaissance planes in the Norwegian port of Bergen. The following day a British force commanded by Admiral John Tovey sailed from the Scottish base of Scapa Flow. It consisted of two battleships (the *King George V* and the spanking new

carrier *Ark Royal*. In the few remaining hours before the German battleship could reach the protective umbrella of Luftwaffe planes based in France, her destiny unfolded. At dusk, before the *Bismarck* reached the arm of sea leading to the anchorage in the French port of Brest, a torpedo hit her rudder. At 8.47am on the morning of 27 May, the *Bismarck* began to be pounded by the combined firepower of the British naval units, which reduced it to a helpless wreck. Two hours later it sank. Of a crew of some 2,300 sailors, just 110 were saved.

The sinking of the pride of the Kriegsmarine ended one of the longest naval battles in the war. From that point on, the war in the North Atlantic was waged almost exclusively by Karl Dönitz's submarine fleet.

(Above:) The profile of the battleship. (Left:) Bow view. The Bismarck *was the pride of the German Navy.*

WEAPONS

DÖNITZ'S 'WOLF PACKS'

The man who was chiefly responsible for the strategy to throttle the British economy by blocking the flow of supplies on the Atlantic routes was Admiral Karl Dönitz, commander of the German submarine fleet. His U-boats (an abbreviation of *Unterseeboot*) were the main threat to American convoys bound for Britain. In September 1939, the Germans had 57 submarines; by July 1942 that figure had risen to 140. Their attacks on Allied shipping reached a peak in the winter of 1942/43. Operating both in the Arctic (against ships bound for ports in northern Russia) and in the North Atlantic (from French and Norwegian bases) the

U-boats – Type IX vessels with a cruising range of 20,000km – moved in 'packs'. Upon receiving orders from base, they gathered in specific areas of the ocean and inflicted heavy losses on merchant shipping and escort units. The 'packs' launched night attacks, preferably against the wind and preferably on the surface, so as to exploit their greater speed with respect to the escorts. Surface attacks became gradually more risky as Allied airpower increased and special anti-submarine units, equipped with advanced technology (including asdic, which could pinpoint submerged submarines, and depth charges), were formed. A turning point in the submarine war came when the Allies discovered the key to decrypting 'Enigma', enabling them to direct many of their convoys away from areas where the 'wolf packs' were operating.

(Top:) Admiral Karl Dönitz. (Below:) A U-boat leaving its base on the French coast for the North Atlantic. (Bottom left:) German Navy magazine.

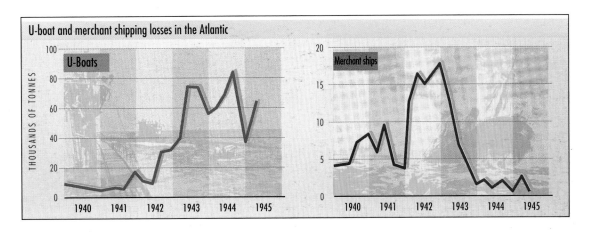

U-boat and merchant shipping losses in the Atlantic

11 March 1941. With this act, one of the most significant political events of the entire conflict, America became *de jure* 'the arsenal of democracies'.

The President had full powers to make American resources available to states whose protection was deemed necessary to America's security, and the faculty to decide which nations should benefit (initially Great Britain, but later China and the Soviet Union as well). These nations could purchase materials on the basis of a promise to pay at the end of the war. In exchange, American capital was allowed into markets that had until then been controlled exclusively by the British. In

the meantime, the British economy was entirely oriented towards war production. The Anglo-American Chiefs of Staff also agreed on guidelines for cooperating in theatres of war in Europe, Africa, East Asia and the Pacific. Priority was given to the maritime security of the North Atlantic (the main focus of the conflict remained the European seaboard of the Atlantic) and it was established that the defeat of Germany was the Allies' prime objective – the concept known as 'Germany first'.

Militarily, Great Britain had responsibility for the Mediterranean, and the North Atlantic became a strategic link between the two countries.

ROOSEVELT AND CHURCHILL.
The key features of the American President's vision of the future world order emerged at a meeting between the two statesmen at Placentia Bay, Newfoundland, in August 1941. Given the economic potential of the United States, Roosevelt wanted a new framework of international relations where in the future there were no restrictions on American goods.

The long-term Anglo-American agreement gave no role at all to Russia in this 'anti-Hitler coalition'. It was the German invasion of the Soviet Union on 22 June 1941 that led to a de facto alliance between the three Allied powers, though this was never formalized at a diplomatic level.

THE BATTLE OF THE ATLANTIC

Even more than the war in the North African desert and the Mediterranean, Britain's survival depended on the North Atlantic convoy routes. The U-boat campaign against the Allied convoys ran in Germany's favour until at least the middle of 1942. Between January and March 1942, German submarines sank 1,250,000 tons of mercantile shipping, which, on an annual basis, was four times greater than the previous year. From their bases on the

French Atlantic coast, U-boats headed out into the waters of the North Atlantic to hunt convoys leaving Halifax (Nova Scotia) for Britain. Besides submarines, the Germans also had a flotilla of armed merchant raiders, which posed a serious threat to Allied shipping in the most far-off corners of the ocean. In the second half of 1942, Allied losses diminished and the United States speeded up its shipbuilding programme: its shipyards

**ON PATROL IN THE
ENGLISH CHANNEL.**
*British patrol boats
armed with Lewis
machine guns patrolling
the Channel waters.*

BRITISH DESTROYERS. *Equipped with new devices that were effective in hunting down German submarines in the North Atlantic, the escort ships proved invaluable in ensuring the safe passage of Allied convoys.*

ENIGMA

Similar to a typewriter, Enigma was an electromagnetic device used by the Germans to encrypt their documents. One of the wars within the war was the struggle by the British to crack the secret of this device, which had been perfected and sold by the German engineer Arthur Scherbius in 1929. All of Germany's land, sea and air forces were equipped with Enigma. Its strength lay in the fact that, on pressing a key, a system of meshed wheels was activated in such a way that one letter was never paired with another even after the same combination had been struck a countless number of times. If used properly, this scrambling device was indecipherable. However, the system had a weakness: in order to decipher the message the receiver had to know the exact position of the disks at the beginning of the coded transmission. To set up the machines, they had to use code words capable of synchronizing the rotors of the different machines, transmitters and receivers. Some of these were generally very simple, for example that related to the day of the month. More confidential messages were encrypted two or three times in a row before being transmitted, using different codes each time. The task of cracking the secrets of Enigma

was entrusted to the British Government's Code and Cipher School at Bletchley Park near London. In July 1941 the British captured the codebooks used for transmitting weather reports from the German ships *München* and *Lauenburg*, and from then until the beginning of 1942 were able to work out the position of the U-boats.

The battle waged by the team of codebreakers and analysts, led by the mathematician Alan Turing (recruited for his talent as a chess player), only really began to pay dividends at the end of 1943, when the decryption work was transferred to the United States and 40 primitive computers were perfected that were capable of working at the same time. At the beginning of 1942 the Germans started using a new and more sophisticated version of Enigma, and the U-boats once again became a serious threat for the Allies' eastbound Atlantic convoys. But in October of the same year the British captured codebooks from an enemy submarine that was sinking off the Egyptian coast. The Battle of the Atlantic was definitively won.

(Above:) An Enigma machine.

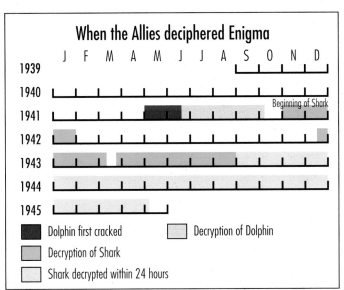

When the Allies deciphered Enigma

	J	F	M	A	M	J	J	A	S	O	N	D
1939												
1940												
1941												
1942												
1943												
1944												
1945												

Beginning of Shark

■ Dolphin first cracked   Decryption of Dolphin

■ Decryption of Shark

Shark decrypted within 24 hours

(Right:) **CHURCHILL'S CELEBRATED TRIBUTE TO THE BRITISH PILOTS.**

(Far right:) **INFORMATION LEAK.**
A poster featuring a drowning sailor warns of the serious danger of loose talk.

turned out three Liberty ships (10,000t vessels) every day.

Furthermore, even though more advanced German submarines came into service, the Admiralty and the RAF developed new techniques for defending the convoys, deploying escort support groups and hunting down the 'wolf packs' with long-range armed reconnaissance planes. The reversal in the trend of the war in the North Atlantic was the result of technical, political and military factors. The use of asdic (a sonar device fitted on Allied destroyers and used for locating submarines), the increasingly extensive air cover provided by American Catalina flying-boats (about 1,100km from the British Isles, 1,000km from Canada and 650km from the southern coast of Iceland) and closer cooperation between Washington and London (the American Navy was authorized to escort non-American shipping) enabled the Allies to protect the Atlantic convoys more effectively. The price paid on both

sides in the Battle of the Atlantic was terrible. Between September 1939 and the middle of 1943, 696 of the Kriegsmarine's 830 submarines were sunk, with 25,870 casualties out of total crew figures of 41,000. The Allies lost 2,452 merchant vessels (about 13 million tons of shipping) and 175 warships.

THE ALLIED CONQUEST OF NORTH AFRICA

November 1942 saw a further British-led offensive in North Africa: a large-scale Allied landing (Operation 'Torch') in Algeria and Morocco. Having entered the war at the end of the previous year, the United States chose this as their first direct military operation in the Mediterranean. Montgomery's attack took the Axis forces by surprise. In Rommel's retreat, 40,000

ON WATCH.
Lookout duty on an escort ship.

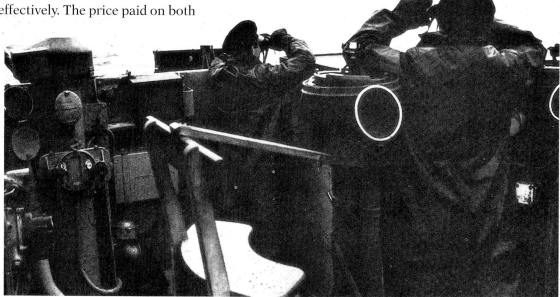

WAR ARCHIVES: THE SUBMARINE WAR

Submarines were used extensively by all the main belligerents, both for attack and for transport purposes. Strategies varied according to the objective. The introduction of technical innovations, which increased submarine speeds and extended the amount of time they could remain submerged, and the development of radar detection systems were of decisive importance in the submarine war. The main objective of the German units was to hit Allied (especially British) merchant shipping. Over 2,000 Allied ships, the equivalent of about 14.5 million tons, were sunk in the course of the conflict. German losses were also significant, amounting to about three-quarters of the entire submarine fleet. The Japanese produced a large number of vessels, which they basically employed to destroy enemy warships. Some models were later used to carry supplies to garrisons holding out on islands surrounded by the Americans; others, weighing more than 6,500t, were capable of transporting up to three bombers and had a radius of action of 37,000 nautical miles.

AGAINST THE DEFEATISTS.
The outcome of the war in Africa sharply eroded consensus for the Fascist regime among Italians.

troops fell into enemy hands. On 23 January 1943, the British 8th Army captured Tripoli and Italy lost the last scrap of its African empire. Two large Allied armies occupied the North African coast: Montgomery's 8th Army in Libya and Eisenhower's 1st Army in Algeria. Rommel's armoured units, retreating east, had no option but to join German forces sent from France to Tunisia to defend the Atlas Mountains. When Rommel arrived in Tunisia, he had almost 30,000 Germans and about 48,000 Italians under his command.

At the beginning of February 1943 the Axis forces amounted to just 100,000 men, and there was also an enormous difference in the armoured strength of the two sides. Despite this, Rommel gave yet another demonstration of his tactical prowess by launching a surprise attack against the American 1st Armoured Division, with an encircling manoeuvre that only confirmed his remarkable ability to concentrate inferior forces at a precise point in order to exploit a temporary margin of superiority.

Worn down by the slow but unstoppable Allied advance, in the spring of 1943 the Axis forces were in a critical condition. On 13 May, overwhelmed by superior enemy forces and with no further supplies, the units of the German General Jürgen von Arnim and the 1st Army commanded by the Italian Giovanni Messe surrendered after a major battle on the outskirts of Tunis. A quarter of a million German and Italian troops surrendered – the first capitulation of a German force since the beginning of the war. The Mediterranean was then reopened to Allied shipping and the

TALLY OF KILLS.
The pilots of the RAF, who became known as 'the Few', were not all British. There were also Canadians, Australians, South Africans, New Zealanders and American volunteers, along with Poles and Frenchmen. (Photograph by Robert Capa.)

(Left:) **UNITED WE WIN.** *All American workers, including blacks, were urged to make a supreme effort.*

(Far left:) **THE BOMBING OF ROTTERDAM.** *The suffering inflicted on the civilian population by Allied bombing raids in Holland was severe, as depicted in a poster distributed by the Germans.*

Italian Navy ceased to be an active combat force. The opening of a second front took the pressure off the besieged Russians as Nazi troops were re-stationed.

If the result of the long African campaign was a major humiliation for Hitler (though he was convinced that the outcome of his design to achieve continental dominion would be won or lost on the Russian steppes), for Mussolini it was a total political and military disaster. Driven by a desire to save face in Africa, Hitler and Mussolini had divergent views on future developments in the conflict. Hitler's delay in sending troops to Rommel had made it impossible to exploit fully a long series of partial victories, and, following the capitulation in Tunisia, Germany and Italy were deprived of a large number of experienced

troops, which could have been used to block the imminent invasion of Sicily.

Both countries paid heavily for their erroneous evaluation of the capacity of the Axis forces to defend Tunisia, at a time when the Allies' air and sea forces had put an almost complete block on the strip of sea separating Sicily from North Africa.

The 'soft underbelly of the Axis', as Churchill defined fascist Italy, had no choice but to continue the war as a satellite nation of Nazi Germany. A few months later, the Allied landings in Sicily bore out the British Prime Minister's prediction that the Mediterranean was a gateway – peripheral, but nonetheless important – to Europe, which was still under the heel of the Nazis.

LANDING EXERCISES. *British soldiers conducting exercises on the North African beaches in 1943. The opening of the 'second front' in Europe was the subject of lengthy negotiations between Roosevelt, Churchill and Stalin.*

Barbarossa and Pearl Harbor

The sixth months between the Nazi invasion of the Soviet Union, the Japanese attack on the American base of Pearl Harbor, and Italy and Germany's declaration of war on the United States were a decisive phase in the world conflict. From then on two conflicts were waged: one for the control of Europe and the other, between the United States and Japan, for strategic domination in the Far East. The attack on the Soviet Union marked the beginning of the greatest land war in history, not only in terms of the number of casualties on the East front through to May 1945, but also due to the scale of the forces involved and the strongly ideological nature of the clash, with Nazi Germany pitted against Stalin's Russia, and the Third Reich's declared intention to wipe out the Soviet Union as a national, economic and social entity. The direct involvement of the world's leading power, with the opening of a new theatre of operations in Asia *(p.96:)* **INJURED PILOT.** *American airman after a mission.*

(p.97:) **PEARL HARBOR IN FLAMES.**

(RIGHT:) WE OF THE WESTERN FRONT. *Wehrmacht publication.*

and the Pacific, marked the founding of an 'anti-Hitler coalition' that was to obtain victory in 1945. Through its global military commitment, the United States achieved undisputed supremacy in the air and at sea and, with its crucial industrial, food, financial and logistical resources, became the powerhouse of the Allies. The industrial might of the United States at the end of the war bore out Roosevelt's prediction that the catastrophe of the conflict would pave the way for the 'American century'.

HITLER'S OBJECTIVES

Operation 'Barbarossa' (from the nickname of Frederick I, the king of Germany and Holy Roman Emperor in the 12th century) was intended by Hitler to establish

the 'world dominion of the Reich' by gaining control of eastern Europe. Unlike the French campaign, the Soviet Union was to be conquered with the same cruelty that had characterized wars in the Middle Ages, and was not just to be defeated militarily. The invasion of June 1941 was part of Hitler's plan for continental dominion whereby the Reich would stretch from the Atlantic to the Urals. It represented an upping of the stakes inherent in the notion of a 'total war', the aim of which was to destroy any military power to the east of Germany and to bring about the 'final solution of the Jewish question in Europe'.

German planners reckoned it would take ten weeks to

MUSSOLINI AND HITLER. *In the period between the German invasion of the Soviet Union, the Japanese attack on Pearl Harbor, and Italy and Germany's declaration of war on the United States (December 1941), Hitler's plan for a worldwide lightning war came about. However, the Reich's attempt to annihilate the Soviet Union and avoid America's entry into the war failed.*

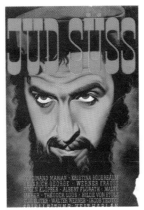

ANTI-SEMITIC PROPAGANDA.
The posters for The Wandering Jew *and* Jud Suss, *the making of which were ordered by Joseph Goebbels, the German Minister of Propaganda. The two films had the declared aim of instilling a hatred of Jews amongst the Germans.*

LEADERS

HEINZ GUDERIAN

Born in 1888 into a family that descended from Prussian landowners, Heinz Guderian was one of the best of Hitler's generals at putting into practice the principles of 'lightning war'. He served in the Great War and was promoted to the rank of general in 1938. In the same year he published a book entitled *Achtung Panzer*, in which he argued that, in a concentrated attack, armoured units were the main offensive weapon and that other forces should be subordinate to them. He commanded an armoured division in the attack on Poland, led the 2nd Panzer Army during the invasion of the Soviet Union, and obtained a string of brilliant successes in the field, at the head of a force that soon called itself the Guderian Panzerarmee. He advanced close to Moscow, but was then ordered to head south towards Kiev to support von Rundstedt. He disagreed with Hitler over this instruction and was dismissed for having wanted to stick to the original attack plan. In February 1943 he was recalled by Hitler and made Inspector-General of Armoured Troops. On 1945 he was appointed Chief of General Staff to replace Kurt Zeitzler, but a few days later was sacked by Hitler; he was taken prisoner by the Americans on 10 May. He died in 1954.

ERICH VON MANSTEIN

Born in the year 1887, tenth child of an aristocratic Prussian family, Erich von Manstein was a career soldier from 1906 onwards. In 1940 he

distinguished himself by making a big impact with his armoured forces in Army Group A's attack on the French and British. He was the supreme German exponent of mobile warfare. During Operation 'Barbarossa' his armoured group advanced 330km in just four days. In 1941 he took command of the 11th Army (in von Rundstedt's Army Group South), with which he overran the Crimea and pushed as far as the Caucasus. The capture of Sebastopol in July 1942 won him the rank of field marshal. In November he assumed command of Army Group Don, operating around Stalingrad. After the surrender of Paulus in March 1943, Manstein, at the head of the new Army Group South, launched a German counter-offensive at Kharkov, obtaining a partial success. An exponent of the war of movement, he fell out of favour with Hitler when the military situation on the Russian front required the application of what Manstein defined as a 'mobile defence' against the counter-attacking Red Army. From March 1944 he no longer played any part in the conflict. He was sentenced to 18 years in prison by a British military court in 1949, but served only four years. He died in 1973.

(Above:) Guderian. (Left:) Von Manstein.

wipe out the Soviet military apparatus with a *Blitzkrieg*. The military objectives went hand in hand with the political ones, namely to gain total control of Europe and thereby force Great Britain into an armistice before (as was considered inevitable) the United States came into the war. Hitler tried to encourage Japan to attack the Soviet Union as part of a global alliance, but to no avail.

Japan's Foreign Minister, Josuke Matsuoka, who until then had negotiated with the Axis countries, was deprived of all authority in July 1941 and Japan then gave priority to expansion in South-East Asia (the 'Great East Asia Co-Prosperity Sphere'). This inevitably meant a conflict with the United States and so Japan decided to cover its back by maintaining neutrality with the Soviet Union.

THE WORDS OF THE FÜHRER.
Young German soldiers on the Russian front listen to a speech by Hitler. A few months before the start of the Russian campaign, Hitler said to his generals: 'The war against the Soviet Union will be such that it cannot be fought in a knightly fashion; it is a war of ideology and racial difference . . . All the officers must rid themselves of all old-fashioned ideology.'

THE *BLITZKRIEG* IN THE EAST

Before the invasion, Hitler declared that the war with the Soviet Union was a 'war of ideology and racial difference'. The ultimate aims were: to enslave the Slavic peoples and erase them as a political entity with a state of their own; to conquer the extensive territories of the east; and to open up 'living space' for German colonists. The Germanization of the lands to the east of the Reich stemmed from an ideological and racial concept. The role of the *Blitzkrieg* in this was to transform European Russia into a German colony and to wipe out entire populations, national entities and racial communities. The continent was to be Germanized through the application of terror and the extermination of the Jews in eastern Europe and the occupied Soviet territories.

Operation Barbarossa

(Left:) **GERMAN PROPAGANDA.**
This German poster reads: 'By making arms for Germany, the Ukrainians will contribute to defending their homeland from the Russians.'

(Far left:) **HOLY RIVER.**
Russian poster from 1942: 'We'll defend Mother Volga!'

was the turning point in the war, and not only in military and strategic terms. The war in the east swept away all humanitarian principles and rules of international law. The subjected populations were not recognized as having any rights whatsoever; no international convention or rule of war would be respected; and the entire wealth of the conquered territories would be put at the service of the German war machine. The Third Reich had no intention of 'liberating' the local populations, as those people in the Baltic and the Ukraine who hoped to gain freedom from the Soviets were to discover. All the battles were conducted with a ruthlessness never hitherto seen in the course of the conflict. Moreover, the mass executions that commenced in the first few days of the invasion, the

massacre of Russian prisoners and the systematic extermination of the Jews by Heinrich Himmler's SS units (by the end of 1941 they had already killed half a million people), and the assassination of political commissars and communist leaders showed that war was conceived as a systematic preventive measure to be used in the clash between peoples and races.

Far from being a military requirement, genocide was deeply engrained in the Nazi ideology of war, a 'total war' from which no civilian must escape and which reduced to ruins the areas the Wehrmacht had to conquer for subsequent Germanization. The results of this grand design were horrifying: by the end of the conflict, the total number of victims in the Soviet Union alone was about twenty million people.

GERMAN INFANTRY.
Coming up behind the armoured divisions, the infantry advanced at an incredible pace: at the height of summer, and with at least 20kg of equipment on their back, the German infantrymen marched an average 25km each day.

BATTLES

OPERATION 'BARBAROSSA'

The surprise attack that was launched against the Soviet Union on 22 June 1941 along a front extending from Finland to the Black Sea involved over three million German soldiers (153 divisions, of which 15 were mechanized and 19 armoured), 600,000 vehicles, 3,600 tanks and over 2,700 planes. In addition to the German army forces, there was a contingent of about 500,000 soldiers made up of Romanians, Slovaks, Finns, Hungarians, Italians and French and Spanish 'volunteers'. The Red Army fielded two and a half million men on the Western front. A similar number was deployed in the Caucasus (against Great Britain, considered a potential enemy by Moscow) and the Far East (against the Japanese). The main attack was made by Army Groups North (Wilhem von Leeb), Centre (Fedor von Bock) and South (Gerd von Rundstedt), which headed for Leningrad, for Moscow and towards the Ukraine and the Caucasus, respectively. The plan of the German High Command was to wipe out the bulk of the Russian forces with a series of encircling manoeuvres in the first three weeks of operations, and applying *Blitzkrieg* principles on such a huge scale produced stunning results. Surprise German air attacks destroyed about half the Russian air force within a week. The mobility of the German tanks (which advanced about 80km a day in the first few weeks) breached the Soviet defensive lines: between 9 and 19 July the Germans took 300,000 prisoners and captured 3,200 tanks and 3,100 heavy guns in a pocket at Smolensk (half-way between Moscow and the German–Russian border). On 10 July, Army Group North occupied Lithuania and reached the river Luga, just 100km from Leningrad. Army Group South, heading for the Crimea, proceeded more slowly because Soviet resistance was stiffer. Aided by Guderian's Panzer group, von Rundstedt obtained one of the most crushing military victories in the war: on 26 September he closed a pincer movement around Kiev, wiping out five Russian armies, capturing 665,000 prisoners (the largest ever bag of prisoners in the history of war operations) and 884 tanks. The Ukraine (the 'granary of Russia'), part of the Crimea and the Donets Basin were occupied. In the first week of October, Army Group Centre completed another encircling movement around Bryansk, capturing 660,000 prisoners, 1,242 tanks and 5,412 heavy guns. At the end of October the blistering German advance came to a halt. The Wehrmacht was worn out and had suffered about half a million casualties. However, although the Russians had lost some four million men, either dead or captured, the Red Army had not fallen apart (indeed, it had been reinforced with the front-line deployment of ten million reservists), Stalin's regime was still intact, and the main objective of Operation 'Barbarossa' – to destroy Soviet military capacity – had not been successfully achieved before the arrival of the rainy season.

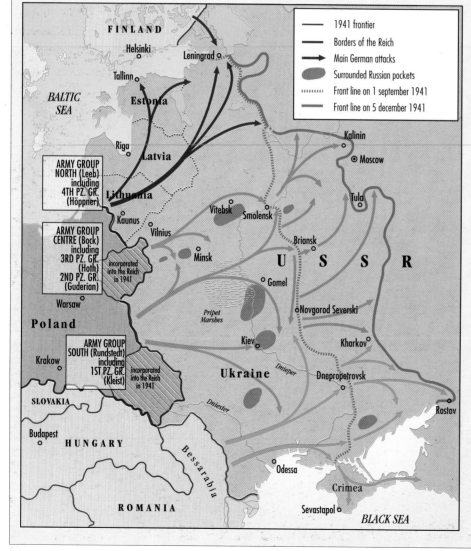

(Left:) **GERMAN WAR PROPAGANDA; HITLER IN A RUSSIAN CARTOON.**

(Below:) **SHATTERED MEN.**
A German officer recalled: 'We saw an immense earth-coloured crocodile marching slowly towards us, from which there arose a quiet murmer. They were Russian prisoners of war...'

SAVING 'MOTHER RUSSIA'

Well trained and well equipped, the German army proved once again that it was a formidable fighting machine. However, its superiority in the field was not enough to achieve the objectives that had been established when the invasion commenced on 22 June. In fact, the outcome of the campaign and of the entire conflict in Europe was determined by the fact that the operation took longer than expected. Furthermore, the strategic dilemma that troubled and divided the German High Command for a whole month – whether to concentrate the weight of the attack in the centre (that is, on Moscow) or to continue the encircling movement on the flanks, heading south-east to the Don basin – was an unexpected benefit for Stalin, giving him valuable time that he exploited to his advantage.

Although caught by surprise, and despite the panic in the country at large, the Russians managed to block the German offensive at the gates of Moscow. The Soviet Union survived thanks to a wide variety of measures that ranged from

L E A D E R S

JOSEPH STALIN

Iosif Vissarionovich Dzhugashvili, known as Stalin ('man of steel'), was born in Georgia in 1879. He was elected General Secretary of the Communist Party in 1922, and after the death of Lenin in 1924 he managed to establish his supremacy in the struggle between the various Bolshevik leaders. The author of a programme of forced industrialization and agricultural collectivization in the Soviet Union, Stalin wielded absolute power, crushing all opposition in the period 1934–37. Until 1939 his 'great terror' policy – an instrument he considered indispensable for bringing about the rapid transformation of society and the economy – swallowed up millions of Russians, who were deported to labour camps. He also purged the top echelons of the Red Army. Caught by surprise by the German attack, he was mainly responsible for the country's military unpreparedness. He was appointed head of the government and Supreme Commander, and presided over the Committee of Defence (also comprising Voroshilov, Beria, Molotov and Malenkov), which ordered total mobilization against the German invader. Stalin also controlled the Stavka (Operations Office), to which the Chiefs of Staff answered. Stalin therefore held all the top positions in the Soviet state. On 3 July 1941, with the country in a desperate situation, Stalin gave a speech on radio in which he presented himself, not as the person who had power of life or death over every Russian, but as the father of a people in danger of being wiped out by the Germans: 'Comrades! Citizens! Brothers and sisters! Men of our army and navy! I am addressing you, my friends . . . A grave danger hangs over our country. How could it have happened that our glorious Red Army surrendered a number of our cities and districts to fascist armies? Is it really true that German fascist troops are invincible, as is ceaselessly trumpeted by the boastful fascist propagandists? Of course not! History shows that there are no invincible armies and never have been. . . . The enemy is cruel and implacable. . . . Thus the issue is one of life or death for the Soviet State . . . The Soviet people must realize this and abandon all heedlessness, they must mobilize themselves and reorganize all their work on new wartime bases, when there can be no mercy to the enemy . . It is not only a war between two armies, it is also a great war of the entire Soviet people against

the German fascist forces. . . . Our war for the freedom of our country will merge with the struggle of the peoples of Europe and America for their independence, for democratic liberties . . . Comrades, our forces are numberless. The overweening enemy will soon learn this to his cost . . . All forces of the people – for the demolition of the enemy! Forward, to our victory!'*

The outcome of World War II gave Stalin undisputed prestige, both at home and abroad, and made the Soviet Union a world superpower in opposition to the United States. The personality cult that built up around him and the system he established survived his death in 1953.

*Translated by and printed in *Soviet Russia Today*, August 1941.

Josif Stalin giving a speech.

(Left:) **SAFE PASSAGE.**
*Bilingual leaflet
distributed by the Germans
to encourage Russian
soldiers to desert.*

(Far left:) **PATRIOTIC WAR.**
*The lightning of the Red
Army impales the Nazi
invader.*

(Below:) **SOVIET T34
TANK.**

relentless patriotic propaganda to the reorganization of the military; the orders given to the political commissars to crush any attempt to desert; the dispatching to the front of generals who had previously been sidelined by Stalin; and even the rehabilitation of the Orthodox Church to foster national unity and a patriotic spirit. 'Mother Russia' was in danger and all means had to be employed to save her.

THE SOVIETS REGAIN THE INITIATIVE

With the arrival on the European front of troops previously stationed in Asia, which increased the Russian forces to more than four million men, the Red Army regained strength. The army

divisions were reorganized and tanks began to roll off the production lines of factories that had been hastily moved beyond the Urals (almost 70% of plant used for military production was saved). The Soviet High Command had new weapons, including battalions of T-34s (the most effective tanks in the war, which often got the better of the short-gun Panzer IV) and Katjuscia missile batteries (known by the Germans as 'Stalin's organs', capable of firing 16 132mm missiles a range of 8,500m in just ten seconds), yet they were unable to break the siege of Kiev. However, they did obtain an enormous political and military result: the bulk of the German forces was drawn away from the capital. The German

PURGES IN THE RED ARMY

The purging of the Red Army's officer class as part of Stalin's policy of terror in 1936–38 was the main cause of the catastrophic state in which the country found itself when Operation 'Barbarossa' was launched: three marshals (out of five), eight admirals, 14 Army commanders (out of 16), nine-tenths of all the army corps commanders and 35,000 officers out of a total of 80,000 were accused of treason or sabotage and executed, mostly without a trial. The most illustrious victim was the Chief of Staff Mikhayl Nikolayevich Tukhachevsky, who had led the Red Army to victory in the Civil War of 1918–20, and had been primarily responsible for reorganizing the Russian military to meet the requirements of modern warfare. The reasons for what amounted to a decapitation of the upper ranks of the Soviet army were largely political: it is reasonable to suppose that large sectors of the armed forces were not in agreement with the policy of forced collectivization that Stalin had embarked on in the Russian countryside. However, over and above all this, what was doubly tragic was the conception of war that prevailed in Stalin's ruling group. In giving the predominant role in the fight to the infantry, the Soviets paid an enormous human cost in the course of Operation 'Barbarossa'.

(Right:) **COMMISSAR OF DEFENCE.**
A political more than a military commander, Semyon K. Timoshenko imposed iron discipline on the Red Army.

(Far right:) **THE RED FLAG.**
Stalin's generals lead the Soviet Union's fightback.

troops were advancing towards Moscow: in early October the advanced armoured units of the Wehrmacht could see the towers of the Kremlin in the distance. They had not suffered losses comparable to those of the Russians, but after an extremely rapid advance they began to suffer from a shortage of basic materials, the enormous length of their supply lines, a lack of rest and the inevitable deterioration in the weather.

On 7 November the traditional parade in Red Square marking the anniversary of the October Revolution was a demonstration (and not only symbolic) of the country's capacity to resist. Although the cold weather assisted German tank operations, there had been a 65% reduction in the number of mechanized vehicles available for the final attack on the capital, and Hitler's generals were themselves doubtful about their chances of completing the

operation within the projected time scale. The massive German thrust across the Russian steppes had come to a halt. The main objectives – Moscow, Leningrad and the Volga – had been reached but not taken.

On 5 December 1941 the Russians attacked the German armies and broke the German encirclement of the capital. This was the first Soviet victory in the war. The push by Zhukov against the Army Group Centre, assisted by Timoshenko on the south-west front and Koniev's forces in the Kalinin area to the north, was a mirror copy of the plan that had enabled the Wehrmacht to inflict enormous losses on the Red Army during the summer. Turning the defensive battle into a desperate attack on the invader, by Christmas the Russian armies had aroused in

GERMAN OPTIMISM.
After marching for hundreds of kilometres, the Wehrmacht came to a halt on the outskirts of Moscow. A war machine that had until that moment been considered invincible had to cope with the adverse weather conditions of the Russian autumn.

WAR ARCHIVES: CIVILIAN MASSACRES

CIVILIANS KILLED BY GERMAN SOLDIERS IN THE CRIMEA IN 1942. Throughout the war on the eastern front countless atrocities were committed at the expense of the civilian population. This photograph shows the lifeless bodies of adults and children massacred by the Germans on their sweep through the area. The purpose of these mass executions was to intimidate the population in the name of a racial ideology that considered the Slav peoples as inferior beings. Terror was applied permanently and without discrimination. For every German soldier killed, thousands of helpless people were shot in reprisal by execution squads from the Wehrmacht, the security forces and the SS. There was no respect of the military code and no pity for a population already tried by the horrors of war. The primary task of the *Einsatzgruppen* ('operative groups') of the Wehrmacht and the SS was to eliminate all captured Red Army political commissars, Jews and partisans in the conquered areas.

FORTRESS LENINGRAD.
The unconquerable bastion of the warrior spirit and of the capacity to resist the Nazi enemy.

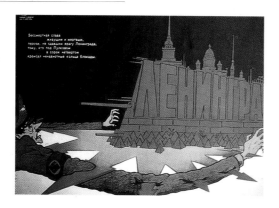

 B A T T L E S

THE SIEGE OF MOSCOW AND LENINGRAD

In the capital 250,000 people, mainly women, dug anti-tank trenches, and General Georgi Zhukov assumed command of the city's defences. Evacuation began on 16 October but Stalin remained at his post. Moscow was the soul of Russia and, as the Russians said, above Moscow there is the Kremlin and above the Kremlin, God. The radio and newsreels transmitted reassuring messages about the bravery of the soldiers and the military capacity of the nation in war. On 8 July 1941, a few days after the German invasion, Leningrad came under siege and was cut off from the rest of the country. Hitler issued orders that the population should be wiped out with every available means. The art treasures of the Hermitage Museum were spirited away to safe zones. In contrast to what was achieved in other areas of the country, the industrial plants were not dismantled and were moved back beyond the Urals.

In Leningrad (formerly the capital of the Tsarist Empire, when it had been called St Petersburg) the entire civilian population was mobilized to defend the city. Almost 1,000km of trenches and earthworks, 650km of anti-tank ditches and 5,000 forts were built. Cut off from the Baltic coast by the German occupation, the city's only link with the rest of the country was across Lake Ladoga. Plied by boats in the summer, during the winter supplies arrived via a 'road' cut into the ice. Leningrad suffered the ravages of hunger and famine, which caused the death of almost a million people before the city was liberated in January 1944. The siege lasted 900 days, and came to an end following one of the cruellest battles in the German-Russian war.

*(Above:) Russian infantry between the houses of a village on the outskirts of Moscow.
(Left:) Members of a battalion of armed workers defending Leningrad.*

AMERICAN FLYING-BOAT.

the German High Command the spectre of the retreat of Napoleon. The Commander-in-Chief of the Army, Walthur von Brauchitsch, was removed from his post and Hitler himself took command of operations. In January 1942 the situation on the front stabilized and both sides waited for the spring thaw.

JAPAN AND THE FAR EAST

In the Far East, events in the European war had created a vacuum that Japan prepared to fill quickly. In the middle of 1940, neither France nor Britain nor Holland was in a position to defend their Asian possessions. Japan's diplomatic and military offensive to build a 'great area of Japanese dominion' and reduce the influence of the European colonial powers had various objectives. Not the least of these was to seize the enormous natural resources of many countries in the Pacific.

Japan had imperial designs on various areas of economic and strategic importance: the essential raw materials of the Dutch East Indies (now Indonesia); the key position of French Indo-China, from whose ports supplies were being sent to the Chinese resistance and the south of which was occupied by the Japanese with the blessing of the Vichy government; Malaysia (the stronghold of Singapore was the fulcrum of the British defences in the Far East); the corridor of Burma, to open up another way into China); and the passage of Siam (now Thailand) as a possible back route for an attack on Singapore.

With this global political and strategic view, that was sanctioned

IN THE GUN-SIGHTS.
In 1941 the Japanese fighters had no Allied rivals.

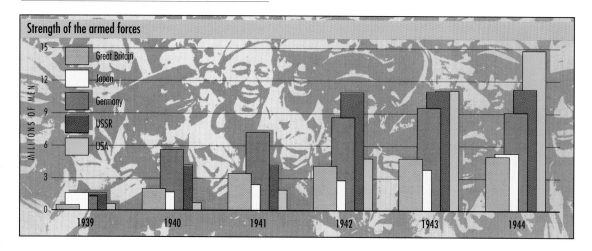

Strength of the armed forces

MILLIONS OF MEN

Great Britain
Japan
Germany
USSR
USA

15
12
9
6
3
0

1939　1940　1941　1942　1943　1944

by the Tripartite Pact, Japan wanted to push Washington into a compromise, the immediate goal of which was to gain recognition of its hegemony over China. Tokyo's bold foreign policy achieved significant results: besides bases in French Indo-China, Japan obtained from the British the closure of the 'Burma road' and the interruption of supplies to the Chinese resistance; and from the Dutch, supplies of oil, rubber and bauxite from the Dutch East Indies. The final but no less ambitious piece in the Japanese imperial puzzle was the Philippines, which had been an American protectorate since the end of the 19th century.

JAPAN AND THE SOVIET UNION

Tokyo's expansionist designs on the Chinese empire were viewed with concern by Moscow. An undeclared war had been fought between the two countries on the Manchurian border in 1938/39, that passed almost

unobserved in the West. Japanese troops had suffered two resounding defeats at the hands of the Red Army and so Japan made diplomatic efforts to neutralize a worrying adversary of its imperialist plans. The aim was to neutralize the Soviet Union and concentrate its efforts on the United States, which Japan viewed as the only true adversary. Siberia was thus excluded from the envisaged 'new order' that Tokyo wanted to establish in Asia, and Japanese diplomacy concentrated on Germany, from which it gained an assurance of an attack on the Soviet Union without this requiring any obligation on Tokyo's part to launch a war against Moscow in Asia. Within the framework of the cooperation between the powers of the Tripartite Pact, Japan, according to Hitler's plans, was to strike at and destroy British power in the Far East. This was followed by a promise that, in the event of a Japanese attack on the United States, the Third Reich would

LEADERS

ISOROKU YAMAMOTO

Born in 1884, Isoroku Yamamoto fought in the 1905 war between Russia and Japan. A naval attaché in Washington, he later became Vice-Minister of the Navy and was opposed to an alliance between Japan and the Axis powers. Appointed Commander of the Japanese Combined Fleet in 1939, Yamamoto was the man who planned the attack on Pearl Harbor – despite his opposition to a war with the United States. He was a prominent figure in the Japanese High Command and a firm advocate of the programme of naval rearmament and of the importance of aircraft carriers in the war that Japan was about to enter. He won a battle against the Dutch fleet in the Java Sea, but was defeated at the Battle of the Coral Sea and at Midway.

On 18 April, American fighters shot down the bomber in which Yamamoto was flying over the Solomon Islands and the plane crashed in the jungle.

A million people attended the admiral's funeral in Tokyo.

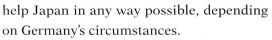

Aichi D3A1.
Prior to the attack on Pearl Harbor, this Navy bomber (nicknamed the 'Val' by the Allies), which had a fixed undercarriage and could carry a 250kg bomb, was used by the Japanese in China.

help Japan in any way possible, depending on Germany's circumstances.

This intricate political and diplomatic tangle unravelled with an unexpected move: in April 1941 Japan and the Soviet Union signed a pact of neutrality that committed the two powers to respect the inviolability of each other's satellite states (Manchukuo and Outer Mongolia). The treaty reinforced those in Japan, and in particular the Imperial Navy, who were pressing for Japan to expand southwards. Having temporarily placed the possibility of conquering China on the back burner, the Japanese government turned to the riches of South-East Asia (Indo-China, Malaysia, Burma, the Phillipines), in order to tackle the chief obstacle to its imperial design: the United States.

Having ensured Soviet neutrality, and strengthened by the war between Germany and Great Britain, Japan aimed to carve up the world into areas of influence. In the 'new world order' coveted by Tokyo, Asia from French Indo-China to the Phillipines would fall under the control of Japan. However, a serious and far from secondary obstacle still had to be overcome: the request by the American Secretary of State, Cordell Hull, that Tokyo leave the Tripartite Pact and withdraw its troops of occupation from China.

AMERICAN PRESSURE ON JAPAN

In June 1941 Roosevelt changed tack with respect to the unresolved strategic vagueness and political caution of American policy in the Pacific until then. Washington

JAPANESE PILOTS.
Japan gave particular importance to training aircrews in its preparations for war.

(Right:) **HITLER ROASTED.** *American playing card featuring the torch of the Statue of Liberty burning the Führer.*

(Far right:) **WARNING.** *The Nazis and the Japanese threaten the United States.*

(Below:) **AMERICAN AIRCRAFT CARRIERS AT SEA.**

began to exercise genuine deterrence, stepping up economic and financial pressure by freezing Japanese assets in the United States and establishing an oil embargo to choke the Japanese economy, and intimating to Japan that it should leave Indo-China and China, accepting the Open Door principle with regard to colonial expansion. The so-called 'China lobby' was a powerful interest group capable of influencing American foreign policy, and it pressed Roosevelt for

further measures to force Japan to withdraw from its conquered territories. Although the diplomatic negotiations between the two powers seeking control of East Asia and the Pacific continued until the end of November 1941, for both nations much more was at stake than a diplomatic carving up of Asia into distinct areas of influence.

For Tokyo – where, with the consent of Emperor Hirohito, General Hideki Tojo had replaced the moderate Fumimaro Konoye as the head of government – there was now no

A MACABRE PARADE.
*In an American cartoon,
Goering precedes
Mussolini and Tojo in
a march accompanied
by Death.*

alternative to a head-on clash with the United States.

Having ruled out the idea of intervention against the Soviet Union and of rescinding its alliance with Berlin, as requested by Washington, Japan speeded up preparations for a military offensive in the Pacific, as a last resort to avoid its economy and energy supplies being strangled. Its plans to create a 'Great East Asia Co-Prosperity Sphere', which would involve breaking British and French imperial dominion, was on a collision course with the economic and military power of America.

WORLD WAR

In the days in which the German offensive was grinding to a halt in front of Moscow, the Pacific became the new theatre of the conflict. With timely synchronism the American government sent Tokyo a proposed agreement which once again called for the abandoning of China. This was considered unacceptable by the Imperial Council. Instead of bowing to the pressure of an ally that had launched Operation 'Barbarossa' without even consulting Japan, and that was now urgently requesting Japanese action on the Russian eastern front, on 7 December 1941 Japan opened hostilities

VICTORS' FLAG.
*After the Manchurian
campaign, Japan wanted
to extend its dominion
over a vast area of Asia.
The imperial ambitions
of Tokyo and Prime
Minister Tojo included
the conquest of China
and control of many
Asian states, which were
intended to be rid of a
Western presence.*

JAPANESE POLITICIANS AND MILITARY LEADERS

HIROHITO (1901–1989)

Emperor of Japan, Hirohito ascended the throne in 1926 following the death of his father, Yoshi-Hito. As a young man he travelled widely in Asia and Europe. Convinced by his advisers to avoid becoming too involved in the country's politics, in the 1930s the royal family maintained a fundamentally passive stance in the face of rising Japanese militarism and expansionism, without seeking to oppose the military in major political choices. Although he was formally the Supreme Commander of the Armed Forces and had extensive powers, during the war he was effectively superseded by the military, which controlled the nation through the Prime Minister, General Tojo. His role was little more than that of a notary, sanctioning decisions taken by others. He remained in Tokyo throughout the war, even during Allied air raids on the city. Finally, partly as a result of pressure from the Prime Minister, Suzuki, he accepted the need for the unconditional surrender of Japan. After the war the possibility of trying Hirohito as a war criminal was considered, but in the interests of the nation's stability it was decided not to depose him. In 1946 the American authorities forced him to accept a parliamentary constitution with a monarchy; the Emperor was no longer to be considered divine and his power derived from the will of the people. In the following decades Hirohito remained detached from events in the country, until his death in 1989.

SANJI IWABACHI (1893–1945)

Promoted to the rank of admiral in 1943 after the Battles of Midway and Guadalcanal, Iwabachi commanded the Japanese naval forces in the Philippines. He died in Manila in February 1945, while the 15,000 men under his command were putting up fierce house-to-house resistance against the Americans and killing, in the space of a month, tens of thousands of Filipinos.

MINEICHI KOGA (1885–1944)

After playing a significant role in the capture of Hong Kong and the Philippines, Koga became the Commander-in-Chief of the Japanese Combined Fleet in May 1943, following the death of Yamamoto. He abandoned an offensive strategy in order to concentrate on building up a system of fortifications to defend the islands. He died when the plane carrying him to Singapore to organize the defences there crashed.

KUNIAKI KOISO (1880–1950)

General Koiso commanded the Japanese army in Manchuria from 1932 to 1934, and was Minister of Colonial Development from 1939 to 1940, and then Governor General of Korea. In October 1944 he was appointed Prime Minister to replace Tojo, and remained in office until April 1945, trying to create the conditions for a negotiated peace. He was sentenced to life imprisonment for war crimes.

YOSUKE MATSUOKA (1880–1946)

Japan's ambassador to the League of Nations, Matsuoka defended the invasion of Manchuria by Japanese troops. He was Foreign Minister in 1940–41 and signed the Tripartite Pact with Germany and Italy. In April 1941 he also signed the non-aggression treaty with the Soviet Union. He resigned before Pearl Harbor. At the end of the war he was accused of war crimes, but he died before coming to trial.

KANTARO SUZUKI (1867–1948)

Suzuki distinguished himself in the Russo-Japanese War of 1904–5 and became an admiral in 1923. He was appointed Prime Minister in April 1945 as part of an attempted compromise between the various political factions. Officially he stated his wish to continue the war, but in fact worked to create the conditions for the Emperor to accept peace. He resigned on 14 August 1945, and in the next few years had to face the hostility of militarists, who accused him of being responsible for the nation's surrender.

HIDEKI TOJO (1884–1948)

The son of a general, for many years Tojo was a military attaché in Germany. From 1937 he commanded the Japanese army in China. An advocate of total war, he became the Army Chief of Staff in 1938 and the Minister of War in 1940, when he formed the alliance with Germany and Italy. Prime Minister from October 1941, he also held the posts of Minister of War, of Industry and of Education. He was the person who decided on the attack on the United States at Pearl Harbor and was the real leader of Japan until July 1944, when he resigned after the loss of Saipan. At the end of the war, following a suicide attempt, he was condemned to death for crimes against humanity and was executed in 1948.

Hirohito in a photo from the early 1930s.

(Left:) **THE JAPANESE OCTOPUS EXTENDS ITS TENTACLES.**

(Far left:) **UNITED WE ARE STRONG.** *Allied propaganda poster after the outbreak of hostilities in the Pacific.*

in South-East Asia and the Pacific by mounting a surprise attack on the American fleet at Pearl Harbor in Hawaii. It was a resounding success for Japan and 'an infamous day' for America. The next day the United States and Great Britain declared war on Japan. On 11 December, Hitler and Mussolini declared war on the United States, even though the eventuality of Japan being an aggressor state had not been contemplated in the Tripartite Pact.

The war thus became a truly global conflict. The United States was committed on two oceans, even though the North Atlantic was the key to the Anglo-American strategic defence system. The Western powers would be engaged on widely distant fronts, but it was the United States that had to shoulder the main burden of the war in the Pacific. The Soviet Union, sticking to the pact of neutrality it had signed with Japan, could use all its human and material resources against Germany, and

throughout the war it would fight on just one front. From now on, the outcome of the conflict was to be determined by the course of three major campaigns: air and sea operations in the Pacific and South Asia; the land war on the Russian front; and the German submarine campaign in the North Atlantic.

The line-up of the two sides in the conflict was now definitive. On one side there were the powers of the Tripartite Pact, although effectively they amounted to just Germany and Japan, given that at no stage of the war would Italy be capable of fighting independently. On the other side there was the coalition between Great Britain, the United States and the Soviet Union. However, there was one gap in this. In fact, Japan was not the common enemy of the Americans and Russians, and there was in fact no state of war between Moscow and Tokyo until August 1945.

AMERICAN PATROL BOAT IN THE PHILIPPINES.

BATTLES

PEARL HARBOR: A JAPANESE TRIUMPH?

The plan of attack drawn up by Admiral Isoroku Yamamoto counted on the big advantage of surprise to destroy the American Pacific Fleet. Protected by clouds and strong squalls, and maintaining strict radio silence, the Japanese formation commanded by Rear-Admiral Chuiki Nagumo (six aircraft carriers, two battleships, two heavy cruisers, one light cruiser, nine destroyers, three submarines and eight support vessels and tankers) took up position 250 miles to the north of Pearl Harbor. Aboard the carriers there were 392 planes, a mixture of torpedo-bombers, fighters and bombers. Operation 'Z' (the code hoisted to the masthead to signal Admiral Togo's order to attack the Russian fleet in the Battle of Tsushima in May 1905) was launched on 7 December 1941. At 7.49am on a quiet Sunday morning, the American ships anchored in Pearl Harbor were struck by an incredible hail of fire from the skies.

The first wave of attackers – 181 planes

in all, a mixture of torpedo-bombers and dive-bombers escorted by Zero fighters, which had taken off from the carriers – sank or seriously damaged the battleships *Utah*, *Arizona*, *Oklahoma* and *California*. Although the planes had shown up on radar, the Americans were caught by surprise. The second wave (180 planes) arrived two hours later and destroyed 11 smaller naval units. However, one unrepeatable opportunity was missed, because three American carriers were away from the base and one was in California for repair. Furthermore, the Japanese failed to destroy the navy's arsenal and fuel storage deposits (equivalent to the total reserves possessed at that time by Japan). The island of Cahu, where the deposits were located, was not occupied, because Japan's ground troops were engaged in operations that began at the same time in the southern Pacific Ocean. The five suicide midget submarines that were supposed to have sunk the rest of the shipping in the base were destroyed. Only 29 Japanese planes were shot down. In less than two hours a large part of the American Pacific Fleet was put out of action. The total American losses were disastrous: three battleships sunk and six seriously damaged, five cruisers put out of action, and 188 planes destroyed or damaged. It was a humiliation without precedent in the history of the United States. The Japanese fleet returned home undisturbed, the master of the western Pacific.

(Above:) The battleship Arizona *on fire after the attack. (Left:) Columns of smoke rise from the American base after the first Japanese air raid.*

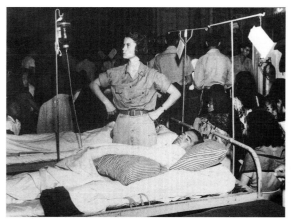

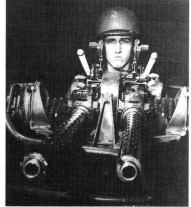

(Left:) **ANTI-AIRCRAFT DEFENCES.** *Gunner on an American warship.*

(Far left:) **NURSE.** *A nurse tends to servicemen wounded in the Japanese attack.*

(Below:) **OFFICER AT THE PERISCOPE, AND A SINKING JAPANESE SHIP.**

THE JAPANESE OVERRUN THE PACIFIC

The attack plans of the Japanese had been drawn up with a view to establishing a new order in East Asia. To defend the territories it planned to conquer (Malaysia, Indo-China, Burma, the Philippines and Borneo), Japan built an enormous defensive perimeter in the Pacific. This comprised a chain of positions that started from the Kuril islands off Siberia and extended south to take in the Wake Islands (American), the Marshall Islands, the Gilbert Islands (British), the Bismarck Islands (Australian), northern New Guinea (Australian) and the Dutch East Indies, extending as far as British Malaysia. A few day after Pearl Harbor, the Royal Navy units guarding Singapore (the 'Gibraltar of the Far East', as the British proudly called it) – including the modern battleship, the *Prince of Wales* – were destroyed in a combined attack launched by Japanese submarines, bombers and torpedo-bombers.

Following its strike against Pearl Harbor and the destruction of the Royal Navy units, Japan controlled the waters of the Far East and of the western Pacific and

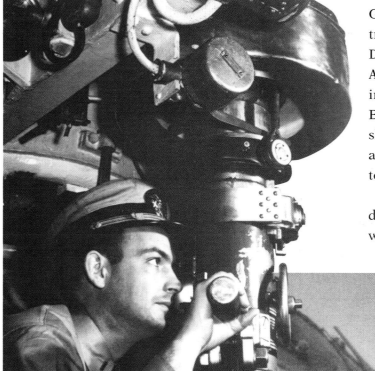

WEAPONS

AIRCRAFT CARRIERS

Aircraft carriers marked a turning point in the history of naval warfare, forcing major changes in rearmament plans, logistics and military strategy. Their contribution proved fundamental in both the Atlantic and the Mediterranean, but it was in the Pacific that they really established themselves as an incomparable offensive weapon.

The first carriers were built by the British in 1918. The Treaty of Washington (1922), which placed restrictions on the tonnage of carriers and the number that each country could have, hindered postwar rearmament plans, which aimed to build large vessels that were better able to cope with the powerful new planes that were being produced. Notwithstanding this, various types of aircraft carrier were available in 1939; some were ships that had been converted from other uses (cruisers, transatlantic liners, merchant ships). The top models had a speed of over 30 knots per hour and were equipped with heavy anti-aircraft guns and solid armour. Only three powers were able to exploit the new weapon: Great Britain (which initially had seven), the United States (seven) and Japan (six). The two carriers that Germany had started to build never became fully operational, and Italy did not have time to finish the modification of two liners.

In 1940 the Royal Navy launched the first of three *Illustrious*-class carriers, which were 225m long and had a tonnage of 20,700t. The decision to fit heavy

armour on the deck limited the ship's transport capacity (33 planes). The Americans and Japanese opted for less heavily armoured models capable of carrying more planes: the *Yorktown* class (1937–41) could carry 96, the *Essex* (from 1942) 91 and the *Shokaku* 72 (1941). In the Pacific war, where fighting often took place far from any land bases,

it was essential to have a greater number of planes than the enemy. Subsequently larger, more heavily armoured carriers were produced: in 1944 the Japanese brought out the *Taiho* (30,300t, 260m, 53 planes) and also the *Shinano* (55,800t, 265m, 70 planes), and in 1945 the Americans commissioned the *Midway* (42,650t, 295m, 137 planes). Many other smaller models performed essential emergency and escort duties. The type of planes varied according to the tactical deployment of the carriers. In the Atlantic and Mediterranean, the British carriers mainly had a support role, so they loaded planes suited to a range of tasks. In the Pacific, where the carriers clashed directly, the United States mainly used fighters, reconnaissance bombers and torpedo-bombers. The first successes of the Japanese were

also due to the technical superiority of their planes: they had a cruising range of over 1,100km and were capable of impeding enemy aerial recognition. The large number of carriers sunk caused great difficulties, because they were expensive and complex to build. After three years of war, Great Britain only had two carriers left, while the United States lost three in the first year and Japan three in the Battle of Midway alone. In the conflict as a whole, the supremacy of the Americans' carrier-building capacity proved decisive: they made over 100, compared with Japan's 14. At Pearl Harbor the six Japanese carriers were vital and made it possible to hit the American base with 189 planes. In the Battle of the Coral Sea (May 1942), for the first time in history, the two naval formations fought at such a distance that they could not see each other or use traditional guns. The biggest clash between aircraft carriers took place in the Battle of the Philippine Sea (19 June 1944): Japan fielded six (with 342 planes), the United States 15 (956 planes). The Japanese lost three carriers and the others were rendered practically unusable because almost all of their planes were shot down. In the final stages of the war, the perfecting of radar equipment and anti-aircraft defences helped the American carriers to ward off the threat posed by kamikaze attacks.

Fighters on the deck of the American aircraft carrier Bunker Hill.

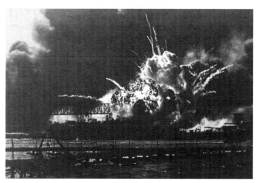

(Left:) **INFAMOUS DAY.** Poster exhorting Americans not to forget 7 December 1941.
(Far left:) **THE SHAW TORN APART BY EXPLOSIONS.**

(Below:) **THE HIRANO FAMILY.** Thousands of Japanese residents in the United States were interned by the American authorities.

could now execute its plans for expansion on land. At the end of 1941 Japanese forces overran Burma. Thus in the space of just six months Japan was the master of half the Pacific and its army had captured the major Allied strongholds.

Thus 1941 ended with results that clearly favoured the nations of the Tripartite Pact: they dominated almost the whole of Europe, the richest regions of the Soviet Union, much of eastern Asia and the most densely populated provinces in China. For the German, Italian and Japanese coalition there was the prospect of further territorial gains, and thanks to the superiority of the Japanese Imperial Navy, the American Pacific Fleet was temporarily crippled. However, the failure to destroy the American's aircraft carriers would weigh heavily on the course of the war between Japan and America.

THE NAZI EMPIRE

The area of Europe under the administration of the Reich (which, in Hitler's plans, was to be completely Germanized) reached its maximum extent at the end of 1942. The heart of this area was 'Greater Germany', which prior to the outbreak of the war had absorbed Austria, the Sudetenland, Bohemia and Moravia and also included part of Poland (ruled by a general government), Alsace and Lorraine (taken from France in 1940), Luxembourg, Slovenia and some areas of Belgium (Eupen and Malmédy). Around this there were a number of 'satellite countries' – nations that joined the Tripartite Pact (Italy, Hungary, Romania, Bulgaria, Slovakia and Finland). Another 'level', which excluded Denmark, Holland and Vichy France (governed by regimes that maintained a relative autonomy from Berlin), included territories and countries that had been occupied, such as northern France and Norway, plus Croatia and Slovakia (Reich satellite states), the human and material resources of which were susceptible to forms of enforced collaboration. Eastern Poland, White Russia, the Baltic States and the Ukraine, all invaded in 1941 and collectively renamed *Ostland*, were ruled as colonies by Reich administrators. The economic and demographic reorganization of many areas of the Continent was based on the indiscriminate exploitation of both human and material resources and was directed towards satisfying Germany's war needs.

For the eastern European territories occupied by German troops, the Nazi administration devised a plan to deport 30 million 'racially undesirable' people beyond the Urals. However, due to the way the conflict developed, this plan was never realized. The tragic fate of the Jewish population in these territories was execution in concentration camps or the ghettos. In the occupied territories of the Soviet Union, random massacres were carried out not only by the SS, who were mainly responsible for the repression and the policy of racial extermination, but also by the Wehrmacht. The latter was the primary guarantor of the Nazi state during the war. The fact that this war was conducted in the name of a racial ideology and the continental supremacy of the Reich meant that no mercy was granted to the enemy or the populations in the occupied territories.

(Below:) German soldier on guard duty at one of the bridges in the Belgian city of Bruges.

- Axis powers
- Axis satellites
- Occupied countries
- Allied powers *(unoccupied territories)*
- Neutral

HANS FRANK, THE GOVERNOR OF POLAND. *A German jurist, Frank was the person most responsible for the massacres in Poland and for the deportation of over 80% of the Polish Jews to the extermination camps. He was sentenced to death at the Nuremberg trials, during which he begged for clemency.*

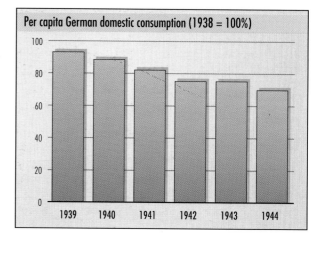

Per capita German domestic consumption (1938 = 100%)

biological annihilation of the Slavic populations, thus enabling Germany to establish its dominion over an almost endless stretch of territory. Ultimately, however, the course of the war on the Russian front prevented these plans from being fully achieved.

In occupied Poland the principle of racial superiority was exercised through the destruction of state organs and the national culture, as well as through physical annihilation of broad sectors of the population. The SS 'operative groups' (*Einsatzgruppen*) and units of the Wehrmacht adopted a policy of terror and extermination: intellectuals, clergymen and a large number of Polish Jews were either executed or confined to ghettos. In the Baltic republics, massacres were carried out by special squads with the help of local militia. During the invasion of the Soviet Union the massacres were conducted on a much

wider scale, and in the name of not only racial but also ideological hatred: operative groups numbering about 3,000 men followed the front-line German troops and had the task of shooting en masse any political commissars of the Red Army who had been taken prisoner, as well as partisans and Jews. By the beginning of 1942, around 600,000 people had fallen victim to this systematic extermination of the population. Captured Russian soldiers were deported to the concentration camps, where most of them died from starvation or exhaustion.

THE REQUIREMENTS OF A PROLONGED WAR

All the measures adopted at the beginning of the conflict – propaganda, industrial production and the repression of any form of dissent – were aimed at ensuring that the German public was fully behind the war effort. When food rationing was first introduced, the Reich exploited its

(Right:) **MEMBER OF THE 'ADOLF HITLER' SS DIVISION.** *The motto of the Waffen-SS volunteers during the Russian campaign was: 'Enjoy the war, peace will be terrible.'*

(Far right:) **SKI UNIT IN NORWAY.**

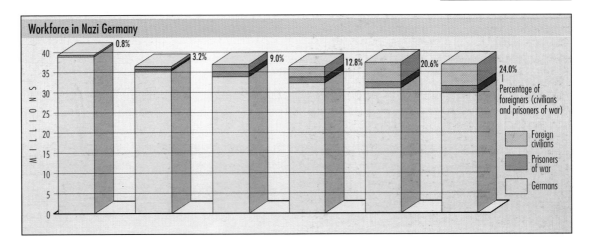

Workforce in Nazi Germany

0.8% 3.2% 9.0% 12.8% 20.6% 24.0%

Percentage of foreigners (civilians and prisoners of war)

MILLIONS

Foreign civilians

Prisoners of war

Germans

occupation of much of continental Europe to ensure that the population living within the borders of Germany enjoyed a better standard of living than those in the rest of the continent.

Military conscription led to a shortage of workers, so in order to increase war production the Reich indiscriminately exploited men and resources in the occupied territories. Germany had few metals and minerals, but eastern Europe had plenty and so the Reich's administrators in *Ostland* took over private businesses, and the management of industrial plants (factories, mines, steelworks, oil wells) was entrusted to state organizations that acted as branches of the Reich's industrial system. If there was a unanimous conviction that Germany would win the war up until 1941, by the middle of 1942 it had become evident that the *Blitzkrieg* in Russia had failed and that Germany was not capable of sustaining a prolonged war. The

peak of the Reich's production drive was in 1944, involving more than 28 million German citizens (split equally between men and women, which represented a massive increase in the number of female workers in the war industry) and approximately 7 million foreign workers (5.3 million forced workers and 1.8 million prisoners of war). In 1943 approximately 750,000 workers arrived from Belgium, Holland and France. There were 10.6 million Germans in the armed forces in 1944.

MASS FORCED LABOUR

One of the key reasons for the Reich's capacity for military resistance was the ruthless exploitation of human resources and materials in the general climate of terror created by Nazism in eastern Europe. Fritz Todt, the Armaments Minister from 1940, rationalized the use of enormous masses of foreign labour (prisoners of war and

WORK VOLUNTEERS.
German officer inspects a unit of young Dutchmen who have volunteered to work for the Reich.

(Right:) **ALBERT SPEER.**
Previously responsible for orchestrating mass Nazi Party gatherings at Nuremberg, and the leading theoretical exponent of the Third Reich's architecture, Speer designed the new Chancellery building in Berlin.

(Far right:) **UNTER DER LINDEN.**
Monumental decorations along one of the main road. in the German capital.

deportees), who worked to meet the Reich's war needs in conditions only slightly better than those in the concentration camps.

After Todt's death, the new plenipotentiary-general for labour mobilization, Fritz Sauckel, made heavy use from March 1942 onwards of prisoners of war and forced labour, much of which was supplied from east Europe and Russia. In the middle of 1942 there were already 2.5 million foreign workers in Germany. More than half of the almost 5 million Russian soldiers taken prisoner died from exhaustion or starvation, and the same fate awaited around 3 million Ukrainians transferred within the borders of the Reich. It was thanks to the indiscriminate exploitation of this slave labour that, notwithstanding the war, the German population had a higher standard of living than the British.

Albert Speer, previously the architect of the Nazi regime, took over from Todt and personally managed the work of the entire labour force of the Reich (frequently clashing with Sauckel) until the end of 1944. Thanks to his direct and periodic contact with Hitler, he was able to set up a central planning office for the total mobilization of available resources for use in the war economy.

Through these measures he reorganized the agricultural labour force and achieved greater industrial efficiency. These were the factors that were responsible for Speer's so-called miracle: in fact, Germany was able to respond to the heavy Allied bombing with an increase in productivity that was not limited exclusively to the key sectors of the war industry.

GERMAN CUSTOMS OFFICER.
Checks at the German–Belgian border to prevent crossing by escapees or resistance fighters.

(Left:) **ALFRED ROSENBERG.**
Rosenberg was considered the 'intellectual leader' of the Nazi Party. Hitler admired his hatred of the Jews and Bolsheviks.

(Far left:) **FRITZ SAUCKEL.**
Plenipotentiary-general for labour mobilization, Sauckel encouraged the inclusion of women in Germany's war industries.

THE FATE OF THE 'SUBHUMANS'

The different components (military, geopolitical and racial) of the Reich's imperialistic plan were all aimed at ensuring a dominant role for Nazi Germany within the confines of its empire. The supremacy of German stock, previously theorized by Hitler in his book *Mein Kampf* (*My Struggle*), was to be exercised over those who were considered racially and genetically inferior: Jews, Slavs, gypsies and homosexuals. Russia's destiny and that of the other eastern Slavic countries was to become a colony of the Reich. A tragic fate was reserved for the local populations: they were either deported or they were physically eliminated.

In the Nazi racial hierarchy the Slavic populations of eastern Europe were to be subjected to forced Germanization, turned into slaves and made to leave the area (because they were decimated by disease or transferred beyond the Urals) when the new Germanic colonists arrived. The German policy in the east was founded on the principle of coercing the populations that they considered *Untermenschen* (subhumans). The local farmers had their farms taken away and were replaced by Teutonic colonists; and even when property rights were respected, the German

ANTI-SEMITISM IN PARIS.
Children crowd in front of a fence barring the passage of Jews. The Vichy regime expelled Jewish citizens from schools and state jobs, expropriated their property and assets and allowed them to be deported to the Nazi death camps. One in five Jews who had previously resided on French territory were missing at the end of the war.

ROUNDING UP JEWS IN THE GHETTO.
Jews in the Warsaw ghetto being forced to leave their homes.

(Below left:) **JEWS LEAVING THE LODZ GHETTO.**

(Below right:) **HEINRICH HIMMLER.**
The ruthless organizer of the massacre of the Jews (bottom right).

occupiers demanded part of the harvest as rent. If the legitimate owners refused, their property was confiscated and they were deported to a forced labour camp.

THE WANNSEE CONFERENCE

In the new European order envisioned by Hitler, anti-Semitism was closely correlated with the containment of the communist 'threat'. The failure of the blitzkrieg on a world scale, combined with recognition of the impossibility of a quick German victory over the Soviet Union, paved the way for the concrete actuality of the Reich's racial assumptions: the systematic elimination of all the European Jews and a 'scorched earth' policy in the occupied territories, without any regard for the populations that lived in these areas. The genocide of the Jews was

(Left:) **ITALIAN ANTI-SEMITISM.**
Following the introduction of a 'racial policy' in 1938, Italian Jews suffered discrimination and persecution.

(Far left:) **MARTIN BORMANN.**
Head of the Chancellery from 1941 and Hitler's personal secretary, Bormann was condemned to death in absentia at the Nuremberg trials.

(Below:) **JEWISH FAMILIES FROM EASTERN EUROPE.**

considered a prerequisite for the perpetuation of the racially based Thousand-Year Reich and was assigned absolute priority over all other objectives, even military ones. After 1941 the number of European Jews that found themselves under German jurisdiction rose from 3.5 to 8.5 million. A 'temporary solution' to the 'problem' of the Polish Jews had been internment in the ghettos that had been created in all the country's major cities, but this was now replaced by mass physical liquidation.

The postulate of German racial supremacy was closely linked to the theory of 'living space': the total annihilation of the Jews, who

were regarded as a source of infection capable of undermining the German state, was judged to be a necessary condition for the absolute domination of the German race over other European cultures. The theory of racial supremacy had already begun to be applied in practice in the form of eugenics, euthanasia and female sterilization. Even among the 'Aryans' there were some people whose right to live was denied: the mentally ill, epileptics, people with handicaps or hereditary defects and those with terminal illnesses.

The extermination programme was worked out at a conference on 20 January 1942, when the high-ranking

YELLOW STAR.
All Jews in Germany and in the territories occupied by the Third Reich in Europe were obliged to wear a yellow star.

THE UPRISING IN THE WARSAW GHETTO

Established in October 1939, the War-saw ghetto held around 450,000 people, who were isolated from the rest of the city by a wall. The Germans divided the city into three zones: one for the Polish population, another for the Germans and a third for the Jewish population. In the spring of 1942 the Wehrmacht began deporting the population of the ghetto to concentration camps: by the end of September some 300,000 Jews had been deported, loaded into railway wagons and taken to Treblinka, where they were killed in gas chambers. The only chance of avoiding certain death was a revolt. An armed organization headed by Mordechai Anielewicz fomented a popular insurrection, which was quashed in May 1943. About 3,000 SS troops, backed by artillery and tanks, attacked the ghetto as a prelude to the final deportation of its population. They encountered fierce resistance from about 1,000 Jewish militiamen, armed with pistols, machine guns and Molotov bombs, who defended the ghetto for weeks. About 14,000 Jews and some 400 German soldiers died during the revolt. Anielewicz committed suicide on 8 May. The ghetto was finally taken by the Germans and

razed to the ground. Nothing remained except for an appalling mass of rubble.

(Above:) The insurrection in the Warsaw ghetto. (Below:) The wall marking the edge of the zone reserved for the Jews.

(Left:) **ADOLF EICHMANN.** *Eichmann organized the 'final solution to the Jewish problem'. He was condemned to death by an Israeli court in 1962.*

(Far left:) **REINHARD HEYDRICH.** *Chief of the German State Police and of the SS's Security Service and 'Protector' of Bohemia and Moravia, Heydrich was killed by the Czech resistance.*

(Below:) **BUCHENWALD CONCENTRATION CAMP.**

members of the SS, the police, ministerial departments, the Nazi Party and the General Government of Poland gathered on the Wannsee banks near Berlin. The 'final solution to the Jewish problem' was the bureaucratic expression adopted by the German hierarchy in planning the suppression of millions of Jews in the gas chambers of the extermination camps. Heinrich Himmler was also made 'Commissar for the Consolidation of the German Race', and it was his two closest collaborators, Reinhard Heydrich (Chief of the German State Police) and Adolf Eichmann (responsible for the Jewish section of the same

body), who calculated the number of Jews that would have to be exterminated – around 11 million. Shortly afterwards, the decision was taken to extend the policy of extermination, already in progress in the eastern territories, to western Europe. In 1942 deportations began in Slovakia, followed by the rounding up of Jews in Paris and Amsterdam and the mass removal of people from the Warsaw ghetto. Greek Jews were deported in 1943; and in October, German soldiers also swooped on the ghetto in Rome.

THE CONCENTRATION CAMP SYSTEM

The camp of Dachau, built in 1933 close to Munich, was the first in a long list of concentration camps to which political dissidents and 'antisocial' elements were deported without any intervention on the part of the judiciary authorities. After the beginning of the war the state secret police (*Geheime Staatspolizei*, abbreviated to

MAIN EXTERMINATION CAMPS

FINLAND 15
NORWAY 728
ESTONIA 1000
SWEDEN
DENMARK 77
Memel 8000
LATVIA 80,000
Danzig 1000
LITHUANIA 135,000
HOLLAND 106,000
Bergen-Belsen
Ravensbrück
East Prussia
Treblinka
USSR 1,000,000
BELGIUM 24,387
Sachsenhausen
Chelmno
POLAND 3,000,000
Sobibor
Lublin-Majdanek
GERMANY 160,000
LUX. 700
Flossenbürg
Auschwitz-Birkenau
Belzec
Theresienstadt
Dachau
CZECHOSLOVAKIA 277,000
FRANCE 83,000
SWITZERLAND
Mauthausen
AUSTRIA 65,000
HUNGARY 200,000
ROMANIA 469,632
Jasenovac
Stara Gradiska
YUGOSLAVIA 67,122
BULGARIA
ITALY 8000
ALBANIA 200
GREECE 69,221
TURKEY
Dodecanese (Italy)
Cyprus (GB)

1937 frontiers
■ Death camps
69,221 Number of victims

THE SYMBOL OF GENOCIDE

In 1940 the largest and most efficient of all the concentration camps opened in Silesia (southern Poland), becoming, with time, the symbol of genocide: Auschwitz–Birkenau. The camp quickly became an extension of the modern industrial production system, where the raw materials were millions of human beings and the final result was death through hardship or in the gas chambers. Forced labour and planned mass extermination went hand in hand, and were the only alternatives available to prisoners who were brought here in sealed railway wagons.

The Auschwitz–Birkenau complex consisted of three camps. The largest was Auschwitz I, which had a gas chamber and a crematorium used to kill Russian prisoners and the terminally ill. The second was Birkenau (Auschwitz II, 2 kilometres from the main camp), where the

mass extermination of Jews and gypsies took place. This was divided into two bunkers, where about ten gas chambers, each measuring about 240 square metres, were in operation. The prisoners were asphyxiated with a pesticide called Zyklon B. The chambers remained in use until January 1945. Birkenau also had four crematory ovens at its disposal. Six kilometres from Birkenau was the industrial complex (Auschwitz III) of IG Farben (at Monowitz), where slave labour was responsible for producing methanol and synthetic rubber.

The commander of the camp, Rudolf Höss, supervised the selection of Jews deported here from every corner of Europe (Poland, France, Holland, Greece, Germany, Italy, Norway, Yugoslavia, Hungary and Belgium, as well as ghettos in the territories occupied by the Wehrmacht), the organization of the labour force and the extermination procedures adopted by the SS. Prisoners suitable for work lived in horrifying conditions: crowded into barracks, they were

decimated by infectious diseases, had barely enough food to avoid starving, and lived in terrible hygienic conditions. In 1943 Birkenau held its maximum number of prisoners: 200,000. Auschwitz–Birkenau was discovered in January 1945 by the Red Army as it advanced towards Germany, by which time about 2 million people had been sent to their deaths.

Recent studies of the organization and functioning of this mass extermination have conclusively discredited all 'revisionist' attempts to play down or even to deny the existence of this enormous death industry, with which the Nazi regime tried to wipe out a whole people for racial reasons. Auschwitz remains a warning to the collective conscience and memory of the civilized world.

(Above:) A view of the Birkenau concentration camp. (Left:) Prisoners in the concentration camp of Ebensee, Austria.

(Left:) **ZYKLON B.**
Zyklon B was used in the gas chambers to asphyxiate deportees.

(Far left:) **INTERNATIONAL JEWRY.**
German anti-Semitic propaganda poster: 'Behind the enemy powers are the Jews.'

Gestapo), the criminal police of the Reich (*Kripo*) and the Nazi party security organs (*Sicherheitsdienst*, abbreviated to SD), to which the military police (*Feldgendarmerie*) would also be added, deported tens of thousands of people from the Russian and Polish occupied territories to concentration camps. Men, women and children were forced to work in conditions that were the equivalent of a death sentence. After Dachau there were the camps of Sachsenhausen, Buchenwald, Flossenbürg, Mauthausen (close to the Austrian city of Linz) and the exclusively female prison of Ravensbrück. These were followed by the construction of, amongst others, Chelmno, Belzec, Sobibor, Treblinka and Majdanek, all of which were extermination camps in the real sense of the word.

Different categories of prisoner were identified by different-coloured badges: red for political prisoners, pink for homosexuals, green for common prisoners, purple for Jehovah's Witnesses, black for antisocial elements, yellow for the Jews. The population of the camps increased horrifyingly with the arrival of prisoners of war and the nucleus of populations from the eastern territories. In 1942 the management of the camps was handed over to the SS, which organized the internees' forced labour. War industries often opened factories near the camps; IG Farben, for instance, had one near Auschwitz.

After the Wannsee conference the extermination of the Jews became systematic. Preceded by the 'night and fog' order (a coded expression meaning 'in all secrecy') in 1941, which ordered the transfer of all suspects to concentration camps, the policy of racial annihilation went

INHUMANE CONDITIONS.
Women cooking in a concentration camp alongside a pile of shoes taken from deportees.

(Right:) **TRUST THE GERMAN SOLDIER.** *Poster in French.*

(Far right:) **WAFFEN SS.** *Poster encouraging young people in the occupied territories to enrol in the Waffen SS.*

one big step forward with the construction of concentration camps in eastern Europe, where gas chambers and crematory ovens were used for the mass extermination of all prisoners deemed unfit for forced labour – Jews and non-Jews alike. It is estimated that around 6 million Jews were killed in the Nazi death camps, while around 20 million were deported to the concentration and death camps between 1936 and 1945. Many thousands of people, both Germans and eastern Europeans, with various kinds of responsibilities (transportation, administration, guard duties) were involved in this gigantic project to wipe out the 'inferior race'. In addition to the 6 million Jews who died there were 3.5 million Soviet prisoners, around one million prisoners in concentration camps, some 240,000 gypsies and no fewer than 70,000 mentally ill people, all of whom were the victims of enforced euthanasia.

FORMS OF COLLABORATION

'Collaboration' is used as a derogatory term defining the different forms and degrees of cooperation given to the Reich's forces by the governments of European countries. In the course of the war the shape of collaboration altered, especially in relation to the needs and internal equilibrium of the limited-sovereignty states that lay within the confines of Hitler's continental empire. They all declared their ideological affinities with Nazism, they all persecuted Jews, many sent workers to Germany and, in the occupied zones of northern Europe, they provided soldiers who were drafted into special divisions of the Waffen SS.

(Right:) **CROATIAN MEMBERS OF THE WAFFEN SS.**

(Far right:) **ROMANIAN IRON GUARD WITH A SWASTIKA ARMBAND.** *King Carol used this fascist organization to seize power.*

MED WAFFEN-SS OG
DEN NORSKE LEGION
MOT DEN FELLES FIENDE...

MOT BOLSJEVISMEN

TU DÉFENDS LA BELGIQUE...

...EN LUTTANT AU FRONT DE L'EST!
VIENS À LA SS-DIVISION BLINDÉE «WALLONIE»

(Left:) **BELGIAN SS.**
Created by Léon Degrelle, founder of the Rex fascist movement, the Walloon Legion fought in the Soviet Union and participated in the final defence of the Chancellery in Berlin.

(Far left:) **SS** PROPAGANDA IN **NORWAY.**

Although they all adhered to the principles of Nazism, there was no lack of conflict between the regimes, which all sought Germany's blessing to defend their own economic and geopolitical interests at the expense of their neighbours.

Hitler's stance was based on the conviction that collaborationist leaders and regimes were merely subordinate players in the Reich's game plan for domination. German military strategy remained an exclusive prerogative of Hitler, who, depending on circumstances, reached political, economic and military agreements with governments in the countries occupied by the Wehrmacht. Therefore there was no 'European' Nazi political organization. One of the symbols of European collaboration, and among the most fanatic supporters of fascist, racist and anti-Semitic ideology, was Vidkun Quisling, head of the

Norwegian Nazi movement, who offered his services to Hitler immediately following the invasion of his country. He was initially sidelined but then, at the beginning of 1942, was placed at the head of the government by the Germans. As part of his vision of a Nazi-based European order, Jews and dissidents in Norway were fiercely repressed. His name remains synonymous with the word 'traitor'. In Belgium the fascist Léon Degrelle (head of the Walloon Legion, incorporated into the SS) also supported the notion of a Nazified Europe and a breaking down of national boundaries. In the Low Countries, two movements contended for the favour of Berlin: that of Anton Mussert, founder of the national socialist movement, recognized by Berlin as the 'Führer of the Dutch population',

WALLOON SS SOLDIERS DECORATED ON THEIR RETURN FROM THE RUSSIAN FRONT.

VICHY FRANCE

the 'New European Order' but with an autonomous role. When the severity of the German occupation became more

for mobilizing French labour. Between June 1942 and the middle of 1944, approximately 600,000 French workers were sent to Germany in order to bolster the German war industries. The vicissitudes of the Vichy republic is one of the most evident examples of the mix of opportunism and ambiguity that distinguished a large proportion of the populations in countries that had fallen within the sphere of Nazi domination.

Of all the collaborationist regimes, France was the most complex case. After defeat in 1940, General Pétain headed the new state set up in the unoccupied southern part of the country, which had its capital in Vichy. Its strong corporative and authoritarian traits were a synthesis of fascist, anti-Semitic and nationalistic leanings and of extreme Catholicism, all of which were already widespread in the country during the 1930s. In the varied panorama of French collaboration there were nationalist intellectuals like Robert Brasillach, who gravitated around the weekly *Je suis partout*; the extreme right-wing nationalists of the *Action française*; radicals like Jacques Doriot, who were imbued with fascist ideology; and politicians like Pierre Laval (pacifist, anti-British and a supporter of Franco-German reconciliation). They all opposed the fence-sitting approach of Pétain, who attempted a policy of economic cooperation with the Reich whilst successfully avoiding involvement in the war against the Allies. As one of the former great powers, Pétain hoped that France would be integrated into

marked and as internal resistance grew and the tide of the conflict turned against the Reich, the line of the Prime Minister Pierre Laval, who did not hesitate to hand over French Jews for deportation, prevailed. A forced labour scheme was established at the request of Fritz Sauckel, the Reich administrator responsible

(Above left:) A Vichy propaganda poster featuring Marshal Pétain. (Above right:) Pétain greets the crowds. (Below:) An effigy of Pétain on a poster representing the hardworking French population, upholders of the values of work, family and homeland.

Areas annexed by Germany

Occupied zones

Zones reserved for colonization

No-go zone

Free zone *(occupied in 1942)*

Zones annexed by Italy

Demilitarized zones

Zones under Italian supervision

(Left:) **JACQUES DORIOT.** *A supporter of collaboration with Germany, Doriot fought with the French volunteers on the Russian front.*

(Far left:) **THE COUNTRY UNDER THREAT.** *In this Vichy poster, France is being attacked by rabid dogs embodying the Masons, Jews and de Gaulle.*

who proposed an independent Holland; and the Flemish movement founded by van Thonningen, who supported the need to integrate Holland into the Great Reich.

THE REICH'S SATELLITE STATES

The so-called satellite states (although their status differed) included eastern European countries such as Slovakia, Croatia, Romania, Bulgaria, Hungary and the Ukraine. In the territories of the former Czechoslovakia, dismantled in accordance with the Munich Agreement, Slovakia (which declared itself an independent state in 1939 and was under German protection from the beginning of the conflict) was a semi-totalitarian state

with a corporative and Catholic imprint. The region of Bohemia-Moravia, part of which was annexed by the Reich, was officially called a 'protectorate' and governed by a representative of the Reich and by a Czech president, who was also head of a nationalist party. In May 1942 the area's resistance movement killed the German 'Protector', Reinhard Heydrich. This prompted terrible German repression, culminating in the destruction of the village of Lidice and the execution of many of its inhabitants, because the village was thought to have supported the resistance unit responsible for the murder of the Nazi official.

After the Axis invasion of the Balkans in March 1941, the independent state of Croatia was founded. This included a large minority of Serbs and Muslims. The pro-Nazi regime had its capital in Zagreb, and it was led by Ante Pavelic, whose

ANTONESCU AND MICHAEL OF ROMANIA. *An ally of Hitler, General Antonescu was arrested by the Romanian sovereign in 1944. He was executed as a war criminal.*

MIKLÓS HORTHY.
Horthy ruled Hungary until 1944. Having chosen to side with the Axis powers, he later tried in vain to negotiate a peace with the Russians.

Croatian Ustashe movement supported the Germans and perpetrated massacres of Serbs and Jews. In Serbia, the occupying German regime was heavily repressive.

Of all the Reich's satellite states, Romania was the one that offered Germany the most military cooperation. After King Carol's abdication, power was shared by Marshal Ion Antonescu and the fascist Iron Guard party, and a climate of terror reigned. After the latter had been temporarily sidelined, Antonescu declared war on the Soviet Union and sent 30 Romanian divisions to take part in Operation 'Barbarossa'. They fought in the Crimea and the Ukraine. Antonescu's position was emblematic of the opportunism that characterized other governments in the area as well, namely military support for Germany in exchange for territorial gains at the expense of neighbouring states. In August 1944 Romania made one of the war's most spectacular switches in allegiance: Antonescu

was arrested and his successor accepted the conditions offered by the Russians and declared war on Germany.

In 1941 Bulgaria joined the Tripartite Pact and allowed Axis troops to cross its territory during the invasion of Greece and Yugoslavia, in exchange for the annexation of Thrace and Macedonia. Bulgarian collaboration also took the form of internal repression and persecution of Jews. In the middle of 1943 the country began to make peace overtures in order not to be caught up in the German withdrawal from the Soviet Union.

Hungary, under Admiral Miklós Horthy, immediately sided with Hitler's Germany at the beginning of the conflict and was rewarded with annexation of a part of Slovakia and the north of Transylvania, at the expense of Romania. The anti-Semitic regime's alliance with Hitler

RED ARMY ON THE ATTACK.
In December 1941 the Russians, with the help of forces sent from Siberia, recaptured the territory occupied by the Germans in the final phase of the Moscow offensive.

BADGES OF CROATIAN, GEORGIAN AND ARMENIAN UNITS OF THE WAFFEN SS.

averted the threat posed by the fascist Arrow Cross Party. Horthy first allowed the Wehrmacht to pass through Hungarian territory, and then sent a contingent of 150,000 soldiers to the eastern front.

In occupied Ukraine a nationalist insurrectional army was formed, which, from 1942 onwards, fought for the region's independence from the Soviet Union and collaborated with the German occupiers. Hitler's plans for the region were to eliminate the local population and replace it with German colonizers. However, in this area the situation was even more complicated, because General Andrej Vlasov formed an army and called on Ukrainians to desert from the Red Army and fight against Bolshevism and Stalin's regime.

GERMANY'S SUMMER CAMPAIGN

On the Russian front the Red Army's counter-offensive in the winter of 1941 failed to breach the German defensive system, which was based on a series of fortress cities. However, the German forces were deployed on a front that was thousands of kilometres long and they began to suffer from serious shortages. The air force was no longer able to supply the ground troops adequately, and the

(Left:) **SUMMARY EXECUTION.**
An inhabitant of the western region of Russia waits on the edge of a mass grave for a shot in the back of the head from a soldier in the German 'special units'.

(Far left:) **GERMAN INFANTRY ON THE DON FRONT.**

(Right:) **THE NOOSE OF STALINGRAD.**
In this Russian poster a soldier strangles an invader with a rope symbolizing the river Volga.

(Below:) **AMIDST THE RUINS OF STALINGRAD.**

strength of those forces was greatly reduced; indeed, although on paper the Germans had a large number of divisions at their disposal, in reality they were often only two or three battalions strong. The situation was exacerbated by the inability of the German war industry to build more planes and tanks.

Nonetheless, Hitler decided that the Russian campaign must proceed with rapid advances. The chief objective was the Caucasus (rich in oil, wheat and minerals), even though the new offensive was, in the second phase, to move in two directions. One of these was to aim for the city of Stalingrad and the river Volga (which would serve as strategic cover for the advance into the Caucasus) and then to head north-west to threaten the rear of the Russian army deployed in defence of Moscow. On 7 May 1942 the Germans launched the Crimean attack and within a week had conquered the entire peninsula with the exception of the fortress of Sebastopol, which held out in the south-west.

Meanwhile Army Group South moved against Kharkov and took more than 240,000 prisoners. In July the whole of the Crimea was in German hands, while Friedrich von Paulus's 6th Army moved on Stalingrad. The capture of Rostov on 22 July completed the wide-ranging German manoeuvre and interrupted vital supplies of oil and grain from the Caucasus to the Russian troops.

However, the umpteenth spectacular German advance lacked something that had previously ensured the success of the Wehrmacht: the speed and force of tanks, which in this phase were greatly reduced in numbers in comparison with past operations. Even though the Red Army was forced to pull back, the Russians no longer surrendered in their thousands and morale remained high.

At the beginning of August the German

WAR ARCHIVES: PRISONERS IN THE DEATH CAMPS

THE FOLLOWING ARE EXTRACTS FROM THE TESTIMONY OF RUDOLF HÖSS, THE COMMANDER OF AUSCHWITZ, AT THE NUREMBERG TRIALS: 'The "final solution" of the Jewish problem meant the complete extermination of all European Jews. I was ordered, in June 1941, to create installations for this extermination at Auschwitz. . . . I organized the premises for the exterminations, using Zyklon B, prussic acid in crystals that were dropped into the death chambers through small openings. Between three and 15 minutes were sufficient to kill the people inside. We knew they were dead when the yelling stopped. Generally, we waited half an hour before we took the corpses away. Then our special units would remove their rings and gold teeth. . . . We were ordered to carry out these executions secretly but the horrible nauseating stench caused by the continuous burning of bodies permeated the whole area and in the end the entire population living in the vicinity knew that mass extermination was going on at Auschwitz.'

TANKS FOR VICTORY.
El Lissistskj's poster illustrates the efforts of the Soviet armaments industry.

advance came to a halt when it ran up against the first strongholds of the Caucasus chain, where the effectiveness of Soviet resistance was helped by the fact that they were fighting with locally recruited troops. Although advance units reached the Caspian Sea, the German offensive was stopped about 60km from Grozny and its oil fields.

THE FIRST GERMAN SETBACKS

Meanwhile Paulus's 6th Army was moving towards Stalingrad, but the advance began to lose its original impetus. The German troops were forced to make exhausting marches in the humid August heat of the steppes and Russian resistance became increasingly stubborn. A long war of attrition was about to begin around Stalingrad. For the Red

Army (which benefited from supplies sent from factories located beyond the Ural Mountains and from massive American and British aid, plus fresh troop reinforcements from the Asian territories of Russia), Stalingrad was the main bulwark, both politically and militarily, against the German invasion. Hitler contributed to the unfavourable course of the German campaign with his inflexibility; despite warnings from his High Command that the line of the Don was impossible to defend

FRIEDRICH VON PAULUS.
Paulus commanded the 6th Army on the southern front. After halting the German advance towards Central Caucasus, the Soviets launched an encircling attack on Paulus's troops, who were barricaded in the city of Stalingrad.

(Left:) **IRON CROSS. GERMAN MILITARY DECORATION.**

(Below:) **ENTRENCHMENTS IN DEFENCE OF STALINGRAD.**

in winter, he decided to employ the 6th Army in the battle to defend Stalingrad at all cost. Hitler also refused to take into account the enormous disparity in men and armaments on the eastern front. Logistic problems, scarcity of supplies, the depletion of infantry forces and the fact that German air cover was less than half what it had been at the beginning of the invasion all affected the German troops, whose morale was already beginning to crumble.

At the end of November 1942, the Russians took advantage of the weather conditions during the few weeks between the first frost and the first snow to launch a counter-attack against the flanks of the 6th Army and the 4th Panzer Army, both located in the Stalingrad sector.

Relying on superior operational speed and flexibility of manoeuvre, the Russians made an encircling movement and closed the noose around the German troops, while to the west of the city they began a similar manoeuvre against the Don line held by the Italian 8th Army. The objective of the Russian move was not just to conquer Stalingrad, but was part of a more ambitious plan to threaten the rear of the German armies in the Caucasus. Irrespective of the outcome of the battle at Stalingrad, which became a bitter house-to-house affair, one thing was clear: the narrow margin of combat superiority that the German troops had was no longer sufficient to hold an enormous front stretching from the Caucasus to Leningrad.

TO THE BEACH
To ToKio- 3130-Mi
To Frisco - WHAT THE HELL DO YOU CARE ?
YOUR NOT GOING THERE
GOLDEN GATE in "48"
BREAD LINE in "49"

The war
in the Pacific

After the attack on Pearl Harbor, Japan's objective was to capitalize on the factor of surprise by quickly extending its power in East Asia and the Pacific, and then to force the United States to accept a negotiated peace that ratified Japan's territorial gains. Like the strategy of Nazi Germany, the key to success for Japan was a rapid and spectacular victory, in order to interrupt the flow of American aid to China, to oust the British from Asia and to secure vital supplies of oil, rubber and other primary materials. This plan for continental domination also had a strong ideological component: Japan did not hide its desire to project itself as the liberator of the Asian peoples from centuries of oppression by white colonialism. Counting on a favourable balance of military strength, Tokyo threw caution to the winds, but in doing so made two serious strategic and political errors of judgement. The first was the almost inevitable decision to pin everything

(p. 144) **SIGNS.**
'Street sign' on the island of Tarawa showing the main 'destinations' of American soldiers.

(p. 145) **MARINES ON BOUGAINVILLE (SOLOMON ISLANDS).**

(Right): **MEN AND WOMEN AT WORK IN AN AMERICAN FACTORY.**

on a brief war. The second was the failure to assess the capacity of the United States to react. When the radio announced the attack on Pearl Harbor, the American people abandoned all neutralist reserve and united against the aggressor. America's powerful war and industrial machine was to prove decisive in settling the outcome of the war in the Pacific.

THE BRITISH COLLAPSE IN MALAYA

While the Pearl Harbor operation was underway, Japan launched an attack on British possessions in Asia. Within a few days, the British air and naval forces at Hong Kong had been destroyed by air raids, and on 25 December the Japanese, who had invaded from Canton, captured the British colony. Resistance in Thailand, which had been won over to

the Japanese cause, was little more than symbolic. Less than a week later the Japanese penetrated into northern Malaya and drove the British troops back towards the island fortress of Singapore, where about 5 million refugees took shelter within a radius of some 5km. Singapore was the 'Gibraltar of the Far East' and a symbol of British imperial dominance in the Indian Ocean; the fortress had been completed in 1938 and had powerful guns that made it impregnable to attack from the sea.

The land operations had just commenced, but in the meantime the two ships that were the pride of the British naval squadron in the Pacific had already been

VIEW FROM THE PORTHOLE OF A US COASTGUARD PATROL BOAT.

HOTEL SIGN.
The Raffles Hotel, one of the most celebrated hotels in Asia, was patronized by the British for holidays and leisure purposes until the fall of Singapore. The most serious military defeat in British history was partly due to the fact that the heavy gun batteries of the fortress city were positioned so as to repel an attack from the sea.

dispatched. On 10 December 1941, a combined attack by torpedo-bombers and high-level bombers sank the *Prince of Wales* and the *Repulse*. Having ensured control of the air and the sea, the Japanese increased their troop landings in Malaya. Their land offensive did not take the form the British expected. Japanese tanks and infantry opened a path in the jungle and advanced with surprising speed through the rubber plantations. By mid-January, the Japanese 25th Army under Tomoyuki Yamashita was just a few kilometres away from the island fortress, having covered 700km in just five weeks. Reserves of water, food and

ammunition in Singapore were running out. After heavy fighting, General Arthur F. Percival, who commanded the fortress of Singapore, raised the white flag on 15 February 1942. The disastrous handling of the defensive campaign in Malaya culminated in the surrender of over 80,000 troops – British, Australian and Indian plus some Malay volunteers – to a Japanese force of about 50,000. With this capitulation, the most dishonourable in its military history, the prestige of the British Empire in the Far East plummeted.

THE FALL OF BURMA

At the end of December 1941, the Japanese pushed into Burma, supported by air raids from bases in Thailand that devastated the majority of the port installations in Rangoon. The main objective of the Japanese was to

JAPANESE TWIN-ENGINE BOMBERS.
Powered by Mitsubishi engines, these planes had a bomb-aiming cockpit in the nose and demonstrated their full destructive effectiveness in missions over China.

INDIA
IN THE WAR

When the war broke out in 1939, the Viceroy, Lord Linlithgow, brought India into the conflict without any consultation with the country's political leaders. There were contrasting views within the Indian nationalist movement about the ruling power and the new situation created by world events. Gandhi, leader of the Congress Party, declared his opposition to the war in accordance with the principle of non-violence, and at the end of 1940 he organized a campaign of civil disobedience against the country's forced participation in the war. Some 12,000 Indians were imprisoned as a result. In the meantime, Gandhi had to curb the energetic initiatives of the Muslim League, whose leader, Muhammad Ali Jinnah, wanted a partitioning of the country and the establishment of a new state (which, when India won independence in August 1947, took the name of Pakistan). Muslim League representatives occupied posts in many provincial governments that had been left vacant by Congress Party officials in protest against the British.

At the height of the Japanese victories in Asia, London sent a mission to India to try to mediate amidst the cauldron of Indian politics. The Congress Party continued to reject all negotiations and adopted the slogan 'Quit India' in mass demonstrations that ended with thousands of arrests. In 1942 Gandhi was imprisoned for two years. During these convulsive events in India, the nationalist leader Subhas Chandra Bose (who had abandoned the Congress Party in 1939 and led a campaign against Gandhi's pacifism on the back of the slogan 'Give me blood, I will give you freedom') began conducting anti-British propaganda from Germany, the aim of which was to liberate India with the help of the Japanese.

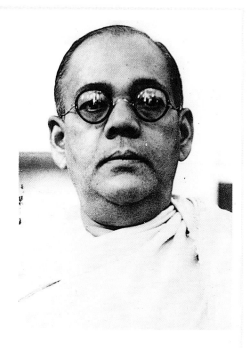

Bose's plan, which led to the establishment of the 'Provisional Government of Free India', seemed for a while to coincide with Tokyo's design to include India, once it had been militarily occupied, in the 'Greater East Asia Co-Prosperity Sphere'. Bose formed three divisions with Indian troops who had been taken prisoner, and they fought alongside the Japanese. However, the course of the war frustrated Bose's plans, and in 1945 he died in an air crash in Formosa after the surrender of his forces in Burma. At the end of the war, the hostility between the Muslim League and the Congress Party was implacable. The 'jewel in the crown' of the British Empire in Asia never became part of the Japanese 'Co-Prosperity Sphere', and more than 2 million Indians fought in the British army during the war.

(Top left:) Gandhi addresses the Indian people. (Top right:) Chandra Bose. (Left:) A cartoon featuring the 'powder keg' of India, contested by all the Allied powers.

JAPANESE ARMOURED TROOP CARRIER.
This vehicle could make rapid progress over poor roads or terrain and was used to transport troops.

interrupt the flow of supplies to Chinese nationalists. These supplies were sent along the railway line linking Rangoon and Mandalay, then across a mountainous region to Lashio, the beginning of the Burma Road, which, after a tortuous mountain route, reached Kunming in south-west China. After blocking a Chinese attack on the northern border, the Japanese soon won over the local population, who were only too happy to see the back of an oppressive and inefficient British administration and to greet the new invaders as liberators. Rangoon fell on 8 March 1942, followed by Lashio on 15 May.

After a retreat of some 1,500km, part of the 60,000-strong British contingent reached Assam (north towards China) and other infantry contingents retreated to safety westwards, beyond the Indian frontier. Air superiority and more effective combat techniques were the key to the success of the Japanese, who gained total control of the country in May. A point of access into India (the jewel in the crown of the British Empire), Burma was to become the theatre of a war fought in extreme environmental conditions, where summer temperatures reached as high as 55°C and as much as 40cm of rain fell every day in the monsoon season.

THE AMERICANS LEAVE THE PHILIPPINES

As part of their plan to establish a solid defensive perimeter in the Pacific, on 8 and 10 December 1941 the Japanese attacked the American island outposts of Wake and Guam. Landing operations also began in the Philippines, which had been an American protectorate since the end of the 19th century and was guarded by the Pacific fleet. Three Japanese armies (the 14th, 17th and 18th) went into action after the air force had destroyed the American planes stationed at Luzon on the ground. Some 30,000

MOBILIZATION OF STUDENTS.
The young also contributed to the war economy. Japanese students filled in for farmers who were away fighting. Men aged between 16 and 40 were militarized and factory workers in essential industries were not permitted to change jobs.

(Right:) **WE CAN DO IT!**
The female aircraft-industry worker was a prominent symbol of patriotic womanhood. This American poster features a strong-looking woman in shirtsleeves.

(Far right:) **THE 'YELLOW PERIL' IN A STRIP-CARTOON MAGAZINE.**

L E A D E R S

DOUGLAS MACARTHUR
Born in 1880, Douglas MacArthur entered the military academy of West Point at the age of 19, graduating in 1903 as a lieutenant in the Engineers. He was injured in World War I. In 1935 he was in the Philippines as military adviser to President Manuel Quezon. When the Japanese attacked the islands, MacArthur made some serious errors in evaluating the enemy's strategy and organizing the American defences. On Roosevelt's orders he abandoned the fortress of Corregidor in March 1942 and made a lucky escape to Australia. When he embarked he made a comment that was to become famous: 'I came through, but I shall return.' The army's Information Office asked him to change the subject of the sentence to make it 'We shall return', but MacArthur rejected the request out of hand. Less than two years later he managed to keep his promise, and was immortalized by photographers as he disembarked in the Philippines wearing his customary sunglasses.

Steeped in military history, MacArthur had a sharp strategic mind, and he found a new way of defeating the enemy. He based his strategy on principles similar to those of judo, namely that the attack should be launched when and where the enemy was off-balance. Having discarded options for making frontal attacks on the Japanese strongholds, MacArthur chose encircling manoeuvres aimed at isolating the Japanese, cutting their lines of communication and supply. He was one of the first to grasp that operations in the Pacific war were in equal measure land-based and sea-based. As a consequence he regarded logistics as essential and did not neglect the importance of the environmental conditions: 'Nature,'

he was later to say, 'is neutral in war, but if you conquer it and the enemy doesn't, it turns into a powerful ally.'

During the course of the war, he was frequently in open disagreement with Chester W. Nimitz, Commander-in-Chief of the Pacific Fleet. In his role as Commander-in-Chief of the Army in the region, MacArthur was one of the leaders of the American comeback. On 2 September 1945 he accepted Japan's surrender on the flight deck of the battleship *Missouri*. In the following years, he was, as Supreme Commander-in-Chief of Allied Forces, Governor of Japan. He oversaw the democratization and demilitarization of Japan, which was occupied by the Americans and by a small Australian force, and he played an active role in the country's economic reconstruction and in the drafting of the new constitution. In 1951 his plan to attack China in order to bring about a turning point in the Korean War and to use the atomic bomb to do so put an end to one of the longest careers in the history of the American armed forces. He died in 1964.

MacArthur with his pipe, made from a hollowed-out corn cob.

FREE TIME.
Sailors from the American battleship New Jersey *applying tattoos during a pause in operations in the Pacific.*

(Below:) **MITSUBISHI ZERO, A6M2 MODEL 21.** *In the first year of the war this plane was the symbol of Japanese air power.*

American soldiers and 50,000 Filipinos were caught up in the rout. After occupying Manila on 2 January 1942, the Japanese introduced martial law. General Douglas MacArthur, who was in command of the archipelago and had wanted to defend it at all costs while waiting for reinforcements (which never arrived), was forced to abandon the Philippines on 11 March and retreat to safety in Australia. Holed up on the fortified island of Corregidor and on the Bataan Peninsula, the remaining American forces held out until early May.

About 50,000 Americans and Filipinos were captured. What awaited them now was the 'death march' to labour camps, where thousands died from illness, hunger and mistreatment. Japan completed its conquest of the archipelago in June. Filipino resistance fighters took refuge in the jungle and began guerrilla operations against the occupying army.

THE DEFEAT OF THE ALLIES IN THE JAVA SEA

The advance of the Japanese war machine seemed unstoppable. While the battle was raging at Singapore, the Japanese also struck at the Dutch East Indies. On 15 December 1941 they landed in British Borneo, taking control of the oil wells there. What was at stake was control of the island of Java, the defensive crux of the Dutch East Indies, an archipelago stretching over 3,000km. The island was rich in oil, rubber, timber and rice, and was a link between Australia and the Dutch empire in the Pacific. After landing at Celebes and Timor, the Japanese forces obtained one success after another, rapidly closing in on the capital, Batavia (now Djakarta).

The decisive battle in this phase of the Pacific war took place in the Sea of Java. The Allied naval forces, under the command of the Dutch Rear-Admiral Karel Doorman, attacked the Japanese invasion fleet that was providing

W E A P O N S

THE ZERO

Built by Mitsubishi, the Zero (Z-00) first saw action over China in the middle of 1940. It had two 20mm cannons and two 7.7mm machine guns. The Americans discovered the full potential of the firepower and speed (over 500km/hour) of this Japanese fighter in the attack on Pearl Harbor. Technologically very innovative, it was built with new alloys which, combined with the lack of armour, made it lighter than other planes; it was very manoeuvrable and proved superior to Allied planes of a similar class in the first phase of the Pacific war. The best carrier-based fighter in the world, the Zero was armed with deadly torpedoes that posed a serious threat to the US Navy, and had an exceptional range of 965km (with extra fuel tanks).

In the first year of the war, the Americans had nothing better witt which to counter it than the F4F Wildcat.

B24 LIBERATOR.
This was the American military plane with the greatest number of versions, and it was also the most widely produced. Built by Consolidated Vultee, it was used in the skies of Asia, Africa and Europe.

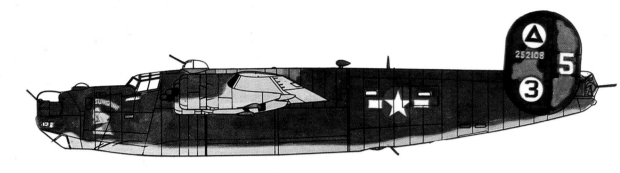

cover for transport ships heading for Indonesia. The odds were weighted heavily against the Allies, who had just 16 ships compared with 52 on the Japanese side; the latter were also faster, more effective and equipped with liquid-oxygen torpedoes capable of a speed of 36 knots. In little more than 24 hours, what became one of the bitterest clashes in the Pacific conflict paved the way for the Japanese conquest of Indonesia.

The Allies (Australians, Dutch, British and Americans) surrendered on 7 March 1942. With the conquest of Malaya and the Dutch East Indies, Japan had achieved an important strategic result: it had obtained control of three-quarters of the world's rubber output, two-thirds of its tin output and a major source of oil.

The next country that had to face the threat of a Japanese attack was Australia.

THE PINNACLE OF JAPANESE TRIUMPHS

With the capture of Rabaul in the Bismarck Archipelago (January 1942), the occupation of Lae and Salamaua on the northern coast of New Guinea (March) and some of the Solomon Islands, Japan's sea defence system reached its maximum expansion. The military might of the Japanese had swept through the Pacific like a tidal wave, from the borders of India to the edge of Australia. The 'white' strongholds (Hong Kong, Rangoon, Manila, Singapore, Java, Corregidor) had fallen one after another. The shockwaves of these

(Right:) **THE DECK OF A JAPANESE AIRCRAFT CARRIER BEFORE THE ATTACK ON PEARL HARBOR.**

(Far right:) **JAPANESE PILOT DONNING HIS HEADGEAR.**

(Left:) **GOD IS WITH US.**
Black soldiers were called upon to do their part in the war.

(Far left:) **STEP UP THE EFFORT.**
Bearing down on the Nazi swastika in the centre of the Japanese flag is the devastating military might of the United States.

(Below:) **JUBILANT JAPANESE TROOPS.**

Allied defeats seemed to mark the end of the European imperialist hold over Asia.

In April 1942 the Japanese navy and air force made a final bold raid, heading for Ceylon with a view to gaining control of the Indian Ocean. The operation was unsuccessful, because the British Eastern Fleet had abandoned the area in time and taken refuge along the African coast. A month earlier, Japanese submarines had pushed as far as Madagascar. Japan now sought a decisive clash with the American Pacific Fleet as a means of securing final victory. It seemed to be within their reach.

THE GREATER EAST ASIA CO-PROSPERITY SPHERE

Following its military successes, Japan could now embark on its plans for military and political subjugation of the region. The concept of the 'Greater East Asia Co-Prosperity Sphere', proclaimed by Tokyo in 1942, clearly revealed Japan's designs for imperialist domination in that area of the world. The notion of 'co-prosperity' had surfaced in nationalist circles of the Japanese army and navy before the war, and reflected the nation's conviction that it exercised absolute primacy in Asia. The nation had to

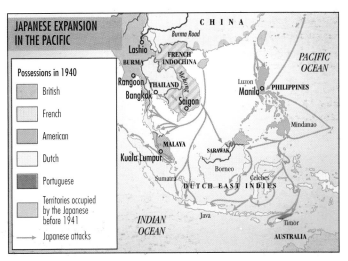

JAPANESE EXPANSION IN THE PACIFIC

Possessions in 1940

British
French
American
Dutch
Portuguese
Territories occupied by the Japanese before 1941
Japanese attacks

CHINA
Burma Road
Lashio
BURMA
FRENCH INDOCHINA
Rangoon
THAILAND
Bangkok
Saigon
Mekong
PACIFIC OCEAN
Luzon
Manila
PHILIPPINES
Mindanao
MALAYA
SARAWAK
Kuala Lumpur
Sumatra
Borneo
Celebes
DUTCH EAST INDIES
INDIAN OCEAN
Java
Timor
AUSTRALIA

(Right:) **BRIDGE ON THE RIVER KWAI.** *A scene from David Lean's celebrated film about British prisoners in Burma.*

(Below:) **LIBERATOR.** *Revolver used by resistance fighters in the war against the Japanese in the Pacific.*

display its moral, cultural and economic superiority (which the armed forces had obtained militarily) over 'Western individualism and materialism'.

It was not long, however, before the 'new order' envisaged in Tokyo's pan-Asiatic policy proved to be quite unlike the independent future – albeit under the protective wing of Japan – to which many populations aspired when centuries of colonial rule ended. Although the European colonialists had been ousted from Burma, Malaya and Indonesia, Japan installed puppet regimes with the task of extracting, at whatever cost, vital resources for Japan's economy. The enforced 'Japanization' of the subject populations disappointed those who had enthusiastically greeted the arrival of the Japanese army and had expected a rigorous, efficient administration. They soon found that, instead of

being liberated, they were now subjected to a rapacious form of occupation.

JAPANESE WEAKNESSES

Japan's stunning military successes were based on shaky foundations. One of the main reasons that had led it to enter the war with the surprise attack on Pearl Harbor was the need to avoid the economic stranglehold deriving from the American embargo on strategic materials. Great territorial gains did not, however, fill the enormous gap in resources between Japan and the Allies, and the Japanese war economy suffered from serious shortages. This was not only due to the failure to build up big stockpiles of raw and other materials to defend and administer the enormous territories (estimates suggest that Japan relied on imports for about 90% of its oil requirements): it was also due to the fact that,

PRISONERS OF THE JAPANESE

The Allied soldiers held in Japanese prison camps were almost always kept in conditions that barely enabled them to survive. The Japanese regarded them as slave labourers and did not concede them the rights stipulated by international conventions. The Japanese took about 200,000 prisoners during the

capture of the Philippines, Malaya and the East Indies. Half of the 20,000 or so Americans died in the following three years. A third of about 60,000 prisoners used to build the 420km railway line linking Burma and Siam (their story was made famous by David Lean's 1957 film *The Bridge on the River Kwai*, starring Alec Guinness) died before the work was completed. The route of the railway crosses one of the most climatically inhospitable regions in the world.

Begun in July 1942, the line was completed in October 1943. The Japanese used Australian, British and Dutch prisoners, plus Malay, Thai and Dutch East Indian labourers. During the war almost a third of the Anglo-Saxon prisoners died in Japanese camps. Many perished as a result of ill-treatment while marching to the camps or from illness, malnutrition and summary execution. The lot of Asian prisoners was even more atrocious: mass execution.

WAR ARCHIVES: LIFE ON AN AIRCRAFT CARRIER

THE CREW OF THE AMERICAN AIRCRAFT CARRIER *YORKTOWN*. The giants of World War II, aircraft carriers resembled floating cities and were designed to enable air attack over a vast range. They were supported by many other ships, which performed escort duties and provided fuel and tactical coordination. Life on board was rigorously and systematically organized, which was essential in order to coordinate the work of thousands of people in various departments and to guarantee an efficient and rapid response in combat or when the planes were landing or taking off. The American *Essex*-class carriers, the most efficient type used in the war, had a crew of 3,240 men and carried six fighter-interceptors, 36 dive-bombers and 18 torpedo-bombers. To repel attack from the air they were equipped with 12 127mm guns, 11 40mm quadruple gun mountings and 44 20mm heavy machine guns.

TRAINING CAMP.
In a war involving large armies, the various governments involved had to balance recruitment needs against the demand for industrial workers. Fifteen per cent of American army recruits aged between 25 and 44 had received a high-school diploma.

although it had conquered the Indonesian oil fields, Japan's war needs were much greater than what was available. About 1,200,000 soldiers were stationed in China, and the puppet governments had a further one and a half million. All these occupied territories needed supplies.

In the year of its maximum output, in 1943, Japan produced less than 9 million tons of steel, compared with 12 million in Britain and 80 million in the United States. Its mineral production (copper, iron, manganese, coal) was on average half that required for its war needs. Food rationing became increasingly strict for the civilian population of about 73 million people, whose needs could not be met either by agricultural production at home nor by the 'rice raids' conducted periodically by the occupation troops to requisition harvests in the Chinese countryside.

Japan's war industries suffered from a lack of skilled labour, and not even the mobilization of women and young people filled the gaps in its industrial apparatus. During the war, the country's gross national product rose by a quarter, but war spending increased fivefold. At the end of the war the population was on the brink of famine. Japan's leaders viewed the war in purely military terms and failed to consider that the defence of the country's enormous territorial conquests depended above all on its economic and production efforts.

The main weak point in Japan's defensive system was therefore its economy. This was even more glaring

THE AMERICAN AIRCRAFT CARRIER *HORNET*.
On 2 April 1942 the Hornet sailed from the port of San Francisco on a reprisal mission to avenge the defeat at Pearl Harbor. A formation of bombers commanded by James Doolittle reached Japan and dropped their bombs on Tokyo, Nagoya and Kobe, and then flew on to China.

(Left:) **UNCLE SAM.**
'Jap ... you're next!'

(Far left:) **RUN THROUGH.**
*American poster showing
the United States stabbed
from behind with a
Japanese katana.*

(Below:) **ERROL FLYNN
GIVES HIS MEN A PEP
TALK.**
Scene from the film
Objective Burma.

when contrasted with the industrial economy of the United States, the most efficient of the century.

Therefore, although Japan's armies had given ample demonstration of their extraordinary combat skills, the country was fatally undermined by serious economic shortages, which, due to a formidable security apparatus, were concealed not only from the nation's population but also from Allied espionage.

AN UNCERTAIN STRATEGY

In order to pursue its policy of expansionism (the slogan coined by Tokyo was 'Asia for the Asians') and to have a free hand in China, Japan had covered its back by signing a pact of neutrality with the Soviet Union in April 1941. Despite the signing of the Tripartite Pact with Germany and Italy in September 1940, and even after the beginning of hostilities in the Pacific, Japan excluded any form of

coordinated initiative with its German ally, which, apart from anything else, did not conceal its interest in the raw materials of Indonesia. In contrast to the cooperation that took place on the Anglo-American side, in Japan's handling of the war and in its subjection of the occupied territories there was no economic or military cooperation with its allies.

After Japan's wide-ranging offensive in the Pacific, its military chiefs debated two strategic options: either to aim to occupy Australia, as urged by General Tomoyuki Yamashita, who had conquered Malaya; or to consolidate Japan's territorial and maritime gains before launching a final offensive to conquer the whole of China, which was Yamamoto's hope. In the end the latter won the day. Yamamoto counted on Japanese naval superiority to take the Midway Islands and win a decisive clash with the American fleet.

THE PACIFIC WAR IN THE CINEMA

The American war effort was actively supported by the powerful Hollywood film industry. From 1943 onwards, operations on the Asian front became the subject matter for films presenting the Japanese as a cruel and treacherous enemy. Walter Wanger's *Gung Ho!* emphasized the blind obedience of Japanese soldiers, while Edward Dmytryk's *Behind*

the Rising Sun attributed most of the responsibility for the war to the Japanese military caste. A harsher tone can be found in *Objective Burma* by Raoul Walsh (1945): set in the Burmese jungle, it starred Errol Flynn as the commander of a squad of troops who repelled a furious night attack by an enemy guilty of all kinds of brutal deeds. A denunciatory stance is also seen in Lewis Milestone's *The Purple Heart*, in which the crew of a bomber shot down by anti-aircraft fire

was tried and condemned to death by a Japanese court. On the other hand, *Destination Tokyo* by Delmer Daves, *Bataan* by Tay Garnett and *Air Force* by Howard Hawks dealt with the solidarity between black and white soldiers, who fought together for the American cause under a common flag.

157

(Right:) **KUOMINTANG PROPAGANDA.**
Chinese nationalist poster: 'The more we fight, the weaker the enemy becomes.'

(Far right:) **FASCIST BRUTES.**
The brutal demons of the American painter, Thomas Hart Benton.

(Below:) **BELL P-39 AIRACOBRA.**
American fighter.

The operational effectiveness of the Japanese armed forces was undermined by its leadership structure. On the strength of its conquests in China and the British colonies, the army was one rung higher than the navy and air force. War planning was therefore carried out first by the Army Command and the plans were then presented to the other two services for approval. The immensity of Japan's territorial gains also had significant logistical repercussions, revealing in particular the shortcomings of the navy. It had the enormous task of defending an almost endless swathe of ocean stretching for thousands of sea miles, which it was unable to patrol adequately. Japan was stretched to the limit in terms of men, logistics and weapons on land, sea and air.

An initial alarm signal for Tokyo came in April 1942, when a surprise raid on the capital by bombers from the American carrier *Hornet* produced major strategic and psychological effects. The heart of the empire had been hit, making an enormous impact on the population and revealing that the eastern flank of Japan's defences was very vulnerable. The success of the retaliatory raid also boosted morale in the American armed forces, which had still been shaky following the disaster of Pearl Harbor. Concerns about possible further raids forced Tokyo to accelerate its plans to block the sea routes between America and Australia. Yamamoto's next objective in the Japanese south-easterly advance was the occupation of the Midway Islands and the southern coast of New Guinea.

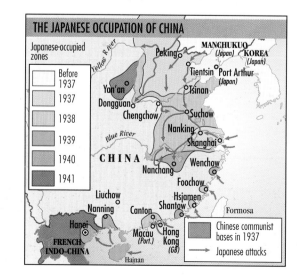

THE JAPANESE OCCUPATION OF CHINA

Japanese-occupied zones

	Before 1937
	1937
	1938
	1939
	1940
	1941

Yellow River

Peking · Tientsin · Port Arthur *(Japan)*

MANCHUKUO *(Japan)* **KOREA** *(Japan)*

Yan'an · Tsinan

Dongguan · Chengchow · Suchow

Blue River · Nanking · Shanghai

CHINA · Nanchang · Wenchow

Foochow

Liuchow · Hsiamen · Shantow

Nanning · Canton · Formosa

Hanoi · Macau *(Port.)* · Hong Kong *(GB)*

FRENCH INDO-CHINA

Hainan

Chinese communist bases in 1937

→ Japanese attacks

(Left:) **THE WAR EFFORT AT HOME.** *Posters urging Americans to contribute to the war effort.*

(Below:) **AMERICAN AIRMEN.**

JAPAN'S IMPERIAL DREAM

Japan's entry into the war was inspired by an ambitious project: to fill the position that had, until the previous century, been occupied by China. Transformation of its spoils from the British Empire into satellite states was the first step in the plan to conquer the most ancient empire in the world. Japan's occupation had divided China into three. The Japanese flag flew in the main coastal cities and the north-east of the country, where there were two governments: Manchukuo's, which had been established in 1932, and the KMT based in Nanking and presided over by Wang Ching-wei (former comrade-in-arms of the nationalist Chiang Kai-shek). The latter controlled the south-west, while the communists under Mao Zedong were based in the Yan'an and the north of the country and had, in the space of a few years, extended the range of their authority.

With extreme brutality, the Japanese occupiers tried to exploit the economic potential of the cities and rural areas. This led to frequent acts of sabotage and a lot of internal migration of the population (terrified by the massacre of

LIGHT SIGNALS.
A signalman sends a message to other units in the American fleet.

W E A P O N S

 THE 'FLYING TIGERS'
Commanded by the American Colonel Claire L. Chennault, the 'Flying Tigers' were a bugbear for the Japanese Air Force in the skies of China. Supported by the nationalist government of Chiang Kai-shek (whose wife put Chennault under her personal protection), this unusual formation of fighters, decorated with bright colours and with enormous shark jaws painted on the nose of the planes, was based near the frontier with Burma. Besides their almost legendary deeds, the pilots were known for the eccentric flying suits and Texan boots that they wore. The majority were Chinese, recruited by Chennault – a flying instructor in the World War I and a former acrobatic display pilot – with the promise of a rapid, highly unconventional training course and a reward for every enemy plane shot down. Divided into two sections, one to defend Rangoon and the other guarding the Chinese border, the 'Flying Tigers' shot down about 400 enemy planes in the course of the war, losing only four of their own pilots. In July 1942 the squadron was incorporated into the US Air Force's China Air Task Force.

0363

(Top:) The profile of the .P-40. (Above:) Chennault with Chiang Kai-shek and his wife. (Left:) A P-40 at the Burmese air base.

F6F TAKING OFF FROM THE AIRCRAFT CARRIER *LEXINGTON* IN THE PACIFIC.

hundreds of thousands of civilians by the Japanese), which upset the traditional equilibrium of the Chinese countryside. The collaborationist government was unable to unite the forces hostile to the communists and nationalists, who for their part were waiting for a favourable moment to attack the Imperial Army.

LONG-RANGE WAR IN THE CORAL SEA

This phase of the conflict was fought at sea. In order to complete its conquest of the Pacific, the Imperial Navy prepared for a final showdown with the American fleet,

counting on its numerical superiority. With its six aircraft carriers it had the largest fleet air arm in the world (about 500 aircraft). The carriers had gathered together prior to the attack planned by Yamamoto. When the Americans deciphered Japanese messages announcing an imminent landing at Port Moresby in New Guinea, two American aircraft carriers (*Lexington* and *Yorktown*) intercepted the Japanese fleet. On 8 May 1942 the two naval squadrons clashed in the Coral Sea at a distance of over 150km. In what was the first battle in naval history to be fought without the contenders being able to see each other, each side lost one aircraft carrier and about 60 planes. The Japanese were technologically inferior and were unable to repair their aircraft carriers for the next battle. So although on paper the Americans came off worse, losing *Lexington*

JUST BEFORE TAKE-OFF.
Plane about to take off from the Yorktown.
This aircraft carrier, which had 42 fighters and 99 bombers, saw action in the Battle of the Coral Sea, during which it was hit by a Japanese bomb. However, it was repaired in record time and participated in subsequent naval operations in the Pacific, before being decommissioned in 1970.

BADGES.
Every large American warship had a badge. The Yorktown's was an eagle on a cannon. A fighter squadron had Felix the Cat.

and *Sims* and with *Yorktown* badly damaged, the more significant result was that the United States had temporarily halted the Japanese advance towards Australia. Yamamoto's strategic objective – the capture of Port Moresby – had not been achieved.

FIVE MINUTES AT MIDWAY

Despite the setback in the Coral Sea, the Japanese maintained the initiative. Yamamoto decided to concentrate his fleet at the Midway Islands (1,600km to the west of Pearl Harbor and an ideal bridgehead for an offensive against the American West Coast) and to confuse the Americans with a diversionary attack on the Aleutians. The greatest concentration of warships ever seen in the Pacific was divided into three distinct combat groups. In the front line were the carriers, followed at a distance of 300 miles by the battleships, and finally the transports

to be used for the Aleutians manoeuvre.

Again, the deciphering of Japanese radio messages offered the Americans a decisive advantage. Aware of his adversary's plans, Admiral Chester W. Nimitz, the Commander-in-Chief of the Pacific Fleet, eluded the trap laid by Yamamoto and sent Task Forces 16 and 17 to Midway. The most memorable air and sea battle in the war began on 4 June and lasted for three days.

The superior strength of the Japanese (11 battleships, four carriers, 22 cruisers, 65 destroyers and 21 submarines against just three American carriers, eight cruisers and 17 destroyers) was, however, undermined by the effectiveness of American aerial reconnaissance. On Admiral Nimitz's orders, the American squadron took up position a long way north of Midway so as to stay beyond the range of Japanese spotter planes. Even before the battle had

'MAGIC'

Unknown to the Japanese, in the first few months of 1941 the Americans managed to crack Japan's diplomatic ciphers, which were transmitted by the so-called 'Machine A'. A more sophisticated version of this, called 'Machine B' (which automatically and electrically transposed the keys struck on the keyboard after having recorded the key of

the cipher, which varied for each telegram), was broken in September 1940 by the rapidly developed 'Purple Machine'. Although this helped the Americans to learn in advance about many of Japan's initiatives before the war, it did not suffice to avert the surprise attack on Pearl Harbor. 'Magic', the American decryption system, was on a par with the British 'Ultra' system used to crack German military codes, and proved crucial in the Battle of Midway. As had happened before the Battle of

the Coral Sea, the Americans managed to intercept a Japanese message revealing their attack plans, which included the diversionary invasion of the Aleutians. After abandoning the option of attacking Port Moresby, which would have paved the way to an invasion of Australia, Yamamoto did not concentrate the bulk of his carrier force for the attack on Midway. By breaking the enemy's military codes, the Americans erased the advantage of surprise on which the Japanese had been relying.

THE PRIDE OF THE JAPANESE NAVY. *Launched in 1940, the* Yamato *was the largest battleship in the world together with its sister ship* Musashi. *It was sunk in April 1945 during the American landings at Okinawa by 12 torpedoes and seven heavy bombs.*

begun, the surprise factor that the Japanese were relying on to bomb Midway had been lost.

Yamamoto's calculations proved erroneous: the Americans did not disperse their fleet, and the strength of the defences at the airport of Midway was much greater than the Japanese had foreseen. In the course of a battle in which the Japanese did not possess radar, and in which the whole fleet had been ordered to maintain absolute radio silence, the powerful Japanese battleships, including the one carrying Yamamoto, never went into action. Contrary to all expectations, it was the aircraft carriers commanded by Admiral Chuiki Nagumo that were the object of a surprise attack by American torpedo bombers. In just five minutes between 10.25 and 10.30 on 4 June 1942, the outcome of the war in the Pacific swung decisively in America's favour.

At the end of the three-day battle, the Americans were not aware of the extent of their victory. The Japanese had lost 3,500 men (many of whom were experienced pilots), four fleet carriers (*Akagi*, *Kaga*, *Soryu* and *Hiryu*), a cruiser and 332 planes; the Americans had lost about 300 men, an aircraft carrier (the *Yorktown*), a destroyer and 150 planes. The tactical errors made by the Japanese commanders were also the consequence of over-complacency about their military strength. The Midway disaster was kept secret from the general public in Japan and survivors returning home were not allowed any contact with their families. The defeat at Midway was the most sudden and dramatic turning point in the war, and in one stroke wiped out Japanese aspirations to take Australia. In September, they were forced to abandon New Guinea.

Six months after Pearl Harbor, Japan's sensational run of naval and land victories ended. From now on the Japanese navy lost the initiative in the Pacific, and the sea war

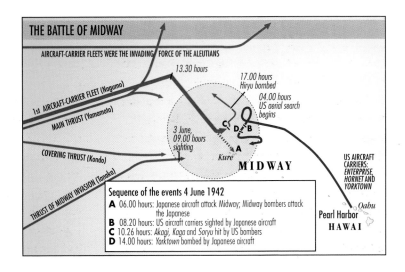

THE BATTLE OF MIDWAY

AIRCRAFT-CARRIER FLEETS WERE THE INVADING FORCE OF THE ALEUTIANS

1st AIRCRAFT-CARRIER FLEET (Nagumo)

13.30 hours

17.00 hours
Hiryu bombed

04.00 hours
US aerial search
begins

MAIN THRUST (Yamamoto)

3 June,
09.00 hours
sighting

COVERING THRUST (Kondo)

C D B

A

Kure

THRUST OF MIDWAY INVASION (Tanaka)

M I D W A Y

US AIRCRAFT
CARRIERS:
*ENTERPRISE,
HORNET* AND
YORKTOWN

Oahu

Pearl Harbor

H A W A I

Sequence of the events 4 June 1942
A 06.00 hours: Japanese aircraft attack Midway; Midway bombers attack the Japanese
B 08.20 hours: US aircraft carriers sighted by Japanese aircraft
C 10.26 hours: *Akagi*, *Kaga* and *Soryu* hit by US bombers
D 14.00 hours: *Yorktown* bombed by Japanese aircraft

ADMIRAL ERNEST J. KING. *Commander-in-Chief of the American Fleet and Head of Naval Operations.*

LEADERS

CHESTER W. NIMITZ

Chester W. Nimitz, who was of German stock, was born in Texas in 1885. After graduating from the Naval Academy in 1905, he served in submarines during World War I.

As head of the US Bureau of Navigation, he had occasion to meet President Roosevelt, who immediately appreciated his worth. Nimitz was optimistic in the face of the Pearl Harbor disaster; after being promoted admiral, he set about rebuilding the American fleet, assisted by an excellent team of staff. He later commented: 'It was by the grace of God that our fleet was at Pearl Harbor on 7 December 1941.'

Affable and with an informal approach, he was, when required, determined and inflexible. In April 1942 he was appointed Commander-in-Chief of the Pacific Fleet. He planned in great detail the air–sea battles in the Coral Sea and at Midway, and the capture of Guadalcanal, and set great store by the reliability of information fed to him by American Intelligence. After Guadalcanal he developed an offensive strategy based on amphibious operations, with a series of landings on Pacific islands. He was also responsible for the submarine campaign that annihilated Japan's merchant fleet and culminated in the economic stranglehold placed on that country at the beginning of 1945. He had to accept Roosevelt's decision (urged by his rival MacArthur) to recapture the Philippines rather than aiming for Formosa and China. In October 1944, Nimitz destroyed the Japanese Combined Fleet at the Battle of Leyte Gulf.

From the island of Guam, which the Americans captured in August 1944, Nimitz directed the landings at Iwo Jima and Okinawa. His great historical merit was to have won, in a period of less than four years, a naval war with a fleet that, at least at the beginning of the conflict, was numerically and militarily inferior to that of his adversary.

When the Chief of Naval Operations, Fleet Admiral Ernest J. King, retired in November 1945, Nimitz was appointed to replace him. He died in 1966.

Admiral Nimitz (right) and General MacArthur.

(Left:) **MAN THE GUNS.** *US Navy recruitment poster.*

(Far left:) **BOMB IN THE SEA.** *Explosion of a Japanese bomb near the stern of an American ship.*

(Below:) **A MARINE TAKES AIM AT A JAPANESE SNIPER.**

was to be marked by a succession of American attacks and stubborn attempts by Japan to contain and halt the inexorable advance of the industrial and military might of the United States.

THE HEROISM OF THE MARINES AT GUADALCANAL

Having halted the triumphant march of the Japanese at Midway, and with command of the land forces assigned to General MacArthur, the United States launched their first counter-attacks. A decision still had to be made about which line of approach to take in order to reach the final objective: the occupation of Japan. Indeed, Japan was over 3,000km from the American bases, and the Japanese defences were organized along an interminable chain of fortified islands. The compromise reached by the American High Command gave the navy and Nimitz responsibility for taking the island of Guadalcanal (east of New Guinea) and advancing into New Guinea, and gave MacArthur's land forces the task of capturing the Japanese base of Rabaul in New Britain. Once Nimitz and MacArthur had reached a compromise agreement on what action to take, the American counter-attack began in the South-West Pacific.

(Right:) **LYING IN WAIT IN THE JUNGLE.**
The Marines were established in 1775. At the beginning of the 20th century they were the symbol of US expansionism in Central America and in Asia.

(Below:) **BADGES OF THE ENGINEERS AND THE 1ST MARINE DIVISION.**

On 7 August 1942 the 1st Marine Division landed at Tulagi, Guadalcanal and other islands in the area. The Japanese garrison (2,200 men) was overcome, but the Japanese navy and air force harried the invading force for months. On the high plains of Guadalcanal – a name that came to be remembered as one of the most famous battlegrounds in the entire conflict – and in the surrounding seas, pitched fighting took place day and night between land, sea and air forces. One of the cruellest clashes between the Marines and Japanese infantry occurred in mid-September: the Marines repelled yet another desperate Japanese attack on positions that had come to be known as Bloody Ridge. The battle continued in October, despite torrential rain.

In February 1943, after six months' hard fighting, the battle for the island finally ended. It was a triumph for the Marine Corps. Though the latter had suffered 1,500 casualties, the Japanese infantry's losses were almost 23,000 and they were no longer invincible. In order to defeat them the Americans had adopted a method that was to be used from now on in the Pacific war, namely the annihilation of the enemy with a massive barrage of firepower aimed at breaching the enemy's defensive perimeter at various points. In addition to Guadalcanal, the Australians and Americans obtained success in Papua, where the Japanese again suffered much heavier losses. MacArthur, who was now Allied Commander-in-Chief of the South-West Pacific, had 460,000 soldiers at his disposition (there were already 380,000 troops on the European front), and now that the threat to Australia had been averted, he could make the next move in his strategy: an Allied attack on the Solomon Islands and the Bismarck Archipelago. Then

WEAPONS

 THE JEEP
General George Marshall regarded the jeep as the United States' greatest contribution to modern warfare. Eisenhower considered it one of the three means of transport that enabled the Allies to win the war, together with the Dakota plane and the landing craft. The idea of developing a fast military vehicle to replace the motorbike was first proposed in the 1930s. After various prototypes had been built, in July 1941 the army ordered 16,000 jeeps from Willys-Overland. They had four-wheel drive and a maximum speed of 60 mph, and they combined power, manoeuvrability and durability, making them ideal for rough terrain. By 1945 some 653,000 jeeps had been produced, the majority of them as part of the aid programme of the 'Lend-Lease' Act approved by Congress in March 1941. The name may derive from the letters 'GP' (General Purpose) or possibly from the go-anywhere, do-anything 'Eugene the Jeep', a character in the comic strip *Popeye*.

(Left:) **BRITISH SURRENDER.**

(BELOW:) IN THE PACIFIC SWAMPS.
Fighting often took place in areas with an unhealthy climate, and which were infested with wasps and malarial mosquitoes. In the Burmese jungle the troops were cut down by dysentery, typhoid, cholera, malaria and red fever. In the forests the soldiers often caught a disease known as 'jungle fever'.

America's policy in the Pacific changed: at a conference in Casablanca (January 1943), Churchill and Roosevelt gave priority to taking the Philippines. The Americans could now hop from one island to another, supported by the new battleships and aircraft carriers being produced with dizzying speed in American shipyards.

A FURTHER BRITISH DEFEAT IN BURMA

In the land war, the British drew up plans for a counter-attack from north-east India. The aim was to recapture Burma with an amphibious attack on Rangoon and joint penetration by British and Chinese troops from the north. Logistical difficulties, a shortage of troops and the lack of support from the Chinese forces under Chiang Kai-shek thwarted the offensive launched by General Archibald Wavell to recapture the coastal region of Arakan. Between December 1942 and May 1943 the frontal attacks made by the British and Indian divisions broke up on the enemy's defensive lines. The superior combat skills of the Japanese infantry in jungle warfare and the heavy losses suffered by the British (also due to malaria) led to yet another British defeat in Asia.

Allies
on the offensive

Once the German and Italian armies had been defeated in North Africa, it was easier for the Allies to turn the conflict in their favour, crushing the powers of the Tripartite Pact one after another. In the first few months of 1943, a war of attrition began in Europe and the Pacific, through which the Allies managed to reverse the tide of the war. They were helped in this by the fact that there was no military cooperation at all between the Japanese and the Germans, who were fighting on opposite sides of the world. As a result of the American victory at Midway and the capture of Guadalcanal, Japan lost its supremacy in the Pacific. On the Russian front the German armies were deployed along a front line stretching thousands of kilometres. The German war machine began to show signs of strain, but at the same time there were tensions between the Allies. Stalin had repeatedly asked the Americans and British to open a 'second front' in *(p. 168)* **GERMAN CHILDREN.**

(p. 169) **HENRI GIROUD, ROOSEVELT, DE GAULLE AND CHURCHILL AT THE CASABLANCA CONFERENCE (1943).**

(Right): **YOUNG GERMAN WOMEN IN UNIFORM.**

(Far right:) **MACABRE TOAST TO HITLER IN A RUSSIAN POSTCARD.**

Europe in order to relieve German pressure on the Soviet Union, which continued to bear the main brunt of the war. The Allies agreed with Stalin, but disagreed about where that front should be opened. The Americans were in favour of invading France, though without departing from a key principle in their approach to the war, namely to intervene only when they had a clear superiority in strength, so as to keep casualties as low as possible.

The British, on the other hand, having seen a drastic reduction in their imperial power in Asia, were keen to defend their primacy in the Mediterranean and regarded the opening of a 'second front' in Italy or the Balkans as an opportunity to attack Nazi Germany from the south. They also urged more systematic bombing of German cities and industrial plants. A major turning point in the conflict came when the German army capitulated at Stalingrad, its first major defeat in the war. Six

months later the Axis was further compromised by the collapse of its weakest partner, Italy.

FINAL OBJECTIVE: 'UNCONDITIONAL SURRENDER'

Confirmation that the Mediterranean, together with the North Atlantic, was to remain the main area of military collaboration between the Anglo-American forces came at a conference between Roosevelt and Churchill (Stalin justified his absence by the need to supervise the battle at Stalingrad personally) and their relative High Commands at Casablanca. The conference (14–26 January 1943) produced a number of strategic and political results. Thanks to their proven diplomatic ability, the British managed to persuade the Americans to follow

CAPTURING THE ENEMY'S FLAG. *American soldiers pose for the camera during the Sicily campaign.*

CHILDREN'S CANTEEN IN GERMANY.

up their commitment in North Africa with an attack on Sicily. Immediate priority was given to: hunting down the U-boats in the Atlantic; heavy daylight and night-time bombing of German cities to bring about the destruction of the 'military, industrial and economic system, and the undermining of the morale of the German people to the point where their capacity for armed resistance is fatally weakened'; and advancing in the Mediterranean in order to knock out Italy, defined by Churchill as the 'soft underbelly of the Axis'. The conference was a success for the British, as it delayed the opening of the 'second front' being urged by Stalin, who, for his part, suspected that the reason why his urgent request had not been met was that his western Allies wanted to make a separate peace with Germany that would be detrimental to Russia.

The political result of the conference was the Allied declaration that they would accept only the 'unconditional surrender' of Germany, Japan and Italy and were unwilling to make concessions. The Allies wanted to prevent any of the defeated nations from negotiating surrender terms, as Germany had done in 1919 by appealing to Wilson's '14 Points' during discussions to work out the clauses in the Treaty of Versailles. The United States and Britain also

WEHRMACHT FIELD GUN AMIDST THE RUINS OF A TOWN NEAR STALINGRAD. *After the German setback in Central Caucasus, Paulus's 6th Army moved to capture the city on the Volga.*

(Right:) **THIS IS THE ENEMY.**
American propaganda.

(Far right:) **ALLIED LIGHTNING.**
In this Soviet poster, the umbrella sheltering Hitler and Mussolini offers little protection against the power of the British, Americans and Soviets.

(Below:) **TOTAL VICTORY AGAINST THE 'ASIATIC HORDES'.**
Joseph Goebbels giving his speech.

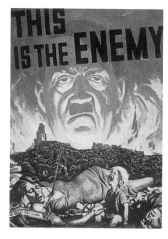

wanted a free hand to organize the future of Germany and Europe. Churchill and Roosevelt undertook to ease tensions with Stalin and to create the conditions for closer cooperation between the Allies after the war. The Americans and the British had divergent views about future military operations: the landings in Sicily were seen by the former as sealing Allied control of the Mediterranean, and by the latter as the first step towards inducing Italy to surrender and therefore to eliminating one of the contenders in the war.

FINAL OBJECTIVE: 'TOTAL VICTORY'

While operations were still underway in North Africa (Montgomery reached the Tunisian border in February 1943), and the outcome of the war on the Russian front hung on the battle going on at Stalingrad, the Reich stepped up measures to mobilize the German people. A

major and very active role in maintaining the internal unity of Hitler's Germany was played by the Propaganda Minister, Joseph Goebbels, who constantly urged the population to stand firm in the face of Allied bombing. The Thousand-Year Reich, he claimed, would achieve final victory over the enemy powers; they were viewed as an expression of international Jewry and Bolshevism and were represented by propaganda as being trapped between Wall Street capitalism and Stalin.

On the tenth anniversary of the Nazi Party's coming to power, and shortly before events on the Russian front resulted in a reverse that was to prove decisive for the outcome of the war, Goebbels addressed the nation and sang the praises of 'total war'. His slogan was a threat for the enemies of Germany, but was also directed against those who

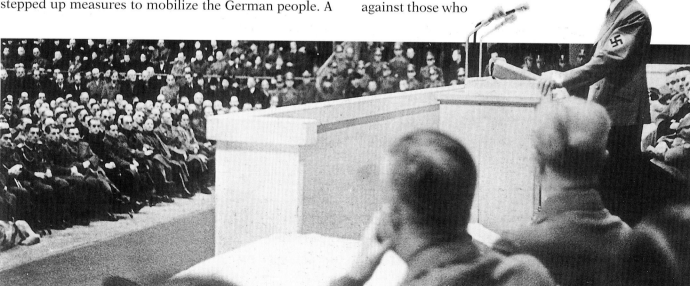

had not done their utmost to support the German war effort. With Nazi propaganda extolling the Reich's mission and the superiority of the German people, this concept of war meant a further and indiscriminate involvement of entire populations and national communities in the process of extermination that was being conducted in Europe in the name of racial exclusivity.

In the mass event organized on 18 February 1943 at the Sports Hall in Berlin, Goebbels entrusted to the unconditional will of the German people the task of taking a big step forwards in the direction of 'total war', with a view to obtaining a victory that would also be 'total'. Praising the sacrifice of the soldiers as proof of the extraordinary qualities of the German people, he conjured up for his audience the threat that the 'steppes' posed for German

and European civilization. The objective, according to the Propaganda Minister, was to close ranks and to act with a spirit of self-sacrifice for the supreme benefit of the nation, through complete mobilization of the country's resources.

Irrespective of the propaganda value of Goebbels' slogans, Germany undoubtedly recognized that the determination of the Allies to obtain the 'unconditional surrender' of the Reich was a prelude to an attempt to wipe out German military power and to destroy the National Socialist regime. Neither the Allies nor the Germans, therefore, contemplated anything other than unconditional surrender or total victory. Shortly before the Stalingrad disaster, the possibility of scaling down the objectives set by Nazi Germany when it entered the war began to gain consensus amongst German

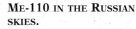

ME-110 IN THE RUSSIAN SKIES.
Various versions were built of this fighter-bomber, which was the backbone of the Luftwaffe's forces during the Battle of Britain. Manned by a crew of two, it had serious shortcomings, including a limited cruising range and a small bomb load.

GOERING AT A DECORATION CEREMONY. *The armoured division that bore the name of the Marshal of the Reich was sent to Sicily to oppose the Allied landings.*

political and military leaders. This was not only in regard to the handling of operations in Russia, where many German generals had for some time been hoping for a more flexible approach.

THE SURRENDER OF PAULUS AT STALINGRAD

In the northern sector of the Russian front, during fighting around Lake Ladoga, the Germans launched a counter-attack and pushed back the Soviets, who had managed to open up a corridor that partially relieved Leningrad (which had been under siege since October 1941). Meanwhile, on the Don front down in the south, the Italian 8th Army was fast disintegrating in the face of a Russian offensive.

In the large Stalingrad pocket, the Soviet armies punched several holes in the defensive perimeter of the 6th Army

under Friedrich von Paulus. The Russian attack began on 19 November 1942, with the breaching of the Romanian and German lines to the north and south of the city. A week later the 6th Army was cut off. In January 1943 the supplies that Goering had promised to fly in were no longer adequate. Almost 20,000 soldiers, a fifth of the remaining combat force, were in improvised hospitals. The prospect of a retreat by Paulus threatened to leave the German armies between the Don and the Caucasus unprotected. The idea of using the few remaining tank units to break out of the Soviet encirclement (enforced by 500,000 soldiers and a third of Russia's total artillery strength) was rejected by Hitler and Manstein, who refused to order a retreat from the Stalingrad pocket.

INSIDE A BATHTUB. *Russian soldier in position amidst the ruins of a house in Stalingrad. Soviet infantrymen were equipped with a sheepskin and felt boots, which enabled them to stave off the cold and to fight in extreme weather conditions. The German soldiers often suffered frostbite in their nailed boots.*

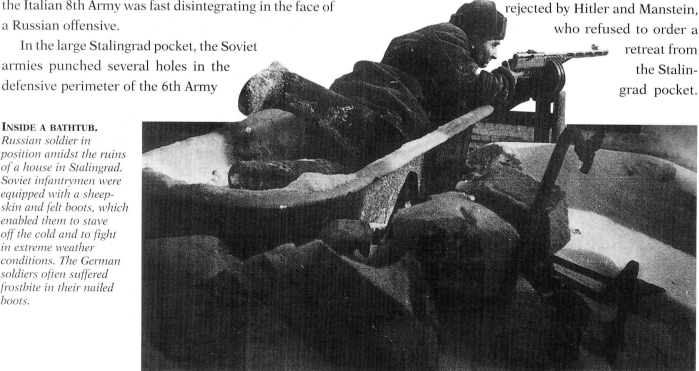

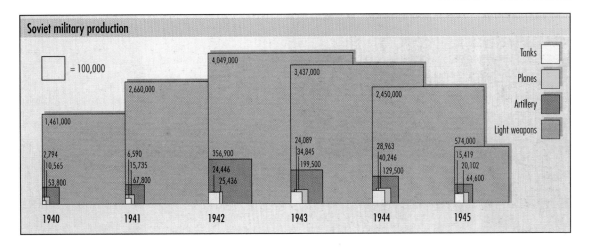

Soviet military production

☐ = 100,000

Tanks ☐
Planes ☐
Artillery ☐
Light weapons ☐

1940
1,461,000
2,794
10,565
53,800

1941
2,660,000
6,590
15,735
67,800

1942
4,049,000
356,900
24,446
25,436

1943
3,437,000
24,089
34,845
199,500

1944
2,450,000
28,963
40,246
129,500

1945
574,000
15,419
20,102
64,600

The tragic destiny of the trapped 6th Army and of Paulus, who was fighting to defend the city and his military honour, was sealed.

In mid-January the Russians started to shell the German positions relentlessly, in order to wipe out what was left of the German army in the ruins of the city. Fighting took place from house to house and in extreme weather conditions, with temperatures falling to minus 30°C. On 30 January, Paulus was promoted by Hitler to the rank of Field Marshal to encourage him not to surrender. However, on 2 February, after the Soviet forces on the east bank of the Volga had crossed the river and the last pockets of resistance around the tractor and Red October factories had been wiped out, Paulus capitulated. Of the 285,000

Germans trapped in the city on the Volga at the beginning of the Russian offensive, 34,000 were evacuated by air and about 160,000 were killed. The 90,000 survivors were sent to Siberia. Few of them would ever return to Germany. In the city that Stalin had decided to turn into the most tenacious stronghold of Soviet resistance, the German army had suffered its first major defeat. It marked a turning point in the conflict. A year and a half after the start of Operation 'Barbarossa', the Soviet Union was saved. This was mainly thanks to the numerical superiority of its troops (over 3 million against 2,600,000 German soldiers), the efficiency of its industry (which had been moved back beyond the Urals) and the aid provided by the Allies (more than 35,000 trucks since June 1942).

SLEDGES FOR TRANSPORTING MEN AND SUPPLIES.
Although temperatures often fell well below zero, the Russians were very skilled at keeping the engines of their vehicles going and preventing their mules and horses from freezing to death.

NIKOLAI VATUTIN.
Vatutin's troops held the south side of the Kursk salient. After recapturing Kiev in 1944, Vatutin was killed in an ambush by Ukrainian nationalist partisans.

THE BATTLE FOR KHARKOV

The disaster of Stalingrad was a big blow for Germany's entire east front and now the German armies were on the defensive for the first time. Both sides were aware that the following two months, before the spring thaw hindered tank movements, would be decisive. A long war of attrition began along the Russian front, which was thousands of kilometres long. Manstein's Army Group Don (renamed Army Group South) was forced to withdraw to Rostov, while the retreat of Kleist's Army Group A from the Caucasus left a long unguarded stretch between his front and Manstein's. Russian pressure on Manstein's northern flank threatened to break the hinge with Army Group B (now called Army Group Centre).

Initially Hitler seemed to accept Manstein's proposal for a flexible defensive strategy to cope with the predicted Soviet offensive, so as to exploit the mobility and tactical superiority of the German armoured units in quick battles. What was at stake was control of the Ukraine. In the middle of February 1943 the Germans were forced to abandon Kharkov, which opened up a gap of some 300km between Army Groups Centre and South. Less than a month later Manstein threw his tank units into an attack on Kharkov (the most hotly contested city in the German–Russian war), halted the offensive of the Russian 3rd Army and conducted an encircling pincer movement against the Soviet forces in the Kursk salient.

A COLOSSAL TANK BATTLE

In the middle of March the Wehrmacht's tank units, which were now equipped with new models (the Panther Mark V, armed with a 75mm gun, and the Tiger Mark VI, with an 88mm gun), pushed the Russians back beyond the east bank of the river Donetz. Shortly afterwards, however, the

WEAPONS

KATYUSHA ROCKET LAUNCHER

The Katyusha rocket launcher was one of the most effective weapons used by the Soviets in the war. It fired 130mm rockets (weighing 40kg and with a maximum range of 40km), which were mounted on a semi-mobile battery. The rockets were positioned in a series of launch tubes known by soldiers as the 'organs of Stalin'. Equipped with an electric firing mechanism, the Katyusha was a formidable artillery weapon used to soften up the enemy prior to an infantry and tank attack. Every Katyusha division could fire 3,840 rockets in a single salvo. This multiple ordnance launcher, which was one of the greatest technological innovations of the Soviet war industry, entered service in 1943 and was used extensively throughout the campaign on the eastern front.

(Left:) **WALTER MODEL.**
*'Hitler's fireman'
committed suicide in 1945.*

(Far left:) **HERMANN
HOTH.**
*Hoth commanded a
Panzer group at Kursk.*

(Below:) **PANTHER G.**
*The most widely used
German tank.*

spring thaw turned the Russian steppes into an enormous marsh, bringing operations to a halt. Alerted about the German plans of attack by their intelligence, the Russians prepared a series of defensive lines staggered over a depth of 160km. Their objective was to absorb the German thrust towards Kursk and then to launch a counter-attack.

In early July, after a pause of more than two months, Hitler ordered the attack. Over 2,000 tanks, 20,000 artillery pieces and more than a million men, supported by 2,000 planes, pushed against the Kursk salient. The 9th Army under Walter Model attacked from the north, while the 4th Panzer Army, commanded by Hermann Hoth, advanced from the south. The Russians concentrated nine armies in the salient (two of these armoured), which were commanded by Georgi Zhukhov and Alexander Vasilevsky. They also had 20,000 artillery guns and mortars, about 1,000 Katyusha rocket launchers, 2,400 planes, 3,500 tanks and semi-mobile guns and 1,300,000 men. Another five Russian armies were positioned near Kursk, ready to intervene as required.

The biggest tank battle in World War II took place between 5 and 16 July 1943. Massed tank units followed by infantry troops slogged it out at close quarters in a hellish din and a cauldron of fire. Fleets of tanks moved across the steppes, their visibility hindered by dense columns of smoke. On 15 July, Hitler had to accept that the Soviet defences had not been breached. The casualty figures were huge on both sides. For the first time the German army had suffered a serious defeat in a large-scale battle. After

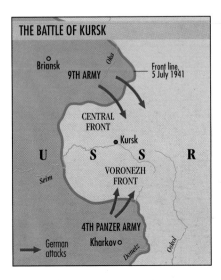

TANK FIRE AT NIGHT.
*The German tank
advance in the Kursk
salient was slowed down
by minefields. Several
months before this major
tank battle, Molotov and
Ribbentrop met to discuss
whether there was any
possibility of putting an
end to the war. The talks
were inconclusive.*

SEBASTOPOL.
The Germans occupied the Crimean city of Sebastopol in July 1942. The Russians recaptured it almost two years later.

L E A D E R S

STALIN'S GENERALS

GEORGI KONSTANTINOVICH ZHUKOV

The son of a cobbler, Zhukov was born in 1896. He joined the cavalry in 1914 and soon rose to the rank of non-commissioned officer. He sided with the revolutionaries in October 1917 and had a brilliant career in

the Red Army. Zhukov was the legendary 'general who never lost a battle'. In 1939 he was in command of the Russian counter-attack against Japan, and in 1940 he was in charge of the Finnish campaign. He coordinated the defence of Leningrad when it was under siege, and halted the German advance on Moscow, before winning a historical victory at Stalingrad. As Commander-in-Chief of the Soviet Armed Forces, he led all the major military operations and advanced across Poland in 1945 to launch the final attack on Berlin. Fearing his popularity, Stalin sidelined him after the war. Minister of Defence in 1955 and a member of the Central Committee of the Communist Party, Zhukov was retired by Khruschev. He died in 1974.

SEMYON KONSTANTINOVICH TIMOSHENKO

Born from peasant stock in 1895, Timoshenko enrolled in the Tsarist cavalry but then became a Red Army officer during the civil war. After serving in the Finnish campaign, he was appointed Marshal and Commissar of Defence and embarked on a radical reorganization of the army. In 1941 he commanded the western front, slowing down the German advance, but in May 1942, when the Germans captured the Crimea and were advancing on Stalingrad, he was removed from his post by Stalin. He died in 1970.

IVAN STEPHANOVICH KONIEV

Born in 1897, Koniev joined the Red Army in 1918. He became a lieutenant-general in June 1940 and commanded the defence of Moscow for several months, then the '2nd Ukrainian front'. Promoted to full general in 1943, his most important victory came at the beginning of 1944, when he defeated the Germans at Korsun on the river Dnieper, in the 'second Stalingrad' of the German-Russian war. During the final offensive against Germany, he commanded the '1st Ukrainian front', which together with Zhukov's '1st White Russian front', completed the encirclement of Berlin. A fierce rival of Zhukov (whom Stalin often preferred), Koniev replaced him in 1946 and was appointed Commander-in-Chief of Land Forces. In 1955 he became Commander-in-Chief of the Armed Forces of the Warsaw Pact countries. He died in 1973.

KONSTANTIN ROKOSSOVSKY

Born in 1896, Rokossovsky was a Red Army officer from a very early age. He fell foul of Stalin's purges at the end of the 1930s, but was brought back in July 1941 and in September 1942 commanded the Don front. He received the German surrender at Stalingrad. Stalin subsequently made him a Marshal of the Soviet Union. After his successes on the 'White Russian front' and in the campaign to liberate Poland, Stalin assigned him to operations in Pomerania and Prussia, and he fought alongside Zhukov in the capture of Berlin. He died in 1968.

(*Left:*) **ITALIAN HELMETS.**
The helmets of a bersagliere and of a non-commissioned officer in the Colonial Militia.

(*Left below:*) **SIDEARM.**
The Beretta was the most well-known semi-automatic pistol used in the Italian army.

(*Below:*) **ITALIAN ARMY (ARMIR) IN THE SNOW.**

their success at Kursk, the Russians definitively gained the initiative, and in August 1943 the Red Army began the march that would lead, less than two years later, to the capture of Berlin.

ITALY AFTER DEFEAT IN RUSSIA

While the Germans were facing defeat at Stalingrad, the tragic destiny of the Italian army in Russia (ARMIR) was also being played out. The ARMIR had been set up by Mussolini to fight alongside his German ally on the Soviet front. In December 1942, the 8th Army, which comprised 230,000 men in ten divisions, was forced to withdraw from the line of the Don as a result of pressure from two Soviet armies. This was the beginning of the rout of the Italian army, which was decimated in the course of a 'death march' of over 350km made in the extreme weather conditions of the Russian steppes. Less than half of the army returned home in April 1943. Three Alpine divisions made a vain sacrifice to protect the retreat of other units, and fought heroically against Soviet tank and artillery units at Nikolajewka.

The death of 180,000 Italians on the Russian front rocked the shaky Fascist regime, and soon afterwards Mussolini's dream of an Italian empire in Africa also vanished. There was muted but growing discontent in the country; defeated on the battlefield, the population was

(Right:) **ALLIED POSTER AFTER THE LANDINGS IN SICILY.**

(Far right:) **CRACK THE AXIS.**
The contribution of war production to final victory.

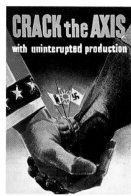

hit by the loss of loved ones and by food shortages, rationing and a burgeoning black market. People began to hold Mussolini and other Fascist leaders responsible for the disastrous handling of Italy's contribution to the war. In March there were strikes in the major northern factories, which resulted in a mixture of repression and economic concessions to the workers. It was the first sign of the impending end of Fascism, now a spent force and caught between the 'internal front' – a resurgence in anti-Fascist resistance movements and widespread popular discontent – and the

course of military operations. The removal of a number of leading members of the regime, which Mussolini pushed through in an attempt to galvanize the nation, was to no avail. In June the British landed on the islands of Pantelleria and Lampedusa, the prelude to the Allied invasion of Sicily.

ARRIVAL OF THE LIBERATORS.
American soldiers on the pier of a Sicilian port. The Allies landed in Sicily a full six weeks after Mussolini had been deposed, because the Anglo-American military chiefs feared that operations in Italy might slow down their plans to invade Normandy and draw troops and equipment away from American operations in the Pacific.

ITALY FROM 25 JULY TO 8 SEPTEMBER

In the summer of 1943, following a succession of Italian defeats and the Allied invasion of Sicily, confidence in Mussolini plummeted and opposition grew, resulting in a latent crisis that led to the fall of the Fascist regime. The country's leading political and military leaders, firmly supported by the king, became convinced that the only way of avoiding the complete collapse of the nation was to remove Mussolini from power.

In a meeting of the Fascist Grand Council that ended in the early hours of 25 July 1943, a motion presented by Dino Grandi (President of the House of the *Fasci* and the Corporations) was approved. This decided on the 'immediate re-establishment of all the functions' of the state institutions and gave effective command of the armed forces to the king. In the afternoon the king told Mussolini he was going to replace him with General Pietro Badoglio, and the Duce was arrested by the *carabinieri*. At 22.45 the radio transmitted the news of Mussolini's deposition and a message from Badoglio announcing the continuation of the war alongside the German ally. Jubilant crowds poured into the streets, acclaiming the king and Badoglio, but in many cases calling for peace and liberty as well. The symbols of the regime were pulled down and the Fascists seemed to melt into thin air.

Badoglio issued a decree dissolving the National Fascist Party and abolishing the Grand Council and the special tribunal. The government wanted to re-establish the continuity of the pre-Fascist state and the Savoy monarchy; it was clear that the risk was that the coup against Mussolini would simply turn into a reshuffle of power within the ruling class. Fearing that mass demonstrations might lead to revolutionary rebellion,

the head of the Army High Command, General Mario Roatta, ordered the army to fire on any demonstration that violated the state of emergency. There were many victims. While the anti-Fascist groups (Communists, Socialists, the Democrazia Cristiana, which arose from the Partito Populare, and the members of 'Justice and Liberty') were reorganizing, the government started secret negotiations with the Allies, and on 5 September an armistice was signed with the Anglo-Americans at Cassibile in Sicily. This was only announced on the radio on 8 September. King Victor Emanuel and the royal family, Badoglio and his generals all fled ignominiously from the capital to Pescara before boarding a ship at Brindisi, well away from the German troops. The army was left without orders and the country was at the mercy of the German troops, who crossed the Brenner Pass on 9 September. On the same day the anti-Fascists set up the National Committee of Liberation, calling on the Italian people to join the 'struggle and the resistance'. The announcement of the armistice led to the disintegration of the Italian army: some 60,000 men were to die or go missing, while 550,000 were deported to Germany. Of the survivors, many headed for home and many others formed partisan groups that injected fresh life into the resistance movement. On 10

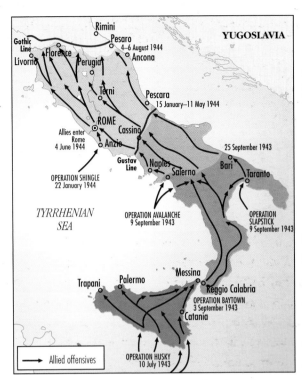

September the Germans secured the surrender of the Italian forces defending Rome. On 12 September a unit of German paratroopers commanded by Major Otto Skorzeny rescued Mussolini, who had been imprisoned in the Abruzzi, and took him to Germany.

Mussolini and Otto Skorzeny before taking off for Germany after Skorzeny had rescued Mussolini from his prison on the Gran Sasso (Appenines).

M4 SHERMAN.
The best known US tank. The Americans named their tanks after generals from the Civil War and World War I.

THE COLLAPSE OF THE FASCIST REGIME

Preceded by heavy shelling, the invasion of Sicily began on 10 July 1943, when the American 7th Army, led by General George Patton and the British 8th Army under Montgomery, landed in the Gulf of Gela and the Gulf of Syracuse, respectively. In a single day more than 150,000 men disembarked on the Sicilian coast from some 3,000 landing craft. The island was defended by the Italian 6th Army, reinforced by some German forces (an armoured and a parachute division), which were ordered by Hitler to fight independently from their ally.

On the slopes of Mount Etna, Montgomery met more resistance than expected on his drive towards Messina, while Patton advanced rapidly towards the north coast of the island. From a military point of view, Operation 'Husky' was not a success: when the Allies entered Messina more than a month later, most of the Axis forces had already crossed unhindered to the Italian mainland.

The political consequences of the invasion, on the other hand, were much greater. It was the final blow for a regime that had been in the balance for some time. On 19 July there was the first Allied bombing raid on Rome: 500 American planes in two waves dropped their bombs on the railway station of San Lorenzo, causing about 2,000 deaths. It caused enormous shock waves in the country. When the radio announced the fall of Mussolini on the evening of 25 July – after he had been outvoted in the last meeting of the Fascist Grand Council, arrested on the orders of King Victor Emanuel III and replaced by Marshal Pietro Badoglio at the head of a new government – the

IN THE COUNTRYSIDE OF SOUTHERN ITALY.
American soldier checks a farmer's house. (Photograph by Robert Capa.)

(Left:) **AMERICANS AT TROINA.**

(Below left:) **QUEUING FOR WATER IN NAPLES.** *(Photo by Robert Capa.)*

(Below right:) **IN MEMORY OF THE FALLEN.** *American soldier mimes the pose of the sculpture of a soldier from World War I, part of a monument in a southern Italian city. (Photo by Robert Capa.)*

people were jubilant. Fascism seemed to have crumbled away, though the Badoglio government declared that it wanted to continue the war alongside Germany.

In the 45 days between the fall of Mussolini and the announcement of Italy's surrender to the Allies (8 September), the Italian nation suffered a profound crisis. With the flight of the king, the army (there were more than a million soldiers on the peninsula) and the state apparatus disintegrated, and Italy was effectively

divided into two. German troops crossed the Alps, disarmed the Italian army in the north and centre of the country, and occupied Rome. Meanwhile the Allies had to deal with stubborn resistance from the six German divisions under Field Marshal Albert Kesselring that had been rushed south to oppose them.

THE MASSACRE OF CEPHALONIA

When the armistice was signed on 8 September 1943, the Italian troops in the Balkans were left with no clear orders from the government or the High Command. In some cases they surrendered to the Germans following negotiations; in others there was fighting that led to the death and capture of Italian soldiers. The most heroic episode,

THE ITALIAN SOCIAL REPUBLIC

The liberation of Mussolini from his prison on the Gran Sasso (Abruzzi) was the prelude to the establishment of a German puppet state in northern Italy. The Italian Social Republic (or Republic of Salò, after the name of the small town on Lake Garda where various government offices were based and Mussolini had his residence) was established on 23 September 1943. Nominally led by the Duce's government, which, with the creation of the Republican Fascist Party (whose secretary was Alessandro Pavolini), attempted to promote a rejuvenated form of fascism, the ISR was not in reality a sovereign state. Its territory was controlled by a German military administration, government acts had to be approved by two German advisers, and the German army effectively controlled the central and outlying offices. Hitler also decided to annex part of northeast Italy.

On 15 November, the party congress in Verona approved the new regime's manifesto. Besides national fascist and republican themes, it also included demagogic socialism and expressed hope for a return to the original Fascism. Shortly beforehand a Fascist action squad had been sent to Ferrara to avenge the killing of a local *gerarca* (Fascist official): 11 people were executed. The next step was a show trial held before a special court in Verona against top Fascist officials who had taken sides against Mussolini on 25 July: Mussolini's son-in-law and former Foreign Minister, Galeazzo Ciano, Emilio De Bono and three other defendants were executed.

The nature of the Salò regime immediately became clear. The economy was subordinated to production for the Nazi war effort, and tens of thousands of workers were deported to Germany or put to work on forced labour projects in Italy. Some 650,000 Italian soldiers captured after 8 September remained in German hands. State powers were at the service of the Nazis, leading to a systematic sacking of the country, ruthless repression of the resistance, the terrorization of the population with reprisals and mass executions, and the stoking of a civil war. An attempt was made to rebuild the army with a call-up in November 1943, but only 40% of young men responded and many of them subsequently deserted. Overall, counting various other military groups, the IRS could initially count on a force of about 200,000 men.

One of the most emblematic events of the 600 days of Salò concerned the Italian Jews ('foreigners' and 'enemies', according to the

Verona manifesto). The Fascist authorities collaborated actively with the Germans to deport them to the death camps, and also organized some independent initiatives of their own. For instance, on 30 November 1943 the Ministry of the Interior decided to set up special concentration camps in Italy. Already undermined by the resistance and by its subordination to the Germans, republican Fascism was definitively overthrown in 1945 by the Allied offensive. Attempts to open negotiations were in vain. On 18 April Mussolini transferred his government to Milan, and on the afternoon of 25 April, the day of the national insurrection, he met representatives of the National Committee for the Liberation of Upper Italy (CLNAI), who requested his immediate and unconditional surrender. Mussolini fled but was captured by partisans near Dongo on the road for Switzerland. He was executed on 28 April, together with his lover Claretta Petacci and a number of top Fascist officials. The next day the bodies were hung up by the feet in Piazzale Loreto in Milan, on display to an angry crowd, on the same spot where 15 detainees shot by the Fascists had been exhibited almost a year earlier. A CLNAI communiqué declared: 'Fascism itself is solely responsible for the explosion of popular hatred, which on this occasion degenerated and led to excesses. These can only be understood in the climate deliberately created by Mussolini himself.'

Propaganda posters of the Italian Social Republic.

WAR ARCHIVES: THE ALLIES IN ITALY

FROM A BROADCAST ON RADIO LONDON, 4 OCTOBER 1943: 'Behind the advancing Allied armies, the amount of liberated Italian territory grows larger by the day. And the more the Germans persist in disfiguring the Italian land with their futile destruction, the keener the sense of liberation and the stronger the sense of distance from the reign of terror, which is gradually sinking into the past. Reason and feeling say that this past will never return again. Italy is no longer alone. . . . The outcome is now certain. The more the Germans stubbornly insist on holding Italy – a task that is superior to their strength – the more certain it is that they will be violently thrown out, and for good. The more ferocious they are towards the Italians, the more they will arouse that ardour for freedom that seemed to have been extinguished in Italy and which is an essential condition for obtaining equality in the society of civil peoples. The generals may do what they will, the politicians can think and say what they want. The spirit of the masses is alive to the future and feels that Italy is no longer alone.'

(Right:) ALBERT KESSELRING.
Field Marshal Kesselring commanded the German troops in the occupation of Italy.

(Far right:) BLACKSHIRT BRIGADES.
The armed forces of the Salò republic made no significant contribution at the front. The republican armed units were used exclusively to repress the resistance movement.

which ended in tragedy, involved the Acqui division stationed on the island of Cephalonia in the Ionian Sea. Following a plebiscite on 13 and 14 September, the division (about 10,000 strong) sent a message to the German Command in which significant reference was made to the collective will: 'By order of the Supreme Command and in accordance with the will of the officers and soldiers, the Acqui division will not give up its arms.' In the terrible clashes that took place in the following days, the Italians resisted strongly but received no outside help and were decimated. Almost all the survivors were executed between 22 and 24 September. Those who did manage to survive joined the Greek resistance.
The Italian-occupied areas of Yugoslavia and France ended up in German hands.

The Italian army disintegrated, and not just at home. About 900,000 men were stationed in France, Yugoslavia, Albania, Greece, and on islands in the Aegean Sea. They suffered the same fate that befell their comrades at home, who were surprised by the armistice on 8 September and were left without orders from above. The majority of them were disarmed by the Germans; others defended themselves selflessly; while more than 600,000 were sent to work camps in Poland and Germany as labour for the Reich's war industries.

THE GUSTAV LINE

Exploiting the physical geography of the peninsula, Kesselring's 10th Army took up positions along the Apennines and the spurs sloping down towards the Adriatic and the Tyrrhenian Sea.

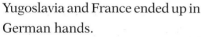

YUGOSLAV PARTISANS HUNG BY THE GERMANS.
The forces led by Tito fought the invaders and rival factions. From safe refuges in the mountains, the partisans waged a guerrilla war and inflicted heavy blows on the German army.

50 AM LIRE.
Banknote issued by the Allied military government, which replaced the worthless national currency everywhere.

On 9 September, the day that the king and the Italian High Command abandoned Rome and fled to Pescara, the American 5th Army commanded by General Mark Clark landed at Salerno. In the meantime, the Italian fleet of five battleships, eight cruisers and 23 submarines left their bases and headed for Malta to surrender to the British. Off the northern coast of Sardinia, the Germans sank the battleship *Roma* with remote-controlled bombs. The captain, Carlo Bergamini, died together with 1,236 members of the crew. On land the Allied advance encountered tenacious German resistance. The British forces moved north from Calabria and met up with the American bridgehead at Salerno, entering Naples on 1 October.

After the Allies had decided against a landing on the east coast of Italy, the main theatre of operations became a strip of territory between Naples and Rome, where the Germans had organized a defensive system known as the Gustav Line. This comprised a string of fortifications running from the Adriatic to the Tyrrhenian – from the Gulf of Gaeta to the mouth of the river Sangro south of Pescara. The Allied bridgehead north of Naples was unable to crush German forces holed up in the monastery of Montecassino, and it required five separate attacks and heavy losses before the Allies finally captured it in May 1944. After the Sangro offensive on the Adriatic coast, Montgomery moved towards the centre of the peninsula to join up with the Americans, but poor weather, the nature of the terrain and delays caused by flooded rivers prevented the Allies from making a rapid advance on Rome. At the end of 1943 the front line was still 100km from the capital.

THE PARTISAN STRUGGLE IN YUGOSLAVIA

The capitulation of Italy had immediate repercussions on the war in Yugoslavia, where there had been an active

---

LEADERS

TITO
Josip Broz (Tito's real name) was born in 1892 in a Croatian village. His mother was Slovenian, his father Croatian. In World War I he was taken prisoner by the Russians. In 1917 he participated in the October Revolution in San Petersburg, and in 1921, after returning home, he went into hiding when the Communist Party was declared illegal. In 1928 he was sentenced to five years' imprisonment, during which he studied Marxism. Later he worked at the Communist International in Moscow. After being appointed General Secretary of the Yugoslav Communists, Tito reorganized the running of the party. When the Axis troops invaded, he could count on an efficient organization with branches in Serbia, Slovenia and Croatia. He was the main leader of the Yugoslav partisans, and when the war ended he headed the Committee for the National Liberation of Yugoslavia. After 1945 he entered into conflict with Stalin and established a Communist regime that differed from the Soviet model. He led Yugoslavia along the difficult path to independence and promoted the country's economic development, placing particular emphasis on self-management. Tito later became the leading figure in the movement of non-aligned countries. He died in 1980.

(Right:) **RATION CARDS IN GERMANY.**

(Below:) **LANCASTER B-1.** *The most famous British bomber.*

resistance movement since shortly after the Axis invasion in 1941. Various partisan groups of different and often antagonistic ideological extraction conducted sabotage operations and mounted ambushes against the occupiers and against the independent Croatian state of Ante Pavelic, which sided with the Axis. The Chetniks ('gang', 'band') led by the Serb nationalist Draza Mihailovic attracted a significant number of men from the former monarchic army and were supplied by the British.

The Chetniks and the Communist-led partisans under Josip Broz (better known as Tito) were implacable enemies. At the end of 1941, the Communists had established the first European free territory in Serbia, which as a whole was under the Nazi yoke. Tito often gained support from Bosnians and Slovenians, who suffered atrocities at the hands of the Ustashe of Pavelic's Croatian government. In Montenegro the Chetniks sided with the Italians in repressing the 'Communist gangs'.

The outcome of the internal conflict between the partisan movements changed suddenly when Italy capitulated. Tito's partisans, who, after repeated German attacks, had

WEAPONS

BRITISH AND AMERICAN BOMBERS

At the beginning of the conflict, Britain had twin-engine bombers (Hampdens and Wellingtons) with a limited bomb load. A new generation of bombers, the four-engined Halifaxes and Lancasters, came into service in March 1942 and were the pride of the RAF. The long-range Lancasters could carry up to 10 tons of bombs (the so-called 'Grand Slam') and were the key players in the night-time missions against Germany's major cities ordered by the head of RAF Bomber Command, Air Field Marshal Sir Arthur Harris. They were equipped with a radar device that enabled the navigator to see an image of the ground below. These bombers were also solid enough to sustain attack from German fighters. The Americans had the four-engine Boeing B-17 (the 'Flying Fortress'), which together with more advanced versions, the B-24 (Liberator) and the B-29, had a number of formidable qualities. Besides their great cruising range, they were fitted with the Norden bomb-aimer, an optical device of deadly accuracy. From 1943 the 8th USAAF stationed in Britain began daytime bombing of Germany.

AFTER AN AIR RAID.
Citizens of Hamburg in a street devastated by Allied bombing.

taken refuge in Bosnia, seized the arms and equipment of the Italian forces and organized a number of brigades with units of the occupying army, who were anxious to make up for the humiliation inflicted on Yugoslavia by Fascist policies. At the end of 1943 the men commanded by Tito (about 150,000) successfully resisted German offensives, though the number of Wehrmacht divisions had risen from six to 13. Tito's was now the only national resistance movement.

The collapse of Italy also undermined Pavelic's fascist regime in Croatia. Here, too, the Communists formed alliances that enabled them to extend popular support for the partisan resistance. Tito and his men fought on various fronts: a war of liberation against the occupying forces; a civil war against the Chetniks, who declared themselves to be the representatives of the

monarchical government in exile in London; and a battle for the future political and institutional organization of the country when the war ended. In 1944 they benefited from the help of the British, who stopped supplying Mihailovic. The latter did not hesitate to stipulate a pact of collaboration with the Germans to fight Tito's Communists. The Balkans, behind the lines of the Wehrmacht retreating from Russia, became an increasingly dangerous region for the Germans at the beginning of 1944.

THE BOMBING OF GERMANY

While the war was going on in Italy, the other main means adopted by the Allies to whittle away the strength of the Reich was carpet-bombing of Germany's major cities. The British and American Commands coordinated bombing raids, which from 1942 onwards hit Germany's major industrial complexes with increasingly destructive force.

GERMAN RAILWAY STATION IN FLAMES.

TAKE COVER FROM SPLINTERS.
Warning to Germans about the dangers of anti-aircraft fire.

UNMANNED FLYING BOMB.
The Luftwaffe started experimenting with the V-2 ballistic rocket at the Peenemünde base in 1943. Of the 9,000 flying bombs launched against Britain from June 1944 onwards, about 4,000 were shot down by fighters or anti-aircraft fire.

This put into effect the orders of the British Air Marshal Sir Arthur Harris ('Bomber Harris'). The aim of the carpet-bombing was to terrorize the civilian population and to destroy Germany's industries. Between March and June in 1942, the bombing of Lübeck, Cologne (1,000 planes destroyed the city centre, saving only its famous cathedral), Essen and Bremen was a taste of what was to come the following year.

The Americans and British divided up tasks in order to demonstrate the terrible destructive capacity they were capable of inflicting on the German cities. The Americans carried out daytime missions while the British operated at night. Between March and July 1943, some 58,000 tons of bombs were dropped on the Ruhr, Germany's industrial heartland. During Operation 'Gomorrah', the RAF caused a four-day firestorm in Hamburg, which reduced the port and the city centre to smouldering ruins and caused at least 30,000 deaths. The same fate later befell Würzburg (4,000 victims), Darmstadt (6,000) Heilbronn (7,000), Wuppertal (7,000), Wesser (9,000) and Magdeburg (12,000). Between November 1943 and March 1944 Bomber Command concentrated its attacks on Berlin. The capital was the target of 16 raids, which caused 6,000 deaths and made 1.5 million people homeless (a million of its 4.5 million population had already been evacuated before this wave of attacks).

Notwithstanding the terrible destruction and death they inflicted, the bombing missions did not achieve the desired effect. The output of the German war industries in 1942/43 disproved Harris's prediction that bombing would instil terror in the population and bring the Third Reich to its knees. In these two years, respectively, 48,000 and 207,600 tons of bombs were dropped on Germany, compared with German production of 36,000 and 72,000

THE TEHERAN CONFERENCE

The first conference attended by all three of the major Allied leaders – Roosevelt, Churchill and Stalin – was held in Teheran from 28 November to 1 December 1943. Codenamed 'Eureka', its purpose was to discuss the final plans for the invasion of western Europe. During the meetings, held in an unusually cordial atmosphere, Roosevelt and Churchill gave Stalin assurances of their intention to open a second front in the West with a landing in Normandy (Operation 'Overlord'). Stalin requested guarantees about the Polish question, that the Soviet frontiers established by the non-belligerence pact with Germany in 1939 and by the treaty with Finland would be maintained, and help for the Yugoslav partisans. The Soviet leader also confirmed that Russia would enter the war against Japan after the defeat of Germany. Aside from the concrete results of the conference, the meeting had great significance in that the three leaders demonstrated to the world their firm desire to achieve victory. In the concluding communiqué, they declared: 'We came here with hope and determination. We leave here, friends in fact, in spirit and in purpose.' Mutual diffidence and suspicion was, temporarily at least, shelved – above all by Stalin, who until Stalingrad had been assailed by the suspicion that the failure to open a 'second front' in Europe was the prelude to a separate peace between the Anglo-Americans and Hitler.

(Left:) **BOMBER COMMAND.** *Sir Arthur Harris (centre, wearing glasses) and his assistants analyse pictures of the effects of RAF bombing raids.*

(Below:) **DESOLATION.** *German town reduced to a pile of rubble.*

tons. By the end of the conflict, German civilian casualties amounted to 600,000 dead and 800,000 wounded; but the Allies did not get off lightly with their strategic bombing, suffering heavy losses due to the effectiveness of German fighters and anti-aircraft fire. The heavy bombing raids did not sap the morale of the German population, which was still influenced by war propaganda promising that the Reich would make a comeback with the use of 'prodigious weapons' capable of wresting air superiority from the Allies and turning the outcome of the conflict in their favour. On 17 August 1943 a raid by 330 bombers devastated the German base on the Baltic island of Peenemünde, where the Germans were testing ballistic rockets. The raid delayed experimentation and building of the V-1 and V-2 rockets, which were launched against Britain the following year. However, it was the raids in the summer of 1944 and the winter of 1944/45 that proved to be the death knell for Germany's war industries.

Leningrad, Rome, Paris, Warsaw

During 1944 the Allies continued to attack in the main theatres of war – the Soviet Union, Italy and the Pacific – where military operations culminated in a spectacular turnaround in the course of the conflict. Although progress was slow in Italy, the advances on the Russian front and in the Pacific led to a drastic shrinkage of the borders of the German and Japanese empires, established several years earlier. The British and the Americans moved towards Germany from the west, while the Russians began to threaten the eastern regions. Having established a clear-cut superiority in numbers, the Red Army became very skilled at seeking out the enemy's weak spots. In September of the previous year, the Russians had crossed the Dnieper, recaptured Smolensk, blocked the escape routes from the Crimea and, in November, retaken Kiev, the capital of the Ukraine. Like a river in spate, the Soviets advanced across the immense steppe lands and, following a powerful push, arrived on the banks of the Vistula near Warsaw in *(p. 192)* **SS soldier being searched.**

(p. 193) **25 August 1945: Paris celebrates.** *(Photograph by Robert Capa.)*

(Right:) **Soviet motorcycle units on the Ukraine front.**

(Below:) **Wrecked German tanks.**

August 1944. In June, the opening of the 'second front' in Normandy paved the way for the liberation of western Europe. The advance in Italy was much less spectacular. In the autumn of 1944, almost a year and a half after the landings in Sicily, the Allies and the Germans were still fighting it out along the Gothic Line.

THE RED ARMY ON THE OFFENSIVE

Exploiting their great mobility and their superiority in numbers and equipment (the Russians outnumbered the Germans six to one), the Soviets launched an offensive in the second half of 1943 that ended two years later with the capture of Berlin. Once the weak points in the German defences had been pierced, the Soviet High Command extended its manoeuvre with a succession of attacks intended to create a chain reaction that would prevent the Germans from rein-

forcing the critical zones. Although the Germans had a narrow margin of technical superiority, they only had limited reserves for their counter-attacks and had to throw in their remaining tank forces in the attempt to break the Russians' incessant encircling movements. The German Army's capacity for effective response was also strongly hindered by Hitler himself, who stuck to the principle of a rigid defence line and refused to authorize any strategic withdrawal. The Red Army launched two major offensives in 1944. In the winter offensive, Germany's Army Group North was breached in three points, and on 26 January the Russians enlarged the narrow corridor that had linked Leningrad to the rest of

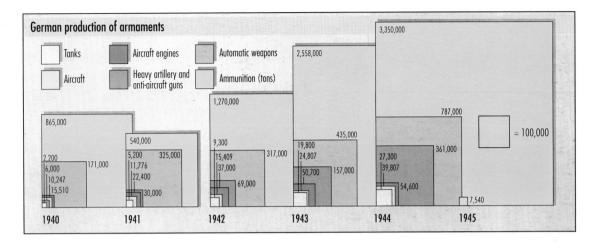

German production of armaments

| Tanks | Aircraft engines | Automatic weapons |
| Aircraft | Heavy artillery and anti-aircraft guns | Ammunition (tons) |

□ = 100,000

1940
865,000
2,200
6,000
10,247
15,510
171,000

1941
540,000
5,200
11,776
22,400
325,000
30,000

1942
1,270,000
9,300
15,409
37,000
69,000
317,000

1943
2,558,000
19,800
24,807
50,700
157,000
435,000

1944
3,350,000
27,300
39,807
54,600
361,000
787,000

1945
7,540

Russia since the beginning of the German occupation. After 1,000 days, the siege of Leningrad, which had become a symbol of Russian resistance, was lifted and the railway link with Moscow was reopened. This change on the northern end of the eastern front had immediate political repercussions. The Finns asked for an armistice, but Moscow's request for a return to the pre-war frontiers was blocked by the fact that the Germans continued to occupy part of Finland. In June the Russians launched a new attack that led to the capture of the isthmus of Karelia and tied up German forces in Finland, which might otherwise have been sent to defend France.

THE COLLAPSE OF THE GERMAN SOUTHERN FRONT

In March 1944 the Russian offensive by Zhukov's '1st Ukrainian front' outflanked the Germans on the river Bug. In the same month Koniev's tank forces reached the river Dniester, advancing along a broad front that made resistance by the Germans, who were heavily outnumbered in troops and weapons, more difficult. The Russians reached the Carpathian Mountains defending Hungary (occupied by the Germans) and opened the door to the plains of central Europe. In the Crimea, the Red Army proceeded rapidly: on 17 April, after devastating shelling with Katyusha rockets, the Russians reached the

FUNERAL CEREMONY. *The incredible resilience of the Russian soldiers was described by a German general as follows: 'The Russian soldier carries a sack on his back with nothing in it except a crust of stale bread and whatever else he can find in villages as he advances, usually a handful of raw vegetables... The Russians are accustomed to living for up to three weeks in this primitive way, and then they just keep going anyway.'*

(Below:) **LIBERATION OF LENINGRAD.** *Red Army infantry fighting in the suburbs of the city.*

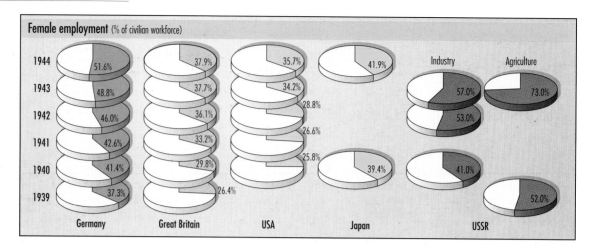

Female employment (% of civilian workforce)

	Germany	Great Britain	USA	Japan	USSR Industry	USSR Agriculture
1944	51.6%	37.9%	35.7%	41.9%	57.0%	73.0%
1943	48.8%	37.7%	34.2%		53.0%	
1942	46.0%	36.1%	28.8%			
1941	42.6%	33.2%	26.6%			
1940	41.4%	29.8%	25.8%	39.4%	41.0%	
1939	37.3%	26.4%				52.0%

outskirts of Sebastopol, taking 37,000 prisoners. Contrary to Hitler's orders, the bulk of the German–Romanian 18th Army was evacuated by sea and on 9 May the city was liberated by the Russians.

In their retreat the Germans adopted a 'scorched earth' policy, destroying factories, villages and bridges, but this failed to halt the advance of the Red Army, whose crack units were followed by infantry deployed along an enormous front. After the Russian spring offensive, Hitler replaced Manstein and Kleist (the two leading exponents of offensive tank warfare) with Walter Model, who was put in command of Army Group North Ukraine (the former Army Group South), and Ferdinand Schörner, a fanatical devotee of Hitler and his regime, who took over Army Group South Ukraine.

THE RUSSIAN SUMMER OFFENSIVE

The Soviet attack was preceded by devastating shelling, and all along the front the German defences became increasingly thin and inadequate. While the collapse of the southern front opened the way for the Russian advance towards Romania and the Balkans, in the centre the Soviets trapped the German forces in a pocket near Minsk. Stalin then ordered his generals to mount a large-scale attack on the White Russian front. Led by Zhukov, the 'Bagration' offensive (named after a Russian general who had died fighting Napoleon in 1812) commenced on 22 June 1944, three years after the German invasion of Russia and a few weeks after the western Allies had landed in Normandy. The wedge of

WOMEN IN THE WAR

Women have always played a part in wars, even though official history has rarely devoted much attention to them. It was only in the 20th century, however, with the advent of conflicts that impinged directly and in a big way on the civilian population and on the pattern of everyday life, that women acquired a more visible role, moving into traditionally male sectors of the 'home front' and assuming a prominent role in the military and logistical apparatus of the various countries. This trend had already emerged during the Great War, but it became more widespread and

with men and in some cases were in the front line, flying planes, driving tanks or serving on ships. About 800,000 Russian women served in the armed forces. In the civilian sector, 55% of the total workforce in the final phase of the war were women. In Great Britain, unmarried women aged 20 to 30 were subject to conscription from 1941 onwards, either in the auxiliary forces (as nurses, office workers, drivers etc.) or in industry. Between 1942 and 1945 some 125,000 women were recruited, while at the same time the age group of women liable to mobilization for work in industry was extended and mothers were included. From 1939 onwards, members of the Women's Auxiliary Air Force (180,000 strong in 1943) performed a

important part in the armed forces and in industry. Both the army and the navy had a women's auxiliary service. Women's experience during the war helped to lay the foundations for the subsequent evolution of their role in American society, which was to become a model for many women in other western nations.

In Germany the prevailing ideology was that women should perform domestic and child-raising functions, and this limited their presence in certain sectors of the war effort. In 1943, women aged 17 to 45 began to be recruited for work in the war industries, but this was never done systematically. However, in 1939 the female workforce was already 37% of the total, a figure that had almost doubled in heavy industry by 1943. In

crucial in World War II. Assessment of its impact on the process of female emancipation and the promotion of sexual equality is at the centre of lively historiographic debate stimulated by a strand of feminist studies. Considering just two aspects of this question, the contribution of women to the labour force and their direct involvement in military operations, attention inevitably focuses on the two countries where the mobilization of women was greatest: the Soviet Union and Great Britain. In the Soviet Union, it was decreed in 1942 that all women aged 16 to 45 could be recruited for war service in any of a wide range of functions. They had parity

range of duties, mainly on the ground (air traffic control, weather reports, preparation of equipment etc.). The Women's Royal Naval Service, or Wrens (70,000 members in 1944), performed analogous duties for the navy. Women also staffed radar stations on the British coast as part of the country's anti-aircraft defences. In 1943, there were over one million women in the Women's Voluntary Services for Civil Defence. Women also distinguished themselves in the 'secret war' and in the intelligence services, both in code-breaking departments and as special agents.

In the United States, women overcame prejudice and suspicion to play an

Japan, the head of the government, General Tojo, refused to introduce military service for women, in order not to upset the existing structure of the Japanese family.

Perhaps an even more extensive role was played by women of all ages in the anti-Fascist and anti-Nazi resistance movements. Male reluctance and pure prejudice did not prevent women from playing a crucial role in the operational efficiency of the various movements, not only in building up and activating networks to support, aid and provide information for refugees and resistance fighters, but also in the front line with specifically military tasks.

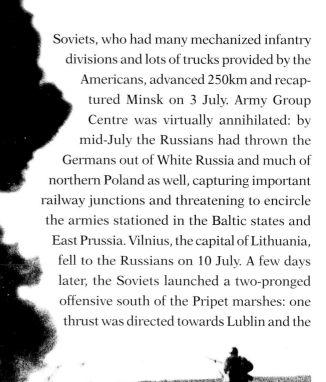

(Right:) **BOAT BRIDGE ON THE RIVER PRUT.** *The war in the vast expanses of Russia was also a battle against the adversities of the terrain. The wet season that arrived with the autumn rains and the spring thaw turned the steppes into an immense marsh.*

(Below:) **MINE EXPLOSION.**

the Soviet attack was in White Russia, north of the Pripet marshes, although in actual fact the offensive extended along a line stretching as far as the Baltic, and was conducted by seven army groups (or 'fronts', as the Russians called them). These were limited in size so as to increase their manoeuvrability. They were opposed by Army Group Centre, commanded by Ernst Busch, who had been forbidden by Hitler to withdraw behind the river Beresina, where there was a more advantageous defensive position.

The Russian plan was to drive in two wedges so as to breach the flanks of the German defences. Within a week the Soviets, who had many mechanized infantry divisions and lots of trucks provided by the Americans, advanced 250km and recaptured Minsk on 3 July. Army Group Centre was virtually annihilated: by mid-July the Russians had thrown the Germans out of White Russia and much of northern Poland as well, capturing important railway junctions and threatening to encircle the armies stationed in the Baltic states and East Prussia. Vilnius, the capital of Lithuania, fell to the Russians on 10 July. A few days later, the Soviets launched a two-pronged offensive south of the Pripet marshes: one thrust was directed towards Lublin and the

KEEP SILENT.
American and British posters warn citizens of being overheard by spies and of squandering petrol by driving alone.

THE SECRET WAR: SPIES

Although the majority of espionage activities during World War II were based on the use of new interception technology, traditional spies continued to play an invaluable role, taking part in a number of adventurous exploits to acquire information of extraordinary strategic value. Talking about Paul Thümmel, one of the best spies in the war, the head of the British Secret Intelligence Service (MI6) said: 'A-54 is an agent at whose word armies march.' A decorated veteran of the Nazi Party and a member of the German military intelligence services, Thümmel began collaborating with Czechoslovakia in 1937. During the war, through the Czech government in exile, he supplied very important information about German plans to the British and Soviet intelligence services. For reasons that remain unknown, he was betrayed and arrested in March 1942. He was executed by the SS a few days

before the end of the war. Richard Sorge (1895–1944, codename 'Ika') was one of the most famous wartime spies. Having joined the Communist Party in Berlin, he was recruited by Soviet Intelligence and sent to Tokyo in 1933. Thanks to his work as a correspondent for German and Dutch newspapers, he gained the trust of the German ambassador in Tokyo. Until 1941 he managed to transmit to Moscow precious information about Germany and, thanks to his agent Ozaki, about Japan as well. In 1941 he informed Stalin that Japan was not planning an attack on the Soviet Union, thereby enabling the Russians to move troops westwards. However, when Sorge gave warning of the imminent German invasion of Russia (Operation 'Barbarossa'), he was not believed. Betrayed by members of his own network, he was captured in 1941 and hung in 1944.
Between 1942 and 1943, while working as a waiter

at the British Embassy in Ankara, the Albanian Elyesa Bazna (alias 'Cicero') managed to photograph hundreds of confidential documents, which he transmitted to the German secret service (the *Sicherheitsdienst*). This information was always accurate, for instance that regarding the Teheran Conference and the Allied air raids on German cities.
There were also cases of German spies who, once discovered, began a risky existence as double agents. For instance, a young Dane named Wulf Schmidt was arrested after being parachuted into England in 1940. He used the trust placed in him by the German military secret service (the *Abwehr*) to enable the British to arrest secret agents sent to Britain by Berlin. Then there was the Yugoslav, Dusko Popov, known as 'Tricycle', an *Abwehr* agent who, after switching to the Allied side, was ordered by his putative masters in Germany to set up a spy network in the United States.

(Above:) An American poster warns people against careless talk. (Left:) Richard Sorge, in a rare photograph from the 1920s.

(Right:) **COLUMN OF SOVIET TROOPS PARADING THROUGH THE STREETS OF VILNIUS.**

(Below:) **LIBERATING FORCES RECEIVING A WARM WELCOME IN A CITY IN WHITE RUSSIA.**

Vistula, the other towards Lviv (captured on 27 July). In six weeks of incessant attacks, the Russian tank forces wiped out 30 German divisions.

Army Group Centre was pulverized, with 350,000 dead, injured or taken prisoner. The German line had been pushed back about 500km, from White Russia to the banks of the Vistula. A year and a half after the turning point at Stalingrad, the Russians had pushed the Wehrmacht out of their territory. Between June and September 1944, the Germans had lost 850,000 men – dead, injured or missing. At the end of 1944 the Russians penetrated into Estonia, Latvia and Lithuania, on the borders of East Prussia, and Hitler's exhausted eastern armies were overrun by the unstoppable drive of the Red Army. The Russians, however, now had to pause for respite, and to reorganize their supply lines before the final phase of their counter-offensive: the thrust into German territory.

THE WARSAW UPRISING

After crossing the 1939 Russian–Polish border in the middle of 1944, on 31 July Rokossovsky's advance units reached the Warsaw suburb of Praga on the east bank of the Vistula. On 1 August, Polish patriots led by General Tadeusz Bór (a pseudonym of Count Komorowski) rose up in arms against the German occupation troops in order to prepare the way for the Soviet entry into the Polish capital. But once again the tragic fate of Poland was decided by inexplicable fence-sitting on the part of the western Allies and the intransigence of Stalin, who refused to give any help to Mikolajczyk (the Prime Minister of the Polish government in exile in London) or to allow American bombers to land at Soviet airfields after parachuting supplies to the resistance in the capital. Moscow recognized only the

LIBERATION OF KÖNIGSBERG.
Inhabitants of the Baltic city talking to a Russian soldier. The arrival of the Soviets in the Baltic nations was followed by ferocious reprisals against anyone who had collaborated with the Germans.

Polish Committee of National Liberation, based in Lublin, as legitimate. This body had already accepted the line of the rivers Oder and Neisse as Poland's western frontier when the war ended. At the beginning of October the uprising was crushed by three SS tank divisions and by brigades of pro-German Russians under the orders of Himmler. Some 250,000 people were massacred and entire neighbourhoods were razed to the ground. Warsaw was devastated.

The Russian advance, which in five weeks had covered about 700 km (the greatest yet achieved by the Red Army), had halted on the outskirts of Warsaw, where the Russians stayed put for six months before commencing the final drive towards Berlin.

THE SITUATION IN THE BALKANS

Following the complete destruction of Army Group Centre, the German position on the eastern front was severely compromised, a consequence of which was the crumbling of the Reich's alliances in the Balkans. On 23 August 1944 it was announced on radio that Romania had signed an armistice with the Allies and joined the war against Germany. General Antonescu, who had led the country since 1940, was deposed and arrested. King Michael I ordered the cessation of hostilities against the Red Army, declared war on Germany and accepted the conditions offered by the Russians, who took the oil wells of Ploiesti at the end of the month, captured the Black Sea port of Constanza and entered Bucharest on 31 August. The German 6th Army (20 divisions) was trapped by the Russians in Bessarabia. In Hungary – where the Romanians reoccupied Transylvania, which earlier in the war had been ceded to Hungary – the Russians recaptured Bessarabia and North

THE LIBERATION OF RUSSIA

FINLAND
Leningrad
Estonia
Latvia
Moscow
Lithuania
East Prussia
Minsk
Warsaw
POLAND
USSR
Kiev
SLOVAKIA
HUNGARY
Transylvania
Budapest
ROMANIA
Bucharest
Belgrade
Sebastopol
BLACK SEA
YUGOSLAVIA BULGARIA

— Front line 22 December 1943
····· Front line in spring 1944
– – Front line at end of 1944
⬤ Trapped German forces
→ Soviet attacks

GERMAN SOLDIER IN ROMANIA.
Following the encirclement of the German–Romanian 6th Army (130,000 men were trapped in a pocket created by the Soviets), the few troops that managed to escape withdrew towards the Carpathian Mountains. This was the Wehrmacht's last line of natural defence to halt the Russian advance towards southern Germany.

THE SHEPHERD AND THE SOLDIER.
In the Sicilian countryside, the Americans – often descended from Italians who had emigrated to the United States – relied on the local population to obtain valuable information about the terrain and the position of enemy forces. (Photograph by Robert Capa.)

Bukovina and had already reached the Carpathian Mountains. In the face of imminent attack, General Lakatos formed a new government and asked the Russians for an armistice. In Slovakia, the partisan resistance was backed by the Russians. In Bulgaria, which had joined the Tripartite Pact in 1941 but had remained neutral towards the Soviet Union, there was a strong and active partisan movement. From the beginning of 1944 Sofia became a target for Allied bombing missions and the Russians entered the city on 18 October. An enormous gap had opened up between the Carpathian Mountains and the mouth of the Danube, and the Russians moved forward unchecked. When they reached the frontier between Romania and Yugoslavia they established contact with Tito's partisans, who, with Stalin's backing, seized Belgrade on 20 October. Yugoslavia had been liberated.

THE ITALIAN CAMPAIGN

In the first half of 1944 the situation on the Italian front (where 18 Allied divisions were pitted against 15 German ones) and in the Mediterranean became a source of bitter contention between the British and Americans. Attacks by the American 5th Army and the British 8th Army ran into tenacious resistance from the German troops commanded by Kesselring. The British still insisted on the feasibility

AMERICAN MORTAR ON THE HILLS AROUND MONTE CASSINO.
From its mountain-top position, the monastery blocked the march of the Allies towards Rome. The Germans turned the mountain into the crux of their resistance on the Gustav Line. On its slopes they built gun emplacements, machine-gun nests and underground cave shelters, and they laid mines all along the banks of rivers in the valley.

L E A D E R S

GEORGE SMITH PATTON

A veteran of the Great War, during which he fought in France, George Patton played an important role in some of the major campaigns of World War II, displaying great prowess

in motorized warfare. After leading the ground troops that captured Casablanca and Morocco, he was put in charge of the American 2nd Corps in

Tunisia in March 1943. Having risen to the rank of lieutenant general, he completed the Sicily campaign in 38 days with the 7th Army. In June 1944 he was at the head of the 3rd Army during the Normandy landings; later his tank units advanced into French territory, capturing Brittany and pushing as far as Orléans before cutting across the country to reach Lorraine. After checking the German offensive in the Ardennes, Patton crossed the Rhine and reached the outskirts of Prague before being stopped for political reasons. He died in Germany in 1945 as the result of injuries sustained in a car crash.

MARK WAYNE CLARK

The son of an Army colonel, Clark had served in France in 1918. On the eve of World War II

he held the rank of major, but from 1942 onwards he had a spectacular series of promotions that led him to become Commander of US Land Forces in Europe. He planned the invasion of North Africa and went to Algeria in a submarine to prepare the operation with the French. He landed at Salerno in September 1943 at the head of the 5th Army, and managed to hold off the German counter-attacks. He also led the militarily unsuccessful landing at Anzio and ordered the bombing of Monte Cassino, for which he was severely criticized. On 5 June 1944 he entered Rome, and then became Commander-in-Chief of Allied Forces in the Mediterranean. After the war he commanded the occupation troops in Austria and UN troops in Korea, before retiring in 1953. He died in 1984.

OMAR NELSON BRADLEY

Bradley commanded the 2nd Army Corps in North Africa, captured Bizerta

in May 1943 and was promoted to lieutenant general. In the summer of 1943 he led the troops in the invasion of Sicily. Together with Eisenhower he planned the Nor-

mandy invasion, during which he commanded the American forces. Once on dry land, his troops joined Patton's to create the largest military force in the history of the United States, which he led in the final attack on Nazi Germany. He captured Brittany, Paris, then Trier and Cologne, before joining up with the Russians on 25 April 1945. After the war, he was chairman of the Joint Chiefs of Staff from 1949 to 1953. He died in 1981.

DWIGHT DAVID EISENHOWER

Born into a modest Texas family in 1890, Eisenhower first studied at the military academy of West Point. He held various

positions, including that of MacArthur's Chief of Staff in the Philippines, before becoming a general in 1941. He was given responsibility for operations planning after the Japanese attack on Pearl Harbor and

played an important role in planning America's intervention in Europe. In June 1942 he went to London as America's commanding general in Europe. Thanks to his consummate diplomatic skills, he managed to overcome the periodic clashes that arose between British and American chiefs and he directed the main military operations: the landings in North Africa and the capture of Tunisia; the invasion of Sicily and the Italian peninsula; and, as Supreme Commander of the Allied Forces in Europe, the Normandy invasion and subsequent operations through to Germany's defeat. On the strength of his enormous prestige, he was elected President of the United States in 1952 as the Republican Party's candidate, and was re-elected in 1956. Under his leadership, the United States continued the policy of 'containing' the Soviet Union begun by Truman. The so-called 'Eisenhower doctrine' involved American military intervention in all Far East countries threatened by communism. Towards the end of his mandate, there was a slight thawing of relations with the USSR, but this came to an abrupt halt with the Cuba crisis, which caused fresh tension between the two superpowers. He died in Washington in 1969.

(Right:) **MEDICAL TREATMENT.** *Treating the wounded on an American landing ship.*

(Centre:) **BAZOOKA.** *The name of this anti-tank weapon, invented in 1942, derives from that of a bizarre musical instrument.*

(Below:) **ALLIES ON THE EDGE OF THE 'ETERNAL CITY'.**

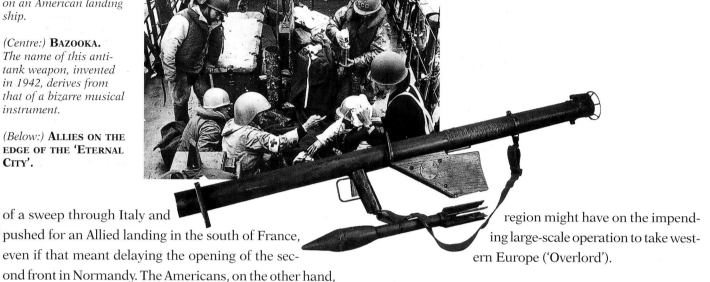

of a sweep through Italy and pushed for an Allied landing in the south of France, even if that meant delaying the opening of the second front in Normandy. The Americans, on the other hand, regarded northern France as the crucial theatre of war. They also felt that the Italian campaign would tie up only a limited number of German troops and that the peninsula's terrain prevented a rapid Allied advance. While the British wanted a prestigious victory in Italy, the Americans feared that the negative consequences of Allied commitments in this region might have on the impending large-scale operation to take western Europe ('Overlord').

THE LIBERATION OF ROME

It seemed as if the stalemate might be broken with the landings at Anzio (22 January), which were to have been followed by an offensive along the Liri valley by Mark Clark's American 5th Army. However, the operation was a disaster. The troops in the Anzio bridgehead were pinned down by constant bombardment from land and air. In the meantime the Allied divisions repeatedly thrown against the

(*Left:*) **MAIMED.**
The effects of war on a Neapolitan child.

(*Far left:*) **MOROCCAN TROOPS AT MONTE CASSINO.**
The French Corps included units of Moroccan troops, who demonstrated exceptional fighting skills.

(*Below:*) **BANDAGED ARM.**
Two American soldiers give first aid to a wounded companion. (Photograph by Robert Capa.)

enemy fortifications for months on end were unable to breach the Gustav Line. It was only after the Benedictine monastery of Monte Cassino had been reduced to rubble by tremendous bombing, and forces comprising American, New Zealand and Indian troops, plus the French Corps of General Alphonse Juin (Moroccan and Algerian mountain troops from the former French army in North Africa), had cleared a passage on 17 May, that Clark's 5th Army was in a position to exploit the situation and cut off the retreating Germans. However, Clark headed for the capital, allowing the Germans to escape. On 5 June the Americans entered Rome, which had been declared an 'open city' and evacuated by the Germans without destruction and with its bridges intact. Operation 'Diadem', which had led to the liberation of Rome, cost the Americans 18,000 men and the British 14,000, while the Germans suffered 11,000 casualties. Although the capture of the city was symbolically important, the strategic results, obtained almost a year after the Allied landings in Sicily, were extremely meagre, especially in view of the fact that it did

205

(Right:) **LANDING SHIP TANK (LST).**
American ship capable of transporting 23,000 tons of men and equipment, with a range of 6,000 miles.

(Centre:) **CANVAS LIFE JACKET.**
Part of the equipment of the American landing troops.

(Below:) **EISENHOWER.**
Instructions to paratroopers leaving for France.

not draw German forces away from France before the Normandy landings. With the Allies now occupying Rome, King Victor Emanuel III abdicated in favour of his son Umberto, who took over as Lieutenant-General of the kingdom, and Badoglio was replaced by the anti-Fascist Ivanoe Bonomi. The government was an expression of the parties belonging to the Committee of National Liberation.

In the autumn the front stabilized along the Pisa–Rimini line. The over-optimistic British hopes of a rapid Allied advance northwards had vanished, and as winter closed in the Germans were in position along the Gothic Line, while the British 8th Army on the Adriatic side was about 100km from the Po. Meanwhile the Germans

(Left:) **LANDING CASUALTIES.** *Corpses of American soldiers lined up on a Normandy beach.*

(Below:) **INTO THE FIELD OF FIRE.** *In the first three hours of the landing operations, the Allies lost 3,000 men on Omaha beach.*

carried out mass executions of any civilians in retreat, especially in the Tuscan–Emilian Apennines. Further operations were put off until the following spring.

THE ALLIED INVASION OF FRANCE

On 6 June 1944, the Allies breached the system of fortifications, obstacles and minefields built by the Germans and known as the Atlantic Wall. Within two weeks they had occupied part of Normandy, though their advance was slower than expected. Fearing a 'second' invasion in the Pas de Calais, Hitler ordered Army Group B to stay put and instructed a handful of Panzer divisions to attack the Allied bridgeheads. In particular, the 12th Division of the Hitler-Jugend SS managed to halt the Allied advance around Caen. Taking advantage of their overwhelming aerial superiority, the British and Americans were preoccupied by the need to land the enormous mass of men and equipment that had arrived off the French coast. Furthermore, they found it difficult to advance through the *bocage*, a bushy tangle of roots that made a formidable natural defensive system.

OPERATION 'OVERLORD'

On the night between 5 and 6 June 1944, a huge fleet of 21 American and 38 Anglo-Canadian convoys set sail from the south coast of England and made for France. In all there were more than 6,483 vessels, carrying or towing 2,000 landing craft and escorted by a formation of nine battleships, 23 cruisers and 104 destroyers. The Allied troops (1,700,000 Americans, a million British and Canadian troops and about 300,000 French, Polish, Belgian, Dutch, Norwegian and Czech soldiers) had about 2 million tons of equipment and 50,000 vehicles of various kinds – tanks, half-tracks, armoured cars, trucks and jeeps. Along the 'Atlantic Wall' – the system of fortified

defences prepared by Rommel – between Holland and Brittany there were 500,000 Germans. The bulk of the German forces (the 15th Army) was positioned around the narrowest point of the Channel, the Pas de Calais, where Hitler thought the Allied landings would take place. The Germans also had ten armoured divisions as back-up, but they were too far from the coast. There was also an enormous disparity in air strength: the Allies had 3,000 bombers and 5,000 fighters, compared with a mixture of bombers and fighters totalling 320 on the German side.

The Commander-in-Chief of the German forces on the western front was Field Marshal Gerd von Rundstedt. When the landings commenced, Rommel was in Germany celebrating his wife's birthday.

Other factors favoured the Allied invasion plans: messages transmitted by the Allies to the French Resistance, though intercepted by German listening stations, were not then forwarded to the military commanders in France. The operation was delayed by 24 hours, due to poor

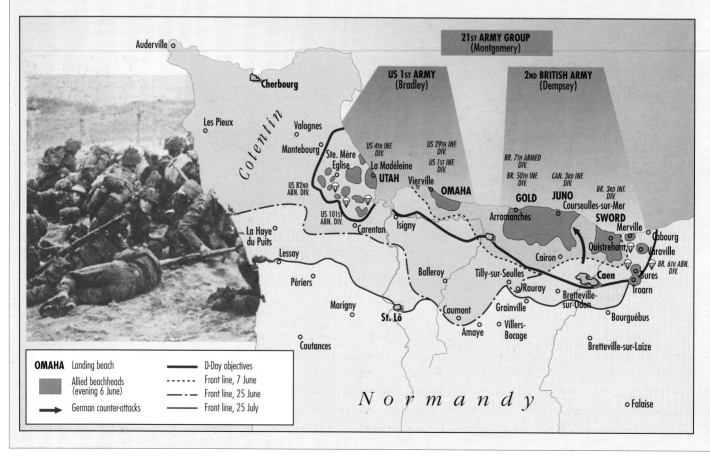

| OMAHA | Landing beach |
| Allied beachheads (evening 6 June) |
| German counter-attacks |

— D-Day objectives
---- Front line, 7 June
—·— Front line, 25 June
—— Front line, 25 July

weather in the Channel. The Supreme Commander of Operation 'Overlord', the American General Dwight Eisenhower (Montgomery had tactical command), chose 6 June on the basis of specific conditions: the low tide in the early hours of

the morning was favourable for landing on the beaches, while the late rising of the moon meant there was more cover for gliders and paratroopers. During the night, the ships that had sailed from various English channel ports converged at a pre-established meeting point ('Piccadilly Circus') and then made for the stretch of coast between the mouth of the Seine and the Cotentin peninsula.

Two hours later the Allied ships began shelling the coastline. At 6.30am the first wave of Montgomery's 21st Army Group hit the beaches, codenamed 'Utah', 'Omaha', 'Gold', 'Sword' and 'Juno'. Coming in behind this incredible mass of military strength were floating concrete wharfs, where ships of up to 10,000 tons could berth, and the segments of an oil pipeline to bring in fuel.

The first soldiers on to the beaches of France were the Americans of Omar Bradley's 1st Army, who landed at 'Utah' and 'Omaha', where sea conditions and

stubborn German resistance caused them serious difficulties. Things went better for

the late morning and Rommel arrived on the scene in the late afternoon. The Germans were still convinced that the Normandy landings were not the main Allied offensive, which they had been expecting for months, and this crucial error was one of the determinant factors in the success of 'Overlord'. In compliance with Hitler's express orders, the armoured divisions stationed in other sectors were not moved to the landing zone, and the Allies were not thrown back into the sea 'by nightfall', as the Führer had specifically requested. By dusk about 160,000 men were on French soil. Although the Allied objectives had been only partially achieved, the operation could certainly be considered a success.

The 'longest day' began at 3.14am on 6 June with aerial bombing of the German coastal defences, followed a few minutes later by Allied parachute drops. About 18,000 out of a total of 20,000 paratroops were able to carry out the mission they had been assigned, which was to disrupt the enemy's logistical network.

General Miles Dempsey's British 2nd Army, which landed on 'Gold', 'Sword' and 'Juno'. A few hours later the British were near Caen, while the Americans were still fighting the infantry and Panzer divisions that had been rushed to the hills surrounding the invasion zone. Hitler was informed of the invasion in

(p. 208 above:) Robert Capa, the American war photographer, who participated in the landings. (Top:) The insignia of British and German divisions who fought in Normandy. (Left:) The first wave of landing troops approaches 'Omaha' beach (photo by Robert Capa). (Right:) The invasion zone in the late afternoon of 6 June 1944.

D-DAY AND THE CINEMA

During World War II, some of the big names of the Hollywood film industry – including Frank Capra, John Ford, Alfred Hitchcock, John Houston, William Wyler and George Stevens – spent time in the front line working on documentaries and reports for audiences at home. Their footage provides valuable testimony for historians, even though the final screened product was almost always the result of reworking and a blending of real images and reconstructed scenes, often designed to achieve a propaganda effect and to avoid an excessively raw and realistic representation of war. Even the most historically reliable films are ultimately the product of a combination of historical documentation and artifice. In the years following the war, the harshest films (the ones that had not been purged through successive reworking) were censored and edited to assuage political fears, and only 'official' versions of major wartime events received an airing. Only recently has there been growing awareness of the wealth of material that is available, much of which is unexplored.

The Allied landings in Normandy were dramatic and decisive for the outcome of the war, and unsurprisingly have attracted great interest amongst post-war film-makers, a number of whom have re-evoked the war years in highly spectacular films. One of the most famous of the celebratory Hollywood films produced in the 1950s and 1960s is *The Longest Day* (1962). This reconstruction of the events of D-Day involved a degree of financial investment and organization of men and materials that was without precedent in the history of the cinema. The four directors who took it in turn behind the camera (Ken Annakin, Andrew Marton, Bernhard Wicki and Darryl F. Zanuck) had at their disposal thousands of men from the US armed forces and a huge number of planes and ships. Leading D-Day figures were played by some of Hollywood's top stars (Richard Burton, Robert Mitchum, John Wayne, Rod Steiger, Henry Fonda and Sean Connery). The plot was based on an account that was written by Colonel Cornelius Ryan, who drew on many personal recollections.

Thirty-five years later, Steven Spielberg also tackled the event in *Saving Private Ryan*. Drawing on consultations with the historian Stephen E. Ambrose, Spielberg's aim was to produce an accurate reconstruction of events. The financial and material resources were once again immense, but Spielberg's perspective in relating the horrors of war was very different. Unlike traditional war

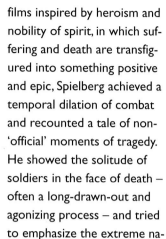

films inspired by heroism and nobility of spirit, in which suffering and death are transfigured into something positive and epic, Spielberg achieved a temporal dilation of combat and recounted a tale of non-'official' moments of tragedy. He showed the solitude of soldiers in the face of death – often a long-drawn-out and agonizing process – and tried to emphasize the extreme nature of all experience of war. Following in the footsteps of Samuel Fuller, who had first-hand experience of war and whose film *The Big Red One* (1980) depicted the landings in a realistic way, Spielberg crammed in, with apparent objectivity, so much violence that he himself wondered how much an audience could take. The film, which lasted almost three hours, opened and closed with two terrible battles, in which the viewer was spared no detail. The first depicted the 'longest day': the orders to advance at all costs, limb-shattering explosions, bloodstained seawater and lifeless bodies on the beach. The second was a pitched battle to gain control of a village and pave the way for the final victory over Nazism. Between these two moments, the film focused on the story of a platoon advancing into enemy territory to save a private: one amongst many, Everyman. The film was incredibly successful, receiving five Oscars and reading many international audiences (above is the Italian poster for the film).

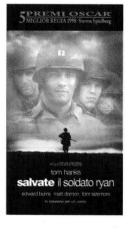

(Above:) Poster for Spielberg's film. (Left:) A scene from The Longest Day.

(Left:) **AIRBORNE DIVISION.**
*American paratroopers in
a village south of
Cherbourg. (Photograph
by Robert Capa.)*

(Centre:) **MILITARY
INSIGNIA.**
*Badges of the Rangers and
the American 1st Division.*

(Below:) **RECONNAISSANCE
MISSION.**
*(Photograph by Robert
Capa.)*

This proved hard going for the armoured vehicles and there were heavy infantry losses. It was only at the end of July, after the Allies had gained a strip of territory stretching from the port of Cherbourg to the city of Caen, that the Americans of Hodges' 1st Army and Patton's 3rd Army managed to breach the front at Avranches and break out into the French countryside. In the middle of August the American 7th Army, assisted by some French contingents, landed on the coast between Toulon and Cannes, with the aim of joining up with forces advancing from Normandy.

DE GAULLE IN PARIS

In mid-August a battle fought in the area between the west bank of the Seine and the Loire wiped out the German 7th Army and the 5th Panzer Army and opened the way to the conquest of France by Montgomery's 21st Army Group. The latter consisted of 37 divisions, including 12 armoured divisions, and the Allies also enjoyed almost total supremacy in the skies. The Germans had 23 divisions, most of which were under strength. On 21 August the encirclement was completed, and Allied artillery and air attacks destroyed an enormous amount of heavy equipment. About

(Right:) **GERMAN PRISONERS.** *A few days after the insurrection by the French Resistance, the commander of the German forces in Paris disregarded Hitler's orders and offered a truce, which was accepted. Paris was free. (Photograph by Henri Cartier-Bresson.)*

(Below:) **THE ALLIES AT THE ARC DE TRIOMPHE.**

50,000 German soldiers were captured and 20,000 died in the Falaise pocket.

The road to Paris now lay open and the columns of General Jacques Leclerc entered the French capital on 24 August. The German garrison contravened Hitler's orders to raze the city to the ground and surrendered the following day. De Gaulle was given a triumphant welcome by the population. The battle for Normandy (6 June to 31 August) cost the Germans 800,000 men, 450,000 of whom were made prisoner. The Allies moved forward rapidly at the beginning of September, and their advance tank units entered Brussels and captured Antwerp. Patton had already crossed the Meuse and was about 50km from the German industrial region of the Saar. In northern France and in Belgium the imbalance in forces was enormous: about 100 German tanks against about 2,000 Allied ones and about 600 planes against more than 14,000 on the Anglo-American side. Notwithstanding the overwhelming superiority in men and equipment, at the end of September the Allied thrust had come to a halt in the swampy strip of land surrounding the Meuse–Scheldt canal, which was defended by German paratroopers.

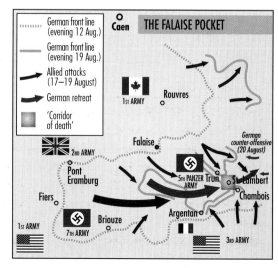

THE FALAISE POCKET

German front line (evening 12 Aug.)
German front line (evening 19 Aug.)
Allied attacks (17–19 August)
German retreat
'Corridor of death'

Caen

1ST ARMY Rouvres

2ND ARMY

Falaise

German counter-offensive (20 August)

5TH PANZER ARMY Trun

St Lambert

Pont Erambourg

Chambois

Fiers

Argentan

1ST ARMY 7TH ARMY Briouze

3RD ARMY

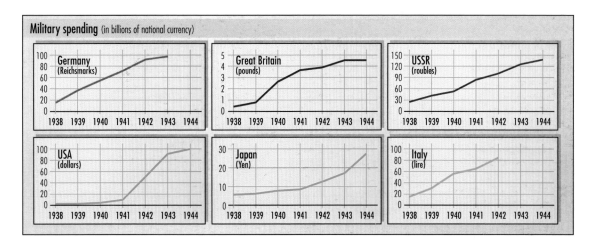

ON THE BORDERS OF THE REICH

The Allies were positioned along a line stretching from the banks of the Scheldt in Belgium as far as the upper reaches of the Rhine on the border with Switzerland. However, their progress was braked by logistical and supply problems and by continuing internal disagreement. Montgomery continued to insist on the priority of 'one shove' on the northern flank of the Allied front in order to occupy the Ruhr (the industrial heartland of Germany). Eisenhower and Patton wanted to cross the western border of Germany. In short, the Allies failed to take advantage of the German collapse to cross the Rhine bridges, which were still intact, and to push deep into Germany.

While strategic bombing of German cities continued (with the same quantity of bombs being dropped in the last three months of 1944 as had been done throughout the previous year), the German Army could still rely on a large number of combat troops, even though they mainly consisted of inexperienced Volkssturm (civilian militia) and army reservists. The Luftwaffe had all but disappeared from the European skies, and what remained of the German navy had a certain freedom of movement only in the Baltic Sea. The German defensive effort on the western front was supported by the recruitment of 25 Volksgrenadier divisions ('peoples' grenadiers') and by the war industry, which, under Speer's leadership, obtained excellent results: production in September 1944 was greater than in any other month in the war.

THE GERMAN COUNTER-STROKE IN THE ARDENNES

In his Berlin Chancellery, Hitler prepared an offensive that was to take place at the same point at which the German tank forces had broken through into France in May 1940:

THE HITLER ASSASSINATION ATTEMPT

On 20 July 1944 an attempt was made to assassinate Hitler. The plot was organized by a group of opponents to the regime who revolved around General Ludwig Beck and the devout Christian Carl Goerdeler, and had some support in the Wehrmacht. The aim of 'Valkyrie', as the plan was called, was to kill Hitler, neutralize the SS and the Gestapo, set up a military government and then negotiate a peace with the Allies. One of the men behind the conspiracy, Colonel Claus Schenk von Stauffenberg, placed a kilogram of plastic explosive, attached to a timer device, under the table around which Hitler held his morning meeting at his Rastenburg headquarters in East Prussia. (Hitler's base, known as the 'Wolf's lair', was a massive underground bunker with walls 10m thick.) Due to a series of circumstances, the effect of the bomb was less than expected. Three of the 24 people present at the meeting died, but Hitler suffered only light injuries. Believing the Führer to be dead, Stauffenberg went to Berlin to lead the military conspiracy and transmitted the order to proceed with the second phase of the plan. Hitler, whose distrust of the upper echelons of the army was reinforced by the incident, quickly exacted his revenge and all the conspirators were rounded up and killed. In many cases they were strangled with piano wire after a summary trial.

(Right:) **SHIELDED BY A SHERMAN.** *American troops entering a French city, covered by the protective flank of a tank.*

(Below:) **AMERICAN INFANTRY ON THE MARCH IN THE INTENSE COLD OF THE ARDENNES FOREST.**

the Ardennes forest. Germany's residual hopes of preventing an invasion of its territory were pinned on the outcome of Operation 'Autumn Fog'. The Allies had been pushing through France for months and had reached the German border, but their advance had come to a halt. In the middle of December, the Germans launched an offensive of their own, in exactly the same place they had chosen for their *Blitzkrieg* four years previously, which in the space of a few months had led to the capitulation of France.

Operation 'Autumn Fog' was centred on the Ardennes forest and was carried out by two reduced-strength Panzer armies (the 5th and the 6th) commanded by two young generals, Hasso von Manteuffel and Sepp Dietrich, respectively, in whom Hitler placed great faith. Exploiting poor weather, the Germans breached the American defences in the Ardennes sector and, partly due to the slowness with which

Eisenhower's Allied Headquarters was informed of the real extent of the attack, achieved a success that was due largely to the factor of surprise. Launched at dawn on 16 December 1944, the German attack consisted of a dual thrust: the first, to the north-west, aimed for Antwerp, while the second was to cross the Meuse and make for Brussels in order to cut the links between the British and the Americans, capture their supply bases and force the Allies to evacuate the continent. The success of the operation depended on the capture of the road junction of Bastogne, where the American 101st Airborne Division, rushed in from Reims, held on stubbornly.

Besides the lack of fuel, which penalized the German tank forces, the attack failed because of the overwhelming disproportion of strength. Nonetheless, this counter-stroke dispelled optimism in Washington and London about a rapid conclusion to the conflict.

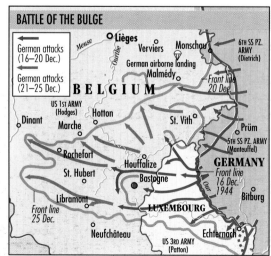

WAR ARCHIVES: COLLABORATORS

In all the nations subjected to Nazi occupation, many men and women worked (with varying degrees of diligence) to promote and sustain Hitler's project for a 'New European Order'. The pejorative term 'collaborator' was used to describe someone who worked for the enemy, was unpatriotic and plotted behind people's backs to betray their fellow countrymen. Collaborators did not regard themselves as victims but fraternized and did business with the occupying forces. Following liberation, the general population's contempt for collaborators and their desire for vengeance often led them to inflict ritual acts of degradation and physical humiliation on former collaborators, often their next-door neighbours, in order to force them to display their guilt in public and symbolically to exclude them from the community. At the end of the war, tribunals in various countries gave legal sanction to the exclusion of these collaborators from society, punishing about 130,000 people in France, 100,000 in Belgium and 110,000 in Holland. However, the initial severity began to slacken off after a few months.

Japan
on the retreat

Although the United States was able to pump a massive amount of men and weapons into the Pacific theatre, there was still uncertainty about which strategy to adopt in order to deal with an enemy that fought with obstinate determination. At the beginning of 1944 the Americans had almost 2 million men in the Pacific (a similar number was already present in Europe), and their aim was to carry out a succession of amphibious operations to wipe out the enemy's strongholds, taking advantage of their air and naval superiority. The Japanese forces were stretched over too large a perimeter (they had 15 million square kilometres of land and sea to guard), and now that the Americans had regained the initiative they were obliged to reduce the defensive boundaries of their maritime empire. However, the American High Command was divided by bitter internal rivalry. On the one hand there was MacArthur, who wanted to organize landings

(p. 216) **Planting the Stars and Stripes on Iwo Jima.**

(p. 217) **Kamikaze dive-bombing the Missouri.**

(Right:) **Anti-Japanese posters.**

(Below:) **Landing on the Lexington.**

on the major Pacific islands (his strategy came to be known as 'leapfrogging') and then to launch an invasion of Japan from Luzon, the northernmost island in the Philippines. Nimitz, on the other hand, favoured an attack through the central Pacific to Formosa and China, which could then be used as bases for launching air strikes at Japan's war industries and as a launch pad for the invasion of Japan. The strategy finally adopted by the Joint Chiefs of Staff was a compromise between these two approaches, and the American war effort continued to be marked by competition between the

navy and the army. The real turning point in military operations in the Pacific was the naval battle that took place off the island of Leyte (Philippines) in October 1944, while the Americans were landing there. Only then were the Americans able to obtain the bases they needed for their proposed invasion of Japan: MacArthur's forces at Luzon and Nimitz's Pacific fleet at Iwo Jima and Okinawa.

Japanese military production					
Tanks	724	1,165	786	342	94
Armoured cars	88	468	629	784	153
Fighter planes	1,080	2,935	7,147	13,811	5,474
Bombers	1,461	2,433	4,189	5,100	1,934
Spotter planes	639	967	2,070	2,147	855
Warships	1	1	–	–	–
Aircraft carriers	5	6	3	4	–
Cruisers	1	2	2	1	–
Destroyers	9	9	15	31	6
Submarines	11	22	40	37	22
	1941	1942	1943	1944	1945

(Below left:) **ANTI-AIR-CRAFT BATTERIES.**

(Below right:) **AFTER THE BATTLE.**
The battle-weary gaze of a Marine after the capture of the Marshall Islands.

GREATER EAST ASIA

Although the Japanese had been defeated at the Battle of Midway and been forced to relinquish their naval primacy to the Americans, they retained control of the territories that they had occupied on the Asian continent. At the end of 1943, after a conference held in Tokyo in November, the Japanese government started energetically promoting the notion of the 'Great East Asia Co-Prosperity Sphere'. The conference was attended by the heads of government of Manchukuo (the puppet state established by the Japanese in the province of Manchuria in 1932), the Philippines, Burma, Thailand and the occupied Chinese territories, who committed themselves to reciprocal cooperation and the defence of their 'independence'. It laid the foundations for an alternative 'bloc' to that of the Western powers, and above all else marked the assumption of an evident and uncompromising anti-colonialist stance that was a challenge to Great Britain in particular. A few years later, after Japan's defeat, the colonial powers would have to take account of this situation when it came to redesigning the political map of postwar Asia. Many of these new states, which had declared war on the Allies and were under the heel of the Japanese occupation forces during the war, freed themselves from their past colonial masters and became independent republics.

A GIGANTIC LOGISTICAL PROBLEM

The sheer immensity of the Pacific posed considerable problems for the Allies, and these did not just relate to the geography and climate of the area. For Japan at the beginning of 1944, on the defensive since its defeat at Midway (six months after Pearl Harbor), its protective barrier of concentric rings gave it a strategic advantage.

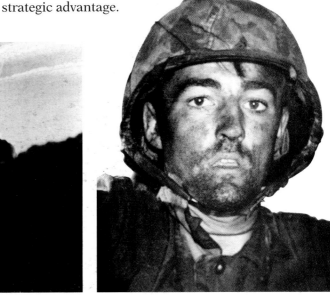

(Right:) **DECEPTIVE SMILE.**
American poster showing a samurai with a dagger hidden behind his back.

(Far right:) **WAR CEMETERY.**
American Marines pay tribute to their fallen comrades.

(Below:) **RADAR ON AN AMERICAN BATTLESHIP.**

The United States, which bore the main burden of the Allied offensive drive, decided against the idea of attacking from the northern Pacific, or a land offensive from the Soviet Union (Russia was not at war with Japan, its prime objective being to defeat Germany), or from China (partly occupied by the Japanese and riven by conflict between nationalists and communists); instead it proceeded simultaneously through the south-west and the central Pacific. From a military point of view, the prime requirement was to seize Japan's sources of raw materials, which the Japanese desperately needed to maintain their military capacity following the nation's rapid conquests in 1942.

The problems faced by the Allies in the Pacific war, and the context in which it took place, were mainly logistical. In addition to the need to get troops and their weapons to the operational zones, the priority for the American High Command was the organization and transport of all kinds of supplies and materials. About 3 tonnes of equipment was required to transport a single soldier to the front, and he needed a further tonne every month – water, ammunition and food – to keep him going. In 1943 more than 5 million tonnes of materials left California. It was therefore essential to set up both fixed and mobile bases to sort the materials, which, amongst other things, also had to service a fleet consisting of hundreds of ships, some of which stayed at sea for up to four months at a time. This, in April 1944, was named the 5th Fleet.

THE PACIFIC FRONT (1944–45)

MONGOLIA
Peking
MANCHUKUO
Korea
JAPAN
Tokyo
Kurile Is.
TIBET
Nanking
CHINA
INDIA
BURMA
INDO-CHINA (Fr.)
Hong Kong
Iwo Jima
THAILAND
Mariana Is.
PHILIPPINES
Caroline Is.
PACIFIC OCEAN
MALAYA
Sumatra
Borneo
New Guinea
DUTCH EAST INDIES
INDIAN OCEAN

Minimum defence line envisaged by Japanese in September 1943

Limit of Allied advance in March 1945

(Left:) **AMERICAN AIRMEN.**

(Below:) **JAPANESE BODIES ON THE BEACH.**

AMPHIBIOUS OPERATIONS IN THE PACIFIC

After occupying Bougainville (the most westerly of the Solomon Islands, politically part of New Guinea) in November 1943, MacArthur landed troops on the western end of New Britain and, having gained control of the Bismarck Islands, left the garrison of 100,000 Japanese soldiers 'to wither on the vine'. This marked the beginning of a new method of waging war, the concept being to cut off and isolate enemy strongholds. The next step was a landing on the Gilbert Islands. Despite heavy bombardment by the supporting battleships (3,000 tonnes of shells in little more than two hours), which was intended to destroy the enemy's defences, the Americans suffered big losses in capturing the well-fortified atoll of Tarawa. The

(Right:) **TANKS AND INFANTRY IN THE JUNGLE OF SAIPAN.**
Considered impregnable by the Japanese, the island of Saipan in the Marianas archipelago was of vital importance for the Americans. Their bombers took off from here for missions over Japan.

(Below:) **BEFORE THE LANDING IN NEW GUINEA.**

5,000-strong assault force was pinned down by enemy fire between the coral reef and the beach for a whole day; 1,000 Americans died and double that number were injured.

The US Navy and Air Force were able to field forces that were enormously superior to those of the Japanese. On the sea, their light aircraft carriers (*Independence* class) carried about 50 planes each and had a top speed of 30 knots, while the new *Essex*-class vessels, which were formed into a fast carrier task force, had even more weaponry and carried about a hundred planes each. In the south Pacific zone of operations, the Americans used an attack fleet to shell enemy positions and prepare the ground for landings by the Marines. The fleet was

P-47 THUNDERBOLT.
American single-propeller plane used principally as a long-range fighter escort in all the theatres of the war. Due to its great acceleration and dive speed, it was also used with increasing frequency for ground-attack purposes.

supported by a mobile Service Force, which consisted of tankers, tenders, minesweepers, lighters, hospital ships, a floating dry-dock and ships for assembling pontoons. The Americans also started using amphibious tracked vehicles to reduce casualties.

In January 1944 it was the turn of the Marshall Islands. The landings were preceded by bombardment (300 tonnes of bombs) and the presence of the American carrier force precluded any Japanese attempt to supply their bases, effectively preventing the Japanese from deploying their sea and air forces. The capture of the Marshalls opened the way for the next objective, the Mariana Islands, in particular Saipan, Guam and Tinian, which the American High Command regarded as the key to gaining access to the western Pacific. These islands would provide a base from which to bomb Japan with B-29s, which until then had only been used from Chinese airfields. In New Guinea,

MacArthur's forces made a series of hops and finally reached the western end of the island, after having dislodged Japanese troops from caves and strongpoints from where they had been defending their air bases. The American successes confirmed the wisdom of following two lines of advance; by alternating amphibious operations with naval moves in the open sea against the Japanese fleet, they disrupted the enemy's defensive system.

NAVAL OPERATIONS AND THE CAPTURE OF THE MARIANAS

The Supreme Command of the Japanese Imperial Navy tried to entice the American carrier fleet into the area east of the Philippines, the plan being to subject it to a deadly two-pronged attack by planes based on the ground in the Philippines and from the 1st Mobile Fleet (the carrier force of the Combined Fleet) commanded by Admiral

BATTLE CASUALTIES.
Bodies of Marines after the battle to capture Saipan. Pictures of soldiers who had died in combat made a big impact on American public opinion, and their publication was subject to censorship by the military authorities.

(Right:) **LANDING SHIPS AND CRAFT ON LUZON.**

(Below:) **PARACHUTE DROP OVER THE PHILIPPINES.**
MacArthur's invasion force landing on the beaches of Leyte was given strong air cover.

Jisaburo Ozawa. But, the air–sea battle in the Philippine Sea in June 1944 ended in heavy defeat for the Japanese. The Americans located the position of the Japanese carriers, and their fighter missions were once again devastating. The battle turned into what came to be known as the 'Great Marianas Turkey Shoot': half of Ozawa's carrier force and two-thirds of his planes were destroyed. In addition to losing a large number of well-trained pilots, the Japanese lost three aircraft carriers (including the brand-new *Taiho*, the fleet's flagship, which was sunk by American submarines) and another three were damaged. The American task force therefore retained a clear-cut superiority in numbers.

Halfway through the following month, after heavy fighting in which the Americans used armoured vehicles equipped with flamethrowers to crush the desperate Japanese resistance, the campaign to conquer Saipan and Tarawa ended. The Americans lost 3,500 men; the Japanese lost 26,000 men and a further 20,000 Japanese civilians committed suicide. The fall of Saipan, which followed the naval disaster in the Philippine Sea, led to Tojo's resignation as the head of the Japanese government. He was succeeded by General Kuniaki Koiso. His first priority was to defend the Philippines at all costs, which was confirmation of the fact that this archipelago was of vital importance for the defence of Japan itself.

THE RECAPTURE OF THE PHILIPPINES

After the air–sea successes and the capture of New Guinea and the Marianas, MacArthur was anxious to make a victorious return to the Philippines once the American High Command had opted not to by-pass the archipelago (as had been requested by

JAPANESE SOLDIERS KILLED BY THE AMERICAN NAVAL BOMBARDMENT OF MINDANAO.

Fleet Admiral Ernest J. King, who wanted to make directly for Iwo Jima and Okinawa). The Japanese, in the meantime, prepared a plan of defence, codenamed SHO-1 ('Victory'). Tomoyuki Yamashita, the conqueror of Singapore, and his 14th Area Army were given the task of defending the land, and a naval operation was devised that was intended to lure the American fleet into a trap. For the second part of this plan, the Japanese, who had little remaining air strength, relied on an old-style fleet consisting of seven battleships and 13 cruisers; this force included the two largest battleships in the world: the 70,000t *Yamato* and *Musashi*, which had 475mm guns and were considered unsinkable. The Americans, for their part, planned to split the enemy's defences in two, in view of the fact that

there were 270,000 Japanese soldiers stationed on the archipelago and that it is 1,500km between the northernmost tip of Luzon and the southernmost tip of Mindanao. On MacArthur's orders, the 6th Army under General Walter Krueger landed on the small island of Leyte on 20 October 1944. The American scheme was to cut communications between Japan and the Dutch East Indies, Japan's principal source of oil supplies.

THE JAPANESE GRAVEYARD IN THE GULF OF LEYTE

Admiral Takeo Kurita's plan was for a decoy force to engage the American force off the archipelago, while another two Japanese formations penetrated into the two navigable channels dividing the group of islands – the Straits of San Bernardino and Surigao – and wiped out the disembarked American troops and the two fleets that

HEADING FOR THE BEACHES OF LEYTE.
Preceded by an intense bombardment, the invasion by 120,000 Americans took place along a front of 29km and involved two distinct landing areas. About 350 troop transports and 400 landing ships of various kinds, protected by the American 7th fleet (which consisted of six battleships, 18 escort carriers and other destroyers and escorts), assembled along the eastern coast of the island.

L E A D E R S

TOMOYUKI YAMASHITA

Born in 1885, Tomoyuki Yamashita attended the military academy at Hiroshima and the Japanese war college. He went on to hold a variety of military posts, and also served in Switzerland, Germany and Austria. In the 1920s he joined a right-wing organization whose objective was to install a military government in Japan and which made a coup attempt in 1936. As he was not directly involved in the plot, he was only punished in ways that put a brake on his career. However, this soon took off again and he acquired considerable standing, especially among the young officers, and in 1937 he was promoted to the rank of Lieutenant General. Fearing his popularity, the Minister of War, Tojo, sent him to Italy and Germany in 1940.

On the strength of his reputation as an able strategist, he was made Commanding General of the 25th Army in 1941. At the beginning of 1942 he conquered Malaya in a campaign lasting just 54 days. His 70,000-strong force chose an unexpected line of advance, opening up a path right through the jungle and overcoming enormous difficulties associated with the environment, and succeeded in a task that was considered impossible. The British, Australian, Indian and Malay troops were forced to give way in the face of fierce attacks by the Japanese, who struck aggressively from all directions and constantly caught them by surprise. Yamashita then proceeded to capture Singapore as well, and in a dramatic encounter issued the British with a bald ultimatum, obtaining their surrender on 15 February 1942. The Japanese took over 80,000 prisoners and captured a large quantity of arms and ammunition. Their own losses were minimal in comparison. One of the biggest British bases in the Far East thus fell. Singapore had been one of the main obstacles to Japanese expansion towards the south-west, and the way now seemed open for the definitive realization of Japan's vision of a 'Greater East Asia Co-Prosperity Sphere'. In his diary, Yamashita was highly critical of the organization and efficiency of the Japanese Army and the competence of some of its generals. He was also obsessed that people were manoeuvring against him in Tokyo and in high political and military circles. While Churchill stood up in the House of Commons to give out the news of a historic defeat, Yamashita, known from then on as the 'Tiger of Malaya', was elevated to the status of national hero by the Japanese press. His fame alarmed those who feared that this might lead to his political ascendancy, and once again he was sent abroad. In July 1942 he was put in command of the armies stationed in Manchukuo, with orders to defend the region against a possible attack from the Soviet Union.

General Yamashita returned to the fore in 1944, when he was appointed Supreme Commander in the Philippines, with the task of performing another miracle, namely to defend the zone from American attack. In the course of the long battle for Leyte, his troops put up tenacious resistance against the American forces. He continued the fight even after receiving the news of Japan's capitulation, and only surrendered to the American General Jonathan Wainwright on 2 September 1945. In the aftermath of the war, Yamashita was accused of war crimes, for not having controlled the 'operations of the members of his command, permitting them to commit brutal atrocities and other high crimes against people of the United States and of its allies and dependencies, particularly the Philippines.' His impassioned defence, which also took the line that the trial procedure was unconstitutional, was not accepted. After being condemned to death by hanging, he appealed unsuccessfully to the American Supreme Court. He was executed on 23 February 1946.

(Above:) Yamashita with his general's sword.
(Left:) Together with the military attachés of Japan's allies in 1942.

(Left:) **FIRE ON THE DECK OF AN AIRCRAFT CARRIER.**

(Below:) **A PROMISE KEPT.**
On 20 October 1944 MacArthur returned to the Philippines, which he had been forced to abandon in 1942. He immediately exhorted the Filipinos to assist the liberators. The recapture of the archipelago engaged the Allied forces until the end of the war.

were protecting the invasion. The Battle of the Gulf of Leyte, was in fact four distinct clashes, starting on 23 October and ending two days later. It was characterized by confused and contradictory interpretations of a succession of signals. This was compounded on the Japanese side by uncertainty on the part of Kurita who, by changing his plans just when SHO-1 was about to be crowned with success, laid the foundations for one of Japan's

worst-ever naval defeats. The *Musashi* was sunk less than 24 hours after the beginning of the battle. Kurita abandoned the attack on the Gulf of Leyte to open up an escape route for his force towards the north.

At the end of the biggest naval battle of all time, involving 282 warships and hundreds of planes, the Japanese Navy was left virtually impotent: four carriers, three battleships, six heavy cruisers, three light cruisers and ten destroyers were sunk. Japan also had almost no naval air force left. The Americans lost three escort carriers and three destroyers, but the US Navy was now in a

(Right:) **AN AMERICAN FIGHTER PREPARES TO LAND.**

(Below:) **HELPING THE WOUNDED ON A BEACH IN THE PHILIPPINES.**

position to push into the China Sea and as far as the coast of Indo-China to strike at enemy convoys. The battle, where the Americans conclusively established their supremacy in the Pacific, also marked the start of a new Japanese offensive tactic: squadrons of kamikaze pilots belonging to a special corps started diving at their targets in planes packed with explosives and fuel.

MacArthur was able to keep the promise he had made two-and-a-half years previously, in May 1942, when he had been forced by the wave of the Japanese advance to abandon the fortress of Corregidor: American landings on the other islands of the archipelago multiplied, and at the beginning of March 1945 the Americans captured Manila, after a strenuous defence by the Japanese had reduced the capital to ruins.

THE CHINESE TANGLE

Although China was not the scene of a direct clash between the Allies and Japan, it was nonetheless of primary importance in the chessboard of the Asian conflict. American submarine activities forced the Japanese to concentrate their efforts in inland areas of China, from where supplies and troops were sent towards Indo-China. The region was also crucial for control of the road leading to Burma and Thailand. China occupied a key place in

DEVASTATING FIREPOWER. *Bombardment by an American battleship off the coastline of the Philippines.*

KAMIKAZE

Legend has it that the *kamikaze* ('divine wind') saved Japan from the invasion of the Mongol fleet in 1281. The Japanese drew inspiration from this in October 1944, when, in the face of the advancing American fleet, they decided to set up a corps of volunteers (known as kamikaze) willing to crash planes packed with explosives on to enemy ships. Animated by a form of mysticism inspired by the code of bushido (the principles of honour and morals developed by the Japanese samurai), they wrapped a white cloth decorated with a red sun around their forehead before setting off on their final mission.

The Americans were caught unawares by the new tactic, and in the Battle of the Gulf of Leyte as many as 250 of their craft were hit. However, they soon organized defences and subsequently only one kamikaze out of eight managed a hit. The final Japanese resource was the *okha* (cherry blossom), a wooden aircraft packed with explosives. In the first stage of their flight the kamikaze glided, before lighting propulsive rockets and launching themselves in a dive at 1,000km per hour. In 82 days of attacks, almost 5,000 kamikaze met a death to which many of them aspired: 'If only we might fall / like cherry blossom / in the spring / so pure and radiant.'

(Above:) A rocket-propelled Japanese plane with a suicide pilot. (Left:) The American aircraft carrier Bunker Hill *in flames after being hit by a kamikaze.*

(Right:) **BURMA ROAD.**
*The Allies sent supplies
to the Chinese along this
mountain road.*

(Centre:) **BURMA STAR.**
*A decoration awarded to
Allied soldiers who fought
in the Burma campaign.*

(Below:) **THE AIRCRAFT
CARRIER *FRANKLIN*
FOLLOWING A HIT.**

Japan's grand imperial design and was a big commitment; also the rivalry between Chiang Kai-shek's Kuomintang and Mao Zedong's communists, and the confused political situation created by Japanese occupation, tied up a large number of troops – 650,000 in Manchukuo, 225,000 in Korea, 325,000 in northern China and 700,000 in Kuangtung (now called Guangdong) to meet the Russian threat.

In April 1944 a force of 1,800,000 Japanese launched a grand campaign ('Ichigo') against nationalist troops to reopen the railway line between Peking and Nanking, and above all to take the bases used by Chennault's 'Flying Tigers' for their air raids. While the nationalist armies were routed, Mao's communists retained control of the 'free territory' of Yan'an, and the Japanese occupation forces maintained control of the rich valleys of the Yellow River and the Yangtze. The casualties of the war in China were horrific – about 10 million – and were largely caused by massacres, which had started with the occupation of Manchuria by Japan and were committed by the Japanese, the nationalists and the 'warlords' alike. Given this tangled situation, the Americans decided to reduce supplies to the nationalists and to give priority to the seas and the islands, continuing their offensive in the Pacific. They were also increasingly reluctant about Chiang having a political leadership role in a China that would sooner or later be liberated by the Allies.

LEADERS

MAO ZEDONG

Mao Zedong was born into a peasant family in 1893. After a patchy early education, he joined the Republican Army in 1911, and then attended the First Provincial Normal School (1913–18). He was influenced by Western thinking and the October Revolution, and in 1921 joined the Communist Party in Peking. He was sent to act as the Party's representative in his home region of Hunan, where he organized peasant associations. In this process he adapted the Marxist–Leninist model and became convinced of the possibility of an independent revolutionary initiative by the rural masses in China. He soon clashed with Communist Party leaders, developing his own revolutionary perspective based on guerrilla activities in the countryside. From 1927 onwards, following the breakup of the alliance between the communists and the Kuomintang of Chiang Kai-shek, Mao led the struggle against the latter, promoting agricultural reform in the occupied zones and linking the armed struggle with the prospect of an economic revolution.

In 1931 Mao founded the Chinese Soviet Republic in the regions of Hunan and Kiangsi. To escape the advance of Chiang Kai-shek's forces, in October 1934 he and his followers began what came to be known as the Long March, a 5,000km journey during which he came to be recognized as the head of the Chinese communist movement. When China was invaded by Japan, he reached a truce with Chiang Kai-shek to organize a joint defence. At the end of the war, the two sides were once again in the throes of a civil war, which ended in 1949 with a complete victory by Mao. This marked the beginning of the long phase of the People's Republic of China, during which Mao devoted himself to building a communist society. There was then a phase in which Mao had to deal with rifts with the Soviet Union, and in which he worked to ensure the independence and prestige of China, which soon became a model for the international communist movement. The 'great helmsman' died in 1976.

CHIANG KAI-SHEK

Born into a trading and farming family in 1887, Chiang Kai-shek did military studies in Japan (1907–11) and took part in the Chinese Revolution of 1911. After a period of exile in Japan, he returned to China in 1918 and began supporting Sun Yat-sen. When the latter died in 1925, Chiang Kai-shek took his place and assumed the leadership of the Kuomintang. His main objective was to free the country from a Western presence and to extend the influence of his movement from the south to the north of the country. With Soviet help, he obtained a series of important successes, managing to reduce the presence of the Western powers. In 1927 he set up a nationalist government in Nanking, broke with the Soviets and initiated a hard battle against the Chinese communist movement. He soon managed to unify the country and was elected President in October 1928. The following years were characterized by the difficult struggle to consolidate the regime, which was hindered by communist guerrilla action and by the penetration of the Japanese into Manchuria and northern China. In 1934 Chiang forced Mao's communists to retreat from Kiangsi, but in 1935, in view of the need to defend the nation against the Japanese, he agreed to join forces with Mao, laying the foundations for a joint resistance movement that lasted until Japan was finally defeated in 1945. During World War II, with the support of the United States, Chiang managed to get China accepted as one of the great world powers. From 1946 to 1949 there was a civil war with Mao's communists, who finally managed to gain complete control of the country. At the end of 1949, Chiang Kai-shek took refuge on the island of Formosa (Taiwan), where he established a nationalist government, which he headed for decades. After nominating his son as prime minister in 1972, Chiang died in 1975.

(Above:) Mao in 1927, at the age of 27.
(Left:) Mao announces the birth of the People's Republic of China in 1949.

(Right:) **LORD MOUNTBATTEN.** *Supreme Allied Commander in South-East Asia from 1943. After the war he became the last Viceroy of India.*

(Below:) **AUSTRALIAN UNITS.**

IMPHAL: A BRITISH FIGHTBACK

In the war on land, the British and Americans were at odds about what strategy to adopt. The former considered Burma essential for recapturing their possessions in Asia (because it was a buffer between India and China, and it also provided access to Singapore and Malaya), while the latter saw it as a strategically vital zone for sending aid to the Kuomintang.

The outcome of military operations in Burma was different from those being conducted in the Pacific. Between 1943 and 1944 the Japanese launched an offensive that took them over the Indian border into Assam, blocking the incipient British plan to retake the northern regions and reopen communications with China via the Burma Road, which wound its way over the eastern ranges of the Himalayas. However, Japanese hopes that their arrival would prompt an insurrection of the Indian population against British dominion were dispelled. The British Admiral Louis Mountbatten, the Allied Commander in South-East Asia, acted to re-establish control over the country and to anticipate the Japanese offensive that was expected in the dry season of 1944, the aim of which was to gain control of the passes linking the Indian region of Assam with Burma. In the middle of March the Japanese 15th Army under General Renya Mutaguchi, which included an Indian contingent recruited by Chandra

WAR ARCHIVES: PRISONERS

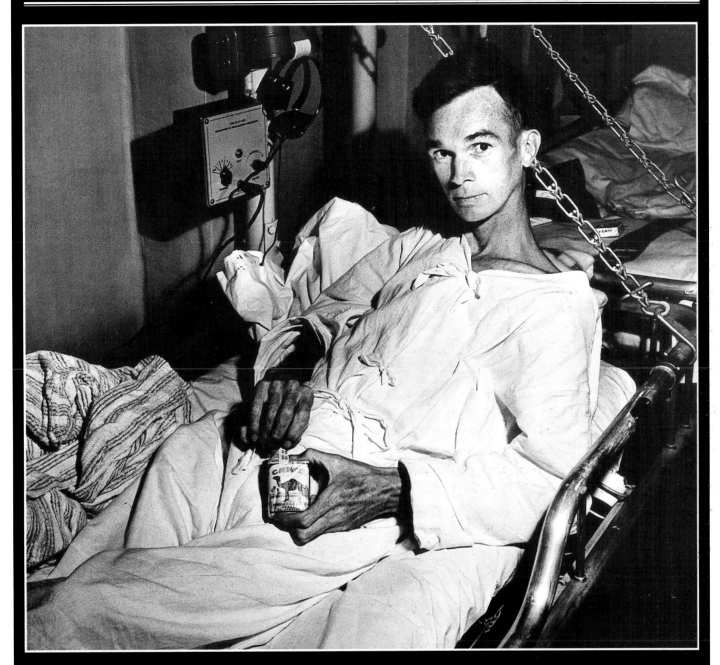

At the outbreak of the war, the treatment of prisoners of war was regulated by various international conventions, such as the Hague Conventions of 1899 and 1907 and the Geneva Convention of 1929 (ratified by all the belligerent countries with the exception of the USSR and Japan). However, the regulations safeguarding the life and dignity of soldiers were repeatedly violated, especially by Germany. Many orders issued by Hitler and other Nazi commanders prescribed the physical elimination of prisoners – a clear demonstration that the violations were preplanned. The Poles and Russians, who were considered inferior beings, were hit worst by these orders. Of an estimated six million Soviets taken prisoner by the Germans, only one million were spared. In the winter of 1941 many were left to die in the open air, without food, on the Russian steppes. At Mauthausen they were executed with a bullet in the neck, triggered by a counterweight attached to a fake device for measuring a person's height.

(Right:) **ONE RUPEE.**
Banknote issued by the
Japanese government
during their occupation
of Burma.

(Below right:) **END OF**
A NIGHTMARE.
Allied prisoners celebrate
after being freed.

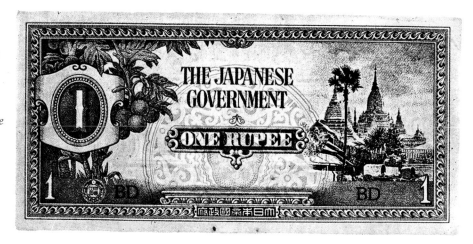

Bose, attacked on the central front and laid siege to the cities of Imphal and Kohima (in Indian territory). After three months of some of the fiercest fighting seen in the Asian war, the British managed to break the siege thanks to a constant airlifting of supplies and also due to the arrival of the monsoon. In an area battered by tropical rains, the Japanese lost more than half (50,000 out of 84,000) of the force that had begun the campaign. The survivors, debilitated by malaria, had to abandon their plan to penetrate into India.

THE RECAPTURE OF RANGOON

Despite their setback at Imphal, the Japanese retained control of Burma. For the Allies it was vitally important to open a corridor in order to supply China, so that Chinese forces there could keep the Japanese armies busy. Mountbatten drew up two plans to shift the Japanese

from Burma: a land offensive in the centre and north of the country (Operation 'Capital'); and an amphibious assault ('Dracula') in the Arakan region on the Bay of Bengal, culminating with an air–sea landing near Rangoon, the idea being to cut off the Japanese retreat as they were pushed back from the north. In May 1944 the British captured the air base of Myitkyna. In October 1944, when the monsoon season ended, the 14th Army attacked from the north. It was commanded by General William J. Slim, who was experienced in fighting in this most inhospitable area of the world and was also considered one of the most brilliant strategists in the war
in the East. In six
months the British
and Indian

THE LIBERATION OF BURMA

→ Allied offensive
— Burma Road
⊽ Allied airborne landings

Bay of Bengala

14TH ARMY Kohima
(Slim)
Imphal
Myitkyina
Kunming
Paoshan
INDIA
CHINA
Kalewa
Shwebo
Lashio
(7 Mar.)
Mekong
Mandalay
(20 Mar.)
BURMA
Akyab
(4 Jan.)
JAP. 15TH
ARMY
Meiktila
JAP. 23RD
ARMY
JAP. 28TH
ARMY
Toungoo
(22 Apr.)
Ramree
Prome
(3 May)
Irrawaddy
Salween
THAILAND
⊽ Rangoon
1 May
OPERATION 'DRACULA'

HIDING PLACE.
Japanese soldier in a cave on one of the Pacific islands. Many years after the war, members of the Japanese Army were found, still alive, on remote islands in the Pacific.

forces reached Mandalay (the starting point of the Burma Road) and, thanks to their air supremacy, pushed back the understrength Japanese 15th Army. After repelling a Japanese counter-attack, the Allies secured control of central Burma and were now about 500km from Rangoon. At this point Mountbatten launched the second part of his plan to recapture the country, and Operation 'Dracula' got under way at the end of April 1945. This was a response to the impelling necessity to capture a port on the Bay of Bengal, so that Slim's army, which was hard pressed by an exhausting campaign, could be resupplied. The American transport planes that had been performing this task until then were to be switched to duties in China. Parachute drops and the landing of amphibious troops at the mouth of the river at Rangoon brought an end to the campaign. In the space of six months (December 1944 to May 1945), the Allies had managed to recapture Burma.

IWO JIMA AND OKINAWA

After gaining strategic control of the Philippines, the Americans turned their attention to Iwo Jima, a volcanic island of just 20 square kilometres and a strategically crucial forward base for the final attack on Japan. The island fortress was defended by a garrison of 20,000 men, commanded by General Tadamichi Kuribayashi. The Japanese resisted incessant aerial and naval bombardment (14,000t of explosives) in fortified positions and caves connected by a network of tunnels. On 19 February 1945, 30,000 Marines began landing on the south-west of the island. After five weeks of bitter fighting, the island was finally taken, thanks to the use of flamethrowers, bulldozers and tanks. Practically the whole of the Japanese garrison was wiped out – just 212 soldiers surrendered. The Americans lost 4,500 men.

The next obstacle on the way to Japan was the island

ON THE BLACK SAND OF IWO JIMA.
The island was a strategically vital objective for the Americans. For months it was used as a base for fighters escorting B-29 bomber formations on missions over Japan.

(Below:)
FLAMETHROWER.
On Iwo Jima the Marines used flamethrowers to crush Japanese resistance and open up a path to Mount Suribachi.

US ship production (July 1940–August 1945)	
Warships	10
Aircraft carriers	27
Escort carriers	111
Cruisers	47
Destroyers	370
Escort destroyers	504
Submarines	217
Minesweepers	975
Patrol boats	1,915
Support vessels	1,612
Landing ships	66,055
TOTAL	**71,843**

of Okinawa, defended by the 32nd Army (150,000 men) commanded by General Mitsuru Ushijima. An American armada comprising 1,300 ships (including 18 battleships, 40 aircraft carriers and 200 destroyers) surrounded the island and began shelling the enemy positions. On 1 April, 60,000 Marines hit the beaches; but the Japanese, rather than engaging the enemy on the shore, decided to fight inland and also relied on kamikaze attacks directed at the American fleet off the coastline. The first waves of suicide attacks (about 700 planes) began on 6 April, but were repelled by American anti-aircraft fire. The next day the battleship *Yamato*, which had also embarked on what amounted to a suicide mission because it only had enough fuel to reach the battle area, was attacked and sunk by 280 American planes, taking its crew of 2,300 with it. Suicide missions against the American fleet were carried out not only by the air force but also by fast patrol boats crammed with explosives. After 80 days of fighting on land, sea and air, Japanese resistance petered out and Okinawa

CROSSES AT DUSK.
The fight to take Okinawa was the Americans' toughest battle in the Pacific. However, the 5,500 American dead were a mere fraction in comparison with over 100,000 Japanese casualties, both military and civilian, who lost their lives in the defence of the island. Many Japanese officers committed suicide.

fell to the Americans. The US Navy suffered its heaviest losses since Pearl Harbor (5,000 men), and the Marines had casualties of 7,000 dead and 31,000 wounded. About 110,000 men of the Japanese garrison were wiped out.

All the generals committed hara-kiri and just 4,000 Japanese surrendered. There were also terrible civilian casualties: approximately one-third of the population of about 450,000 died.

TOO HIGH A PRICE

The Iwo Jima and Okinawa campaigns were an ominous warning for the Americans, now separated from Japan by a single stretch of sea. This was not only because Japanese resistance had become increasingly tenacious and desperate as the battle moved closer to their homeland, but also because the high number of losses (albeit only a fraction of the number suffered by Germany and the Soviet Union

FACE WOUND.
A Marine aids a comrade during a pause in the fighting.

WE'LL MAKE THEM PAY.
The Americans were asked to respond to the cold-blooded execution by the Japanese of shot-down American pilots by stepping up production and joining the armed services.

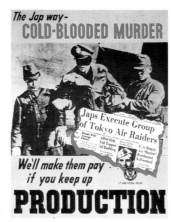

in the drawn-out battles in Europe) profoundly upset American public opinion.

The American successes thus far were no guarantee that the invasion of Japan – geographically similar to the islands that had just been captured – could be achieved without heavy losses. The American Chiefs of Staff estimated that, of the approximately 800,000 soldiers deemed

necessary to conquer Japan, the total number of casualties might amount to about 270,000 men, the same number that America had lost until then on all the fronts of the World War II. It was therefore decided to block all channels of sea supply in the Strait of Shimonoseki between Korea and Japan. In the meantime, Japan's cities were being subjected to devastating bombing raids.

MEN AND EQUIPMENT.
After the capture of Okinawa, US President Truman commented that he hoped there was a 'possibility of preventing an Okinawa from one end of Japan to the other'. In May 1945 the United States was still uncertain about what approach to take in invading Japan.

(Left:) **JAPANESE BOMBERS.**

(Below:) **AMERICAN B-29.**
The largest bomber in the war, the B-29 had a range of over 6,500km.

AIR RAIDS ON JAPAN

In the summer of 1944 the Americans started using the Mariana Islands as a base for strategic bombing. Missions against Japan started at the end of the year, with B-29 bombers taking off from Saipan to hit Tokyo. The first daytime raid on the capital (after the raid in 1942) marked the beginning of a strategic offensive to put a stranglehold on the enemy. The campaign became increasingly intense, culminating in a deadly switch in tactics. Exploiting the weakness of Japanese anti-aircraft fire, the Americans opted for strategic low-level bombing missions at night, similar to the kind they had for some time been running over Germany. This allowed them to hit smaller targets as well. On 9 March 1945 each of the 300-odd B-29s that took off from their bases on Saipan, Guam and Tinian released 8 tonnes of incendiary bombs on Tokyo in the space of three hours. A fifth of the capital was destroyed by flames and 185,000 civilians died. In the days that followed – while the American flag was flying over Iwo Jima – Osaka, Nagoya and Kobe received the same treatment. Besides causing a mass exodus of the civilian population towards the countryside and paralysing Japan's industry, it also left many people with few illusions that it would be possible to negotiate anything other than an unconditional surrender with the American military power.

From Yalta to Hiroshima

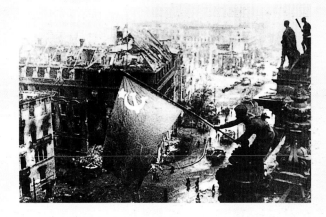

In the final year of the war, as Germany and Japan were
heading towards military defeat, the Allies began to lay the
foundations for a new world order. By the end of 1944 the
Soviet Union had occupied much of central and eastern
Europe, thereby reinforcing its position in relation to the Americans and British, who were still on the banks of the Rhine. The
Italian campaign, which had become a secondary concern after
the landings in Normandy, ended in April 1945 with the liberation of Italy and the surrender of the German forces there. More
or less at the same time, the Third Reich finally came to an end
with the capture of Berlin by the Soviets. In the Pacific and in
Asia, Japan was now cut off from its Asian territories, and its military capacity was at a low ebb due to American bombing and
a shortage of raw materials. In August 1945 two new developments broke the pattern of military operations and hastened
Japan's unconditional surrender, and with it the end of the conflict. One was the Soviet Union's entry into the war against Japan

(p. 240) **6 AUGUST 1945.**
The atomic mushroom cloud in the skies of Hiroshima.

(p. 241) **THE FLAG OF VICTORY.**
Red Army soldiers on the roof of the Reichstag.

(Right:) **CAPTURED GUN.**
American soldiers stand on a 274mm artillery piece.

alongside its western Allies; the other was the dropping of atomic bombs on Hiroshima and Nagasaki. The destructive capacity of these bombs brought about a peace that was characterized by American military and technological pre-eminence. The greatest catastrophe of the contemporary age ended with a radical change in the shape of the world order, which was to lead to a postwar equilibrium based on two superpowers.

THE FUTURE OF GERMANY

Long before the military campaign against Germany had ended, and at a time when the United States, Great Britain and the Soviet Union were looking for ways of establishing a lasting world peace, the Allied advance effectively prefigured – in both the east and the west – the spheres of influence that would arise from the geography of military occupation at the end of the war, and which would define the nature of postwar Europe. In talks held at Dumbarton Oaks (near Washington DC) in September 1944 to draw up the charter of the United Nations, Henry Morgenthau, the US

Secretary of the Treasury, presented a plan that envisaged the dismemberment of Germany and the destruction of its industrial potential. Some aspects of this plan were later adopted in the partitioning of Germany. A month later Stalin and Churchill agreed on the need to transform the 'zones of operations' in central Europe and the Balkans into 'spheres of influence'; at the end of the war these would confirm Soviet dominance (compensated by

MECHANIZED COLUMN.
American units drive through a German city. One of the obstacles that frequently hindered the Allied advance into German territory was piles of rubble caused by air raids.

RADIO LONDON.
Members of the Danish Resistance listen to the BBC. The broadcasts served a dual purpose: to inform people in the German-occupied countries about the progress of the war and to send coded messages to Resistance groups.

Greece being assigned to the British sphere of influence) over many of the countries in the region. Acknowledging the relative strength of the forces in the field at that moment, Stalin and Churchill agreed to counterbalance Soviet and western influence in Yugoslavia and Hungary.

Having agreed that Germany had to be forced into total capitulation, the 'three great powers' also began to sketch out the borders of their respective occupation zones, and to consider the possibility of giving Berlin a special status that would be guaranteed by the occupation forces of the three Allied nations. A prominent role in European politics and in the administration of postwar Germany was also envisaged for liberated France; de Gaulle, the head of the provisional government, acquiesced to Stalin's request to recognize that the future western border of Poland should be along the line of the river Oder and the river Neisse.

THE WAR OF THE PARTISANS

A contribution to the battle to liberate Europe from Nazi occupation was also made by partisan formations, and civilian resistance played an important role. Many civilians did their bit in the struggle against collaborationist regimes and the Nazi occupation forces, with various kinds of non-violent action – helping Jews and those in hiding, anti-fascist propaganda, strikes and forms of mass disobedience.

A broad-based Resistance movement emerged in response to de Gaulle's appeal to the French to continue the struggle against the Reich after the trauma of defeat in 1940. In 1943 the Resistance groups and the main movements opposed to the Vichy regime joined together to form the National Resistance Council. Sabotage and guerrilla operations were carried out by young French Resistance fighters (Maquis), who then went into hiding to escape capture, conscription and forced labour in

COLUMN OF GERMAN PRISONERS IN THE STREETS OF KARLSRUHE.

(Right:) **WOMAN PARTISAN.**
In Italy women did not just liaise between the various resistance groups. The photo shows a female partisan fighting in the Ravenna area.

(Below:) **SABOTAGE.**
The French Resistance has just sabotaged the railway line.

Germany. There was a similar resistance movement in Italy; set up on 8 September 1943, it included everyone – in the countryside and in the cities, in the north and in the south – who fought against the Nazi occupation and the attempt to re-establish Fascism with the Republic of Salò. The various resistance movements were directed by the National Committee for the Liberation of Upper Italy (CLNAI), which brought together all the anti-Fascist parties under one roof (communists, socialists, liberals, Christian-Democrats, Action Party) and coordinated resistance activities, making a vital contribution to victory by liberating a number of northern cities before the Allies arrived, and restoring moral and political dignity to a population and a nation that had been sorely pressed by the conflict. In the Balkans the Yugoslav partisan movement was the main force in the war against the Axis forces. After Italy's surrender, partisans also made a significant contribution to the liberation of Greece, though the movement was divided. When the Germans withdrew froam Greece, the nationalists and communists began fighting each other, triggering a civil war that did not end until several years after the end of World War II.

THE HOME FRONT IN THE COUNTRIES AT WAR

The effects of the war were devastating not only materially and economically, but also for the morale of civilian populations, which became directly entangled in the war as in no previous conflict. Six years of violence and devastation deeply affected and disturbed the daily lives and the minds of millions of people, splintering family and social ties. Adopting rigid, centralized control, the entire production system and resources of individual nations were mobilized to win the war. New industries, specializing in the production of strategic materials, were established. In Great Britain, the workforce was employed heavily in war industries and the Ministry of Labour moved workers around as required. In the United States the War Production Board wielded almost dictatorial powers with regard to industry, production, raw materials and the distribution and rationing of goods. Women, children and the elderly were employed extensively in factories, in auxiliary activities and services, or in preparing defences against enemy attacks. In the USSR the climate of patriotic mobilization induced millions of workers to toil until they dropped so as to supply the soldiers at the front. The population complied with the directives of the regime and put up with the most acute shortages of basic foodstuffs, though those working in the war industries were given larger rations of food than the average member of the population. In Germany the Nazi regime benefited from its initial supremacy in battle and managed to channel production for war purposes, also offering incentives for working at night or on weekends and holidays. In the second phase, as the war dragged on and military needs grew, the increasing shortage of workers was met through the forcible employment of millions of foreigners and prisoners of war. In 1943 all men aged 16 to 45 who were not in the armed forces, and all women aged 17 to 45, were mobilized for work. In many countries, civil defence systems, for instance the Air Raid Precautions system in Great Britain, were organized to provide protection against air raids or gas attack. Civilian populations were subject to food and petrol rationing, and prices rocketed on the black market. A lot of effort was also made to keep the morale of the civilian population high; in addition to the newspapers, to posters and to the radio, films were made and entertainment and various other kinds of distraction were laid on. Actors and singers contributed to this. Finally, political leaders personally addressed their citizens directly. For instance, Winston Churchill's speeches appealing to the unity of the nation became famous and helped to reinforce hope in victory.

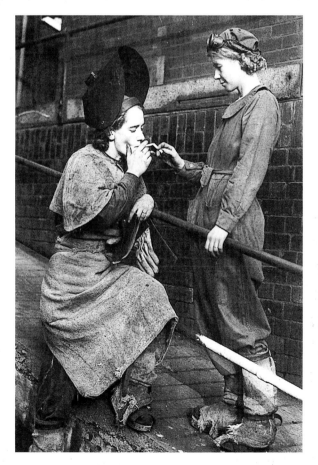

(Above:) Russian blast-furnace worker.
(Left:) English steelworkers having a smoke during a break.

(Right:) **WRECKED GLIDER.**
A medic gives first aid to a parachutist whose glider has crashed in German territory. (Photograph by Robert Capa.)

(Below:) **MEDALS.**
Red Army soldiers proudly display their medals to the citizens of Odessa.

THE RUSSIANS AT THE GATEWAY TO EAST PRUSSIA

In Hungary the Red Army had to struggle hard to open up a passage to Budapest, where the civilian population was suffering terribly. Stubborn German resistance only ended in early February 1945, after two months of bitter fighting. On the Baltic and Leningrad front, the Soviets mounted a successful manoeuvre to isolate the German Army Group North, which was forced to abandon Estonia and was threatened with the prospect of being crushed in an enormous pocket on the Baltic. Soon after that, the gateway to East Prussia opened up before the headlong advance of Rokossovsky's '2nd White Russian front'. At the same time Stalin ordered the other two fronts, Koniev's '1st Ukrainian' and Zhukov's '1st White Russian', which possessed almost a third of the Soviets' total infantry strength and half its tanks, to prepare a major offensive with the objective of reaching Berlin. On 21 January 1945, Rokossovsky occupied Tannenberg, where the Prussian armies had defeated the Tsar's troops in 1914. The German forces in East Prussia fell back to Königsberg, which was promptly besieged by the Russians. With a series of tremendous pushes aimed at crushing the enemy, Koniev moved towards Bratislava, Kraków and the industrial region of Silesia. On 27 January the Russians entered the extermination camp of Auschwitz–Birkenau. With a thunderous bombardment from the Soviet bridgehead on the Vistula to the south of

PROPAGANDA

Both the Allies and the Axis powers used propaganda to reinforce the ideological dimension of the conflict, organizing specific technical systems and departments for the purpose. While the prime objective for the Allies was to rid the world of Nazism, the Axis powers envisioned the establishment of a 'new order' in Europe and in 'Greater East Asia'. Press, poster and radio messages were also used tactically to support military operations, and were aimed not only at the home population (and, in the case of Nazism, the occupied countries as well), but also at the enemy's armed forces and civilian population. In all the belligerent nations, radio was the main instrument of conveying propaganda. Sales of radios, now affordable for the working classes as well, had quadrupled in the years leading up to the war. However, there was a disadvantage: radio also transmitted the messages of the enemy. Steps were therefore taken to disturb enemy radio broadcasts in order to counteract their propaganda messages. The British proved to be masters in spreading a message of hope, of the value of the struggle for freedom, and at reinforcing faith in eventual victory. With the support of the government, the British Broadcasting Corporation (BBC) broadcast its programmes in 23 languages. Black propaganda programmes like Soldatensender Calais, which was broadcasted to Germany, established the BBC's credibility by making detailed reference to the German armed forces, and took advantage of this to add salacious titbits, mostly invented, about the private lives of Nazi officials and military commanders. It has been estimated that in the

ВОДРУЗИМ НАД БЕРЛИНОМ

last year of the war more than 10 million people listened to the BBC's German-language broadcasts.

The major themes of German propaganda were the injustices of the Treaty of Versailles, the global threat of Jewry, the role of the Third Reich in

defending the western world from Soviet communism and the inevitability of German victory. Placed under the direction of Goebbels right at the beginning of the war, the radio and other means of communication celebrated Nazi heroes and the victories of the Reich to the point of veneration, systematically pursuing the goal of shaping public opinion in Germany and the occupied territories. German propaganda made no impact on the enemy troops, and the over-the-top tone and schematic content of the messages were often greeted ironically and with scepticism.

Before the war, the Soviet Union had the most developed propaganda machine (Agitprop). While in the first phase of the conflict its intent was to justify Russia's non-aggression pact with Germany by citing the need to thwart western capitalism, after 'Barbarossa' the focus was on the theme of a struggle to the death against the 'fascist beast'. An appeal was made to all the forces of the Soviet nation, which mobilized en masse for the 'great patriotic war' and put up a strenuous resistance.

The Americans, besides a systematic use of traditional forms of communication, also dropped basic foodstuffs from the air for people in the occupied countries (in packets containing propaganda slogans) and safe conducts for German troops.

(Top:) Russian poster reading: 'Let's set up in Berlin'. (Left:) Churchill and Roosevelt depicted as gangsters by Republic of Salò propaganda.

247

VIKING DEFEATED BY THE COSSACK.
Russian playing card from 1945.

Warsaw, Zhukov also commenced his offensive, which led to the liberation of the Polish capital a few days later.

THE EXODUS FROM THE EASTERN TERRITORIES

Having reached the borders of Brandenburg and Pomerania at the end of January, the Russian armies were just 150km from Berlin, on the banks of the icy waters of the river Oder. Just as Hitler had foreseen a few years earlier, the eastern campaign was proving decisive for the conflict in Europe, and it became a symbol of the tragic fate of millions of helpless civilians. The Reich's dream of conquering 'vital space in the east' had been shattered by the Russian counter-offensive, which had now been under way for over a year, and

REMNANTS OF THE WEHRMACHT.
The main goal of the few remaining forces defending German territory against the Allied advance was to ensure that the British and American armies reached Berlin before the Red Army.

Germany was on its knees in the face of the unstoppable Soviet advance. If German military operations since summer 1941 had amounted to a war of extermination, with blatant and repeated violations of the conventions of war regarding the treatment of soldiers and civilians, the arrival of the Russians in the 'lair of the Fascist beast' was marked by equally horrific atrocities. About 4 million refugees fled westwards from the German territories of Prussia, East Brandenburg, Silesia, Pomerania and Danzig to escape the massacres being perpetrated by the Russians as retaliation for the atrocities carried out by the Wehrmacht and the Waffen-SS in the occupied countries. The Russian writer Ilja Ehrenburg had this to say in the Red Army newspaper:

'We have all too often repeated: universal

BROKEN SWASTIKA.
French poster showing powerful Allied arms tearing apart the symbol of Nazi power.

judgment will arrive! Well, now it has … We do not forget. We march through Pomerania, but before our eyes there is White Russia, destroyed and bleeding … Berlin has not yet repaid us for the torments of Leningrad.'

THE YALTA CONFERENCE

With the Red Army holding positions along the Oder and preparing for a final push towards Berlin – confirmation that the Russians had acquired a head start in the field over their Allies – Stalin, Churchill and Roosevelt met at Yalta in the Crimea for their second summit (4–11 February), following the one in Teheran. At the conference, the 'three great powers' discussed the postwar world order. While Churchill and Stalin shared a vision of a European power set-up based on reciprocal security needs, what Roosevelt had in mind was a global order based on a new international organization founded on

collaboration between the great powers, above all with the Soviet Union, and respecting the principle of self-determination. Roosevelt's view was that the spheres of influence should not be rigidly sealed, nor should they prevent the liberated countries from establishing their own independent forms of government. The fact that the conference took place before the war ended gave the Soviet Union an edge deriving from its military potential. This was confirmed by discussion about the future of Poland, because although the final communiqué was a compromise that talked about setting up a new 'Provisional Government of National Unity' (consisting of the Lublin Committee, recognized by Stalin and by members of the government in exile in London), which was to organize free elections, the application of it all was to be managed by the Soviet Union.

A similar agreement was reached with regard to Yugoslavia, while for the other liberated European states the powers undertook

THE THREE GREAT POWER BROKERS.
Churchill, Roosevelt and Stalin at the Yalta Conference, in the course of which the Soviet leader declared that his country wanted to participate in the invasion of Japan. He neglected to reveal that the Japanese had for some time been sending out high-level feelers with a view to attaining a quick end to hostilities.

WORLD HEALTH ORGANIZATION.
One of the bodies set up after the foundation of the United Nations in San Francisco in 1945.

to organize free elections to form 'governments representative of the will of the population'. Stalin also undertook to enter the war against Japan within three months of Germany's surrender. The three powers reached agreement about the fundamental principles of the Charter of the United Nations; the final version of the text was approved at a conference in San Francisco, where, between April and July 1945, representatives of 50 states signed the 111 Articles of the UN Charter. The Yalta Conference thus ensured collaboration between the powers until final victory had been achieved, and delineated a possible system of collective security in the postwar period.

THE DESTRUCTION OF DRESDEN

The Luftwaffe had by now been virtually wiped out and the Allied bombing offensive continued with increasing

intensity. On 13 and 14 February, British and American planes mounted a three-phase bombing mission with incendiary and fragmentation bombs. Their target was Dresden, which was packed with refugees from Silesia and had no anti-aircraft batteries. When the night and daytime missions ended, the city on the banks of the Elbe had been razed to the ground. A devastating fire burned for days and 35,000 of the 70,000 people in the city were buried in the ruins. A month later another raid wreaked similar mass destruction at Würzburg, and other German cities received the same treatment in subsequent months. The Allies ended their strategic offensive against the German cities in the middle of May. By the war end, about 600,000 people in Germany and 60,000 in Great Britain would have died in air raids.

RATIONS IN THE SNOW.
In the final, cold winter of the war, American infantry queue up for food on the border between Belgium and Germany.

(Left:) **Two armies.**
In this poster, Americans leaving for the front march past soldiers from the 1776 War of Independence.

(Below left:) **Bombed-out Krupp steelworks in Essen.**
In 1945, Allied air power targeted German industrial plants with increasing precision.

GERMANY ON THE VERGE OF COLLAPSE

The Third Reich was on the brink of total collapse. The German Army was hamstrung by a terrible shortage of troops and equipment. Hitler's fanatical desire to resist at all costs had until now translated into a strict ban on any form of strategic withdrawal, which had resulted in the loss of entire armies. Now it drove him to order the mobilization of the civilian population. Squads of women were put to work building trenches, and at the orders of the 'Führer's secretary', Martin Bormann, members of the Volkssturm ('People's Militia') were incorporated into party organizations. All Germans aged between 16 and 60 were conscripted. Hitler now relied on the struggle of the National Socialist 'people's community' and on total mobilization to defeat the 'international Jewish enemy'. However, his plan was undermined by the collapse of the country, which had already suffered terrible destruction and whose armed forces were no longer in a position to resist the impetus of the Allied invasion.

The entire economic infrastructure of the country had disintegrated. Virtually all road communications had been interrupted, and millions of refugees and people who had been bombed out of their homes tried to escape the Russian advance. Germany was crippled. The conscription of thousands of civilians, hurriedly trained and thrown into battle, simply increased the incredible loss of life suffered by Germany in the final phase of the conflict. The desperate order to block the enemy's advance by means of 'obstruction through self-destruction', as Hitler put it in the dark deluded state that characterized his conduct in the final year of the war, led to a growing desire amongst Germans for a rapid Anglo-American advance. Their hope was that the western Allies would arrive in Berlin as quickly as possible, and at any rate before the Russians. The latter

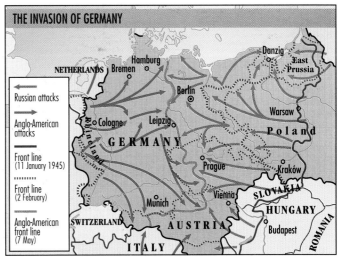

THE INVASION OF GERMANY

Russian attacks
Anglo-American attacks
Front line (11 January 1945)
Front line (2 February)
Anglo-American front line (7 May)

NETHERLANDS • Bremen Hamburg Danzig East Prussia
Berlin Warsaw
Cologne Leipzig Poland
GERMANY
Prague Kraków
Munich Vienna SLOVAKIA
SWITZERLAND AUSTRIA HUNGARY
ITALY Budapest ROMANIA

THE RUSSIANS ENTER VIENNA.
Mechanized Red Army troops fight in one of the squares of the Austrian capital. At the beginning of April the Germans blew up all but one of the bridges over the Danube. A week later the Russians reached the heart of the city and captured the Parliament building.

were already moving into position for the final attack on the capital – 450,000 soldiers, equipped with over 12,000 artillery pieces, 21,000 rocket launchers and 1,500 tanks.

THE ALLIES CROSS THE RHINE

At the beginning of March, Patton's 3rd Army was on the banks of the Rhine, and a few days later the Americans gained control of a strip of territory between Mannheim and Coblenz. Preceded by devastating artillery bombardment, the Allies began to penetrate into German territory with a pincer manoeuvre that trapped 325,000 Germans defending the industrial region of the Ruhr. For the final attack on Germany, Eisenhower gave priority to the southern thrust, giving Bradley's 12th Army Corps the task of taking Dresden and Leipzig, and Montgomery's British and Canadian troops responsibility for Hamburg and Lubeck. In this case again, the Allied advance was slowed down more by the rivalry between the Allied High Commands

than by German resistance, which was sporadic.

In mid-April the American 9th Army reached Magdeburg on the Elbe (the river that had been established as a demarcation line between the American and Soviet occupation zones in Germany), and Patton penetrated into Thuringia and pushed into southern Germany, arriving just 50km from Prague and Vienna. The latter was occupied on 13 April by Red Army units that arrived from Hungary. The Russians established a provisional government in the Austrian capital, and a few months elapsed before they signed an agreement permitting the British and Americans to enter the urban district of the capital, Styria and Carinthia (which had been occupied by Yugoslav partisans).

THE FINAL ASSAULT ON BERLIN

Four days after Roosevelt's death on 12 April, and while the British and American armies were arriving on the banks

RUSSIANS AND AMERICANS.
On 25 April advance units of the Russian 5th Army and the American 1st Army met at Torgau, to the south of Berlin, on the banks of the river Elbe. Germany had effectively been divided into two.

YOUNG PRISONER.
An adolescent conscripted in the last few months of the conflict, taken prisoner by Red Army soldiers.

of the Elbe, the Soviets launched a general all-out offensive, which, in the space of a few days, took them over the rivers Oder and Neisse and into the suburbs of Berlin. A week later, the Russian juggernaut overran the remnants of the 4th Panzer Army and Berlin was cut off as Zhukov's armies closed in from the east and Koniev's from the south. On the evening of 20 April, Hitler's birthday (during which he awarded decorations to members of the Hitler Youth recruited for the final defence of the capital), Zhukov commenced bombardment of the city. Holed up in his bunker beneath the Chancellery, Hitler removed Guderian from his position as Chief of General Staff, Goering

from command of the Luftwaffe and Himmler (who had made a surrender offer to the Anglo-Americans) from that of the SS. There were now no more than 45,000 combatants (with just 50 tanks) still defending Berlin, including a large number of People's Militia and a few thousand Hitler Youth and Waffen-SS volunteers recruited in former Nazi-occupied countries, who put up some final resistance. Berliners had taken refuge in the reinforced concrete air-raid shelters or in cellars, in extreme conditions with no food, electricity, gas or water.

At midday on 30 April, Russian infantry stormed the Reichstag and raised the Red Flag above the dome of the wrecked building. A few hours later, with Soviet units fast approaching the Chancellery, Hitler committed suicide. He left a personal and political testament in which he appointed Grand Admiral Karl Dönitz as his successor and Goebbels as the Chancellor of the Reich. Goebbels, however, and members of his family

THE BATTLE FOR BERLIN.
Eisenhower did not consider the German capital to be of strategic importance and allowed the Soviets to take it. After they had done so, fighting house to house, it became the symbol of their victory.

(Right:) **HOMELESS GERMANS QUEUE FOR A MEAL.**

(BELOW:) PARTISANS IN SIENA.
The 'civil resistance' of the Italians supplemented the 'armed' resistance of active combat units. The effectiveness of the partisan movement in German-occupied Italy was the result of close collaboration between the population and armed anti-Fascist groups.

swallowed poison. Two days later, on 2 May, the commander of the remaining troops in Berlin accepted the Soviet demand for an unconditional surrender.

THE LIBERATION OF ITALY

At the end of 1944 the Allies had been just south of the Gothic Line. The 5th and 8th Armies (about 550,000 men) waited until the spring of 1945 to begin the final offensive against the Germans and the Republic of Salò combatants for the conquest of northern Italy. Aided by clear aerial supremacy, the Allies also benefited from disruptive operations carried out by partisan groups. The Canadian Corps of the 8th Army captured Ravenna and arrived at the river Senio, while the 5th Army was held up near Bologna; and on the Tyrrhenian Sea, Clark's American

forces were already at Pisa. The retreating Germans, who often executed civilians in retaliation for partisan activities, caused heavy Allied losses. The terrain favoured the defenders and the Allied advance proceeded slowly everywhere. This was also because of the fact that the Italian theatre had become of secondary importance after the landings in Normandy.

It was not until the middle of April 1945 that American tanks breached the German defences, whereupon the Allies fanned out into the plains beyond and finally reached the Po. Karl Wolff, the commander of the SS in Italy, started negotiations with the Americans to avoid an insurrection by the Resistance, to safeguard the country's industrial plants and guarantee a smooth handover of power. However, the talks came to nothing. In the

LEADERS

HARRY S. TRUMAN

Born in Lamar, Missouri, in 1884, Truman came from a farming family. He served as an artillery officer in World War I, and then did various jobs and business activities before entering politics as a member of the Democratic Party. Senator for the state of Missouri (1934–44), he contributed to the legislative work promoted by President Roosevelt. In 1941 he acquired considerable political prestige as the head of a Senate national defence investigative committee that uncovered waste and shortcomings in the sector. Elected Vice President of the United States in 1944 on a ticket with Roosevelt, he took over the presidency when Roosevelt died in April 1945. During the few months of his vice presidency, he did not play an active part in political decision making and so found himself, with no specific experience, having to face and make decisive decisions about complex issues in the final phase of the war. Aware of his task, he commented to journalists: 'Boys, if you ever pray, pray for me now.' He continued the line pursued by his predecessor, relying on the support of a small number of advisers. Truman attended the Potsdam Conference, during which he informed the other Allies that the United States had successfully tested an atomic bomb, a project about which he himself had only recently learnt. Determined to accelerate the unconditional surrender of Japan and to save the greatest number of American lives possible, he decided to use the new weapon on the Japanese cities of Hiroshima and Nagasaki. Thereafter he always upheld the wisdom of his decision on the grounds that it was based on purely military considerations. His foreign policy in the postwar period was oriented towards containment of communist expansion and support for the European democracies. In March 1947, he announced to Congress the 'doctrine' that then bore his name. This envisaged aid for Turkey and Greece, began a process of economic and military intervention to support countries threatened by the Soviet Union, and activated the European Recovery Program (Marshall Plan) to finance reconstruction in European countries. In the following years he steered the West through the crucial phases of the Cold War. On the domestic front, he adopted a policy of moderate reformism, during which he had to face opposition from the Republican majority in Congress and from elements within his own party. In 1948, contrary to expectations, he was re-elected. With the creation of NATO, he began building a western defence system, and in 1950 decided to intervene in North Korea, though he rejected General MacArthur's proposals for a broadening of the conflict. When his presidential mandate ended in 1952, he retired from politics. He died in 1972.

Attlee (the newly elected British Labour Prime Minister), Truman and Stalin at the Potsdam Conference in July 1945.

ART WORKS.
During their advance through Germany, the Allies discovered secret stores where the Germans had kept art treasures filched from other European countries.

meantime, the Republican Fascists under Mussolini sought a 'political solution' to the situation, but the Allies were suspicious and the political leaders of the Resistance adamantly insisted on an immediate and unconditional surrender. The convulsive days that followed the rapid advance of the Allies through northern Italy marked the end of the Republic of Salò and with it the tragic finale to Mussolini's life. There was no possibility of negotiating with the Resistance. While the latter began a general insurrection, Mussolini left Milan to try to reach Switzerland, but was stopped at a roadblock near Como and executed by the partisans on 28 April. A few days later his body and that of other Fascist officials were put on display in Piazzale Loreto in Milan. This macabre event – in the city that had been the cradle of Fascism – ended 20 years of dictatorship, five years of war and two years of German occupation. On 29 April the Germans signed an unconditional surrender.

THE END OF THE WAR IN EUROPE

From its seat in Schleswig-Holstein, Dönitz's government made its first moves, with the illusory hope that the Third Reich might survive the disaster of the conflict. Dönitz offered a partial capitulation, hoping to secure guarantees regarding the continuing existence of the state and to allow the largest possible number of refugees and German soldiers in various corners of Europe (about 2 million) to escape from the clutches of the Soviets and reach the area of Germany under the control of the Western powers. But, for Britain and the United States unconditional surrender was the only way of ensuring the application of the principles that had been agreed the year before, and of forcing Stalin to honour his

BRANDENBURG GATE.
After the battle for Berlin, the last survivors of the German army trudge past the symbol of the Reich's imperial grandeur as they make their way to prison camps.

(Left:) **GERMAN GIRLS AND AMERICAN SOLDIERS IN A GERMAN CITY.**

(BELOW:) THE GERMAN SURRENDER.
Watched by a group of Russian generals, Field Marshal Keitel signs the document agreeing to the unconditional surrender of all German forces.

pledge to join in the war against Japan. After arranging with Montgomery the surrender of the German forces in northwest Europe, the total capitulation of the Reich was signed by General Alfred Jodl on 7 May 1945 in the headquarters of the Allied forces in Reims, in the presence of the four victorious powers. The ceremony was repeated two days later in Marshal Zhukov's headquarters at Berlin-Karlshorst.

In the face of the evident intention of the Dönitz government not to abandon the key principles of Nazism, the winning powers dismantled the apparatus of the German state and began to demilitarize and totally disarm Germany, at the same time fixing the borders of the occupation zones. On 5 June 1945 the Allied Control Council of the four victorious powers (in which France had been included a few months earlier), based in Berlin, took over the government of the country on the basis of the 1937 frontiers. In the former capital of the Reich, the demarcation lines of the occupation began to take shape: the eastern sector was to be controlled by the Russians, and the western sector by the Americans, British and French.

THE POTSDAM CONFERENCE

The talks between Churchill (and later Attlee), Stalin and the new American President Harry Truman that took place in the castle of Cecilienhof at Potsdam (17 July to 2 August) were marked by mutual suspicion. If at Yalta the three great

BERLIN IN 1945. ENTIRE NEIGHBOUR-HOODS HAD BEEN DEVASTATED BY AIR RAIDS.

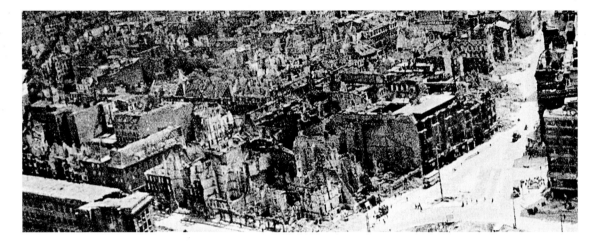

powers had established a framework for cooperation until final victory had been achieved over the Axis forces, at this conference the ideological hostility that had been dampened but not removed by the conflict surfaced once again, given that the two major powers wanted to ensure that their interests prevailed in the new world order, in which Europe was the main source of friction. The issue of the set-up and the territorial boundaries of Poland was a source of conflict, not just because it also related to the definition of Germany's frontiers, but above all because it became emblematic of Soviet behaviour in the countries that it had occupied. Moscow's position, on the other hand, was dictated by the fear that if Russia loosened its control over the sphere of security it had acquired in eastern Europe, it might once again be faced by the threat of a new capitalist alliance.

The Soviet proposal about Poland's western frontier was thus accepted in exchange for a reduction in Russian demands for reparations (which they would only have obtained from Poland and the German zone they occupied), the plans to dismember Germany were shelved and a new goal was established: democratic reconstruction. Truman's design won the day. This envisaged the division of Germany into occupation zones, each of which would be controlled by one of the victorious powers. For his part, Stalin did not bow to Western pressure on Poland even when Truman announced the successful testing of the first atomic bomb. Stalin also undertook to enter the war against Japan shortly. If Potsdam sanctioned the tacit Anglo-American consensus for Moscow's policy in eastern Europe, at the same time it confirmed that the disintegration of the German Reich had paved the way for the control of Europe by the United States and the Soviet Union. The latter was now the major European military power.

RUSSIAN TANKS IN THE STREETS OF BERLIN.

THIS IS OUR CHANCE TO...

LABOUR

FOR HIM

VOTE LABOUR AND WIN THE PEACE!

(Left:) **FINAL EFFORT.**
Japanese poster urging the nation to purchase treasury bonds.

(Far left:) **ELECTION PUBLICITY.**
British Labour Party poster. Churchill was defeated in the general election held in Britain on 7 July 1945.

JAPANESE WILLINGNESS TO SURRENDER

While the Americans continued to advance towards the Japanese homeland, the 'Co-Prosperity Sphere' that Japan had set up in Asia crumbled. In Indonesia a nationalist revolt broke out against Japanese rule, which led to that country's independence. Burma was recaptured by the Allies. In Indo-China the communist resistance of the Vietminh was active in the countryside, and in September they proclaimed the independence of the Democratic Republic of Vietnam. The exploitation of local populations, the rapacious economic policy of Tokyo and brutal repression resulted in forms of protest that opened the way for the Japanese withdrawal.

Exhausted by the conflict, subjected to a maritime blockade and heavy aerial bombing, and with a now almost non-existent fleet of its own, Japan began to look

RETURNING HOME.
Japanese troops on the move. Japan took steps to prepare for an expected Allied invasion of its territory.

(Right:) **IN THE BOMBSIGHT.**
Hiroshima in the sights of the American bomber Enola Gay.

(Centre:) **THE ATOMIC BOMB.**
On 6 August 1945 President Truman declared: 'The world will note that the first atomic bomb was dropped on Hiroshima, a military base.' In actual fact the city, which was razed to the ground, was an industrial centre and was crowded with women, children and the elderly.

for a way out of what was a desperate situation. On 5 April 1945 Moscow surprised Japan by reneging on the pact of neutrality it had signed with Tokyo in 1941. The immediate effect of this move was the fall of the Koiso government and the appointment of Admiral Kantaro Suzuki as head of the government. Suzuki declared that he was prepared to open peace negotiations. But while Tokyo sent out a series of signals that merely indicated their willingness to put an end to the war, in Potsdam the Allies reiterated that Japan had been asked to make an unconditional surrender.

THE MANHATTAN PROJECT

On 2 August 1939, the German physicist Albert Einstein, who had emigrated to the United States, wrote to President Roosevelt, informing him that Nazi Germany might soon be capable of building a devastating weapon that worked by exploiting the process of atomic fission. He then urged him to start a research programme to ensure that the West achieved primacy in this

THE BEGINNING OF THE ATOMIC AGE

While the US Navy and Air Force were in agreement that the naval blockade and strategic bombing that had been adopted thus far were effective means of bringing Japan to its knees, Washington was alarmed by the Army's estimated casualty figures if America were to invade Japanese territory. Having been assured by Stalin that Russia would join in the war in the East, Truman decided, despite the contrasting views of some scientists and military leaders, to use the atomic bomb to accelerate Japan's surrender. The first nuclear bomb was dropped on Hiroshima on 6 August 1945, causing the death of more than 70,000 people (not counting those who died later from the effects of radiation)

field. However, it was only in the summer of 1942 that the American government finally gave the go-ahead for the grandiose 'Manhattan Project', which was directed by General Leslie Groves with the assistance of the physicist J. Robert Oppenheimer. On 2 December 1942 a group of researchers headed by the Italian Enrico Fermi tested a nuclear chain reaction. In the meantime, a laboratory city was built at Los Alamos (New Mexico), employing over 140,000 civillians between 1943 and

1946. In utter secrecy, work began at the beginning of 1943 to study how to build an atomic bomb. This was ready at the beginning of 1945, by which time it was certain that the Germans were a long way off having one of their own. The first experimental plutonium bomb was exploded in the desert of Alamogordo on 16 July 1945, when the Germans had already capitulated. 'Babies satisfactorily born' – this was the cryptic message informing Truman, who was at the Potsdam conference, that the experimental test had been a success.

(Left:) **CONSEQUENCES OF THE EXPLOSION.** *Amongst the most horrific effects of the explosion, a witness recalled 'the disappearance of a man in front of his front door. All that was left was a shadow on the door. Nothing else. A man had disappeared, evaporated. The only sign that he had existed was a shadow.'*

(Below:) **WHAT REMAINED OF HIROSHIMA.**

and the destruction of the city. Three days later it was the turn of Nagasaki (80,000 deaths). In the meantime the Red Army had attacked Manchuria and Korea, and invaded the Kurile Islands. Truman's decision to use the bomb was prompted by military as well as political considerations: to force the enemy into a rapid cessation of hostilities and to induce the Soviet Union to acknowledge America's technological superiority, dissuading it from making demands following its very late involvement in the Asian conflict.

THE END OF THE WAR

The bombing of Hiroshima and Nagasaki induced Hirohito to authorize Suzuki to send a surrender offer to the Allies, and on 14 August the Emperor announced on radio, in what was the first ever public message by a Japanese sovereign, that Japan was prepared to accept unconditional surrender. On 2 September 1945 Japanese envoys signed the capitulation on the deck of the battleship *Missouri*, anchored off Tokyo. Thus four months after the

WAR ARCHIVES: THE RADIOACTIVE HOLOCAUST

At 8.15 on the morning of 6 August 1945, the American bomber *Enola Gay*, piloted by Colonel Paul Tibbets, dropped an atomic bomb on Hiroshima. It exploded 600m from the ground, releasing energy equivalent to 20,000t of TNT. The Japanese city became an inferno. The ball of fire that developed at the centre of the explosion had a temperature of millions of degrees Celsius; it emitted a blinding light and extended for kilometres. The shockwave radiated at a speed of over 1,000km per hour, destroying everything in its path. A few minutes later, a hot wind was generated and developed into a tornado: smoke and rubble billowed thousands of metres into the air and then, as it cooled, fell back earthwards, producing an enormous mushroom cloud. All forms of life in a radius of hundreds of metres were wiped out; 70,000 people died instantly, while a further 37,000 were seriously injured, afflicted by mutilation and major first-degree burns. In the decades to come many more people would die as a consequence of the delayed effect of ionizing radiation.

(Left:) **AMERICAN B-29S DROP CLUSTERS OF BOMBS ON JAPAN.**

(Below:) **SURRENDER OF JAPAN.**
MacArthur countersigns the surrender document that the Japanese envoys had just signed on board the battleship Missouri.

surrender of Germany and six years after Germany's invasion of Poland, World War II was over. After the collapse of Germany, now it was Japan's turn. In China the advance of the Soviets was accompanied by Mao Zedong's communists, who aimed for Nanking and Shanghai and fought the nationalists of Chiang Kai-shek to gain control of the majority of the territory abandoned by the Japanese occupation troops. On 9 September, after the Japanese had laid down their arms in Manchuria, a million Japanese soldiers stationed in China capitulated to the nationalist government. On 12 September, Mountbatten accepted the surrender of the Japanese forces in south-east Asia. The Japanese capitulation opened the way to significant political changes in the region, which would soon lead to the end of western domination.

The legacy
of the conflict

World War II was not just a world war; it was also, and above all, a 'total' war, more so than its predecessor had been. Its effects were felt far beyond the battlefields: it disrupted the lives of hundreds of millions of people in every corner of the planet and caused destruction on an immense scale. It was the biggest and bloodiest war in the history of humankind, ending in the late summer of 1945 after almost exactly six years of fighting, and involving 70 million combatants, of which 17 million died. One in 22 Russians, one in 25 Germans, one in 46 Japanese, one in 150 Italians, one in150 British, one in 200 French and one in 500 Americans perished. Unlike any other conflict in the modern age, the majority of victims were civilians, who died as a result of air raids, deportation and extermination, imprisonment, hunger, forced labour or sheer exhaustion. The largest number of deaths was in Europe, the *(p. 264)* **A RUSSIAN SOLDIER RETURNS HOME.**

(p. 265) **KISSING IN NEW YORK.**

(Right:) **JAPANESE SOLDIERS.**

(Far right:) **ITALIANS CELEBRATE.**

(Below:) **GERMAN FARMERS FLEE FROM THEIR BURNING HOMES.** *(Photograph by Robert Capa.)*

macabre record going to the Soviet Union with 20 million: of these, between 6 and 7 million were soldiers, while the rest were civilians who died either on Russian territory or following deportation to Germany.

The nation that had the highest death toll in relation to the size of its population was Poland. Approximately 300,000 servicemen and almost 6 million civilians (of which almost a third were Jews) were killed by the Germans; but the figures for Poland are difficult to establish accurately, because its postwar borders differed from those of 1939, and deportations were carried out by both the Germans and the Russians. In Yugoslavia there were about a million and a half deaths, a third of which were combatants. Four and a half million Germans died in combat, while the number of civilian deaths came to 600,000.

Japan lost over a million servicemen and 600,000 civilians. The number of deaths in China is hard to estimate but was somewhere between 4 and 12 million, to a great extent the result of massacres and famine. France lost 200,000 servicemen and 400,000 civilians; Britain lost 270,000 and approximately 90,000, respectively. Total Italian casualties, both military and civilian, were about 400,000. The Americans lost about 300,000 servicemen and 5,000 civilians. In the British Empire, including the Dominions (Canada, Australia, South Africa, New Zealand), the overall number of deaths was 85,000; and more than a million people died from famine in India. The gypsies of eastern Europe met the same fate as the Jews and were almost totally exterminated in Nazi gas chambers.

THE IMPACT OF 'TOTAL WAR'

One of the most devastating effects of the 'total war', which affected, albeit to different degrees, both the belligerent and the neutral nations, was the problem of refugees and

(Left:) **ELECTION DAY IN JAPAN.** *In 1947 Japanese women voted for the first time.*

(Far left:) **BLACK WORKERS IN AN AMERICAN FACTORY.**

(Below:) **FINAL CASUALTIES OF THE WAR.** *(Photograph by Robert Capa.)*

evacuees from bombed cities and regions devastated by fighting and foreign occupation. There are abundant examples of the forced migration that, in the space of just a few years, reshaped the human and social geography of Europe and other regions of the world: Germans who had settled in occupied Polish territories in 1939; Poles deported to Siberia by the Russians; Chinese who had fled massacres perpetrated by the Japanese army; German-speaking inhabitants of the Volga basin and Muslim populations in southern Russia, who were forcibly moved at Stalin's orders; the millions of Germans who fled westward to escape the advance of the Red Army; and the Jews who survived the Nazi extermination camps. A signficant indication of this movement of populations was the fact that about 60 million changes of

address, albeit for different reasons, were recorded in Great Britain between 1939 and 1945.

The conflict also wrought significant changes in mental outlook, customs, individual relationships and social conventions. It drove peace-loving citizens to extreme decisions, modified deep-rooted habits, brought different peoples into contact with each other, gave an enhanced role to women and the young, and it forced millions of people to be more aware of the destiny of the world and the outcome of a war that had been fought in the name of democratic principles on the one hand and a racist ideology on the other.

Long periods of separation undermined the stability and conventional structure of the family. The number of divorces in the United States doubled in 1945, while in Britain it increased five-fold. For women, the war brought greater direct responsibility

8 MAY 1945: RED SQUARE IN MOSCOW ON VE DAY.

in areas such as production (including the war industries) and a greater sense of independence. In the United States many black women stopped doing domestic jobs and went to work in industry. In many European nations women had played a prominent role in the resistance against the German occupation. Japanese women, who had been almost entirely excluded from the war industries and confined to agricultural labour, acquired the right to vote a few years after the end of the war.

THE NEW INTERNATIONAL SYSTEM

For the defeated nations the outcome of the war brought major and abrupt changes. Germany, which had failed in its second 'assault on world power', came out of the war with its territory in ruins, with millions of

refugees and homeless people, and with no territorial integrity. The collapse of the Reich led to a traumatic break with the past that was much more clear-cut than in the other Axis countries, though it was evident there too. Italy retained its national unity and was allowed to continue to govern itself, but it no longer had any clout as a European power. The collapse of Japan led to the disintegration of customs and conventions that dated to the medieval period (the Emperor kept his throne but was no longer to be regarded as the incarnation of divinity). The territorial boundaries of the country were maintained, but at the cost of renouncing the military and authoritarian tradition that had taken it into the war. Occupied by the Americans and governed by General MacArthur, after the conflict Japan

BARTERING.
An American and a Russian soldier use gestures to negotiate the sale of a watch in the days following the fall of the Reich. (Photograph by Robert Capa.)

WAR ARCHIVES: VICTORS AND VANQUISHED

IN THIS PHOTO BY HENRI CARTIER-BRESSON, A GESTAPO INFORMER IS HUMILIATED AND SLAPPED AROUND IN A PRISON CAMP THAT HAS JUST BEEN LIBERATED. After years of suffering, humiliation and personal loss, for many people the liberation was not a glorious experience. Besides the bitterness towards those who had preferred not to see or had been complicit with what was going on, there was an awareness that something irreversible had taken place. Reflecting on the experience of the victims, Primo Levi wrote: 'There are those who, in the face of other people's guilt, or their own, turn their backs so as not to see and not to feel involved. That's what the majority of Germans did in twelve years of Hitler, in the illusion that not seeing was equivalent to not knowing, and that not knowing relieved them from their share of complicity or connivance [. . .] The sea of pain, past and present, surrounded us, and its level rose year by year until it almost submerged us. It was pointless to close one's eyes or turn one's back, because it was all around us, in every direction, as far as the horizon. It was not possible for us, nor did we wish it, to be islands; the just amongst us, who were neither more nor less numerous than any other group of humans, felt remorse, shame, in a word pain, for what others and not they had committed, and in which they felt involved, because they felt that what had happened around them, and in their presence, and in them, was irrevocable. It could never be washed away; it seemed to demonstrate that man, the human race, in a word, us, are potentially capable of building an infinite mass of pain; and that pain is the sole force that is created from nothing, without expense and without effort. All one has to do is not see, not listen, not do anything.'

Sentences at the Nuremberg Trials

DEFENDANTS	1st ch.	2nd ch.	3rd ch.	4th ch.	sentence
Hermann Göring	■	■	■	■	Hanging
Rudolf Hess	■	■	□	□	Life imprisonment
Joachim von Ribbentrop	■	■	■	■	Hanging
Wilhelm Keitel	■	■	■	■	Hanging
Ernst Kaltenbrunner	□		■	■	Hanging
Alfred Rosenberg	■	■	■	■	Hanging
Hans Frank	□		■	■	Hanging
Wilhelm Frick	□	■	■	■	Hanging
Julius Streicher	□			■	Hanging
Walther Funk	□	■	■	■	Life imprisonment
Hjalmar Schacht	□	□			Cleared
Karl Dönitz	□	■	■		10

DEFENDANTS	1st ch.	2nd ch.	3rd ch.	4th ch.	sentence
Erich Raeder	■	■	■		Life imprisonment
Baldur von Schirach	□			■	20
Fritz Sauckel	□	□	■	■	Hanging
Alfred Jodl	■	■	■	■	Hanging
Martin Bormann	□		■	■	Hanging
Franz von Papen	□	□			Cleared
Artur Seyss-Inquart	□	■	■	■	Hanging
Albert Speer	□	□	■	■	20
Konstantin von Neurath	■	■	■	■	15
Hans Fritzsche	□		□	□	Cleared
Total guilty	8	12	16	16	
Total not guilty	14	4	2	2	

Verdict
Guilty ■
Not guilty □

sentence
Hanging ■
Life imprisonment ▦
Sentence (years) [20]
Cleared ▢

ch = charge

moved towards social emancipation and the democratization of its political system.

France gradually began to acknowledge that its status as a European and world power had been drastically reduced. Great Britain, which had made an immense military effort and contributed greatly to the Allied victory, had to accept that it was no longer in a position to oversee the new European order and maintain the imperial power it had held until 1939. The 'special relationship' established between Roosevelt and Churchill a few years earlier mutated, and the British found themselves in the role of subordinate partner in the postwar global policy that was exercised by the United States in the military, economic and financial fields.

The postwar world was marked by the undisputed supremacy of a global power: the United States, which was the driving force behind the world economy, possessed the atom bomb and ruled the seas. The Soviet Union, which had suffered the highest loss of human life in the war against Nazism, emerged from the conflict as the real power on the European continent.

ORGAN-GRINDER IN THE SEMI-ABANDONED CITY OF BERLIN.
(Photograph by Robert Capa.)

THE NUREMBERG WAR TRIALS

The international military tribunal of Nuremberg, which comprised judges from the four major victorious nations in the war, was set up to try 22 prominent members of the Third Reich on the following basic charges: crimes against peace ('planning, initiating and waging wars of aggression' or a war in violation of treaties), war crimes (execution of prisoners, torture, bombardment of undefended cities) and crimes against humanity ('assassination, extermination, enslavement, deportation or forcible transfer of population' and other inhumane acts at the expense of the civilian population). The Nazi leaders were charged with being responsible for the death of 12 million people. The trials commenced on 19 November 1945 under the presidency of Lord Geoffrey Lawrence and ended, 403 sessions later, with the sentencing on 10 October 1946. Besides the testimony of numerous witnesses, documents found by the Allies in German headquarters buildings were presented as supporting evidence. These documents also served as the basis for an initial reconstruction of the history of Nazism. The Nuremberg trials were the first fundamental affirmation of a principle that was to become decisive in international law. New classes of crime were

defined, which, by their very nature, could be judged by authorities other than those of the state in which they had been committed. These supranational authorities represented the rights of the whole of humankind. This signalled the rejection of the argument presented by the defence, which, in appealing to a general principle of law, sustained that no one could be incriminated for acts that did not constitute a crime in the period in which they were committed. The defence also claimed that the defendants had had a 'duty to obey' their legitimate superiors. Although the prosecutor requested death by hanging for all the defendants, this sentence was passed for only 12 of them: Goering (who committed suicide after

being sentenced), von Ribbentrop, Keitel, Kaltenbrunner, Rosenberg, Frank, Frick, Streicher, Sauckel, Jodl, Bormann (*in absentia*) and Seyss-Inquart. Hess, Funk and Raeder were condemned to life imprisonment. Other leading figures who had been responsible for Nazism followed the example of Goebbels and of Hitler himself, and took their own lives: Himmler when he was captured and Ley before the beginning of the trial proceedings. The tribunal also outlawed various organs of the regime, including the SS, the Gestapo and the Sicherheitsdienst (secret service). Subsequently there were other convictions by military tribunals in the individual nations concerned, but after the Cold War started, Nazi war criminals benefited from wide-ranging amnesties. It was only after a long delay, and with considerable reserve, that the German judicial system began to tackle the issue of Nazi war crimes, and many of those who were responsible for massacres in the occupied countries remained unidentified.

(Above:) The defendants' bench. (Left:) Von Papen and Schacht (with glasses) eating in prison.

GERMANS QUEUE FOR A MEAL.

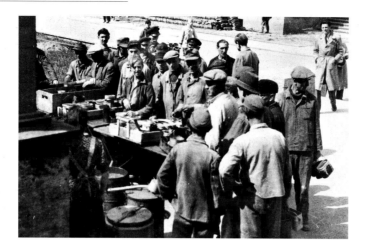

THE TERRITORIAL SHAPE OF EUROPE

Divisions amongst the members of the anti-Hitler coalition over the future territorial make-up of Europe had already emerged at Potsdam, and final definition of the peace terms was postponed until a conference held in Paris in October 1946. Germany's former allies (Italy, Romania, Hungary, Finland, Bulgaria) were required to return to their pre-war frontiers. Italy ceded the Dodecanese to Greece, part of Venezia Giulia to Yugoslavia and the Briga-Tenda area to the French. It also recognized the independence of Albania and gave up all claims to its former colonies, although it retained a mandate over Somalia.

Trieste (returned to Italy in 1954) was divided into two zones, administered by Anglo-Americans and Yugoslavs. Romania recovered Transylvania from Hungary, but ceded Bessarabia to the Soviets, who also acquired border areas from Finland. The new frontiers of eastern Europe were determined by the reality of Soviet military occupation: Poland ceded the Ukrainian and White Russian territories to the Soviet Union and acquired the German regions to the east of the rivers Oder and Neisse. Moscow incorporated part of East Prussia and the Baltic countries into its territory. Germany was divided into four occupation zones (administered by the victorious powers); Berlin,

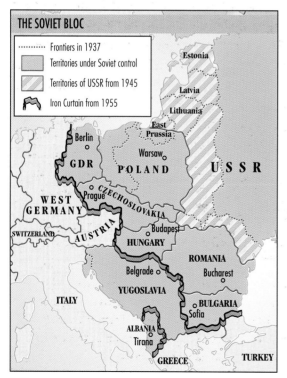

THE SOVIET BLOC

- Frontiers in 1937
- Territories under Soviet control
- Territories of USSR from 1945
- Iron Curtain from 1955

Estonia · Latvia · Lithuania · East Prussia · Berlin · GDR · Warsaw · POLAND · USSR · WEST GERMANY · Prague · CZECHOSLOVAKIA · AUSTRIA · SWITZERLAND · Budapest · HUNGARY · ROMANIA · Belgrade · Bucharest · YUGOSLAVIA · ITALY · BULGARIA · Sofia · ALBANIA · Tirana · GREECE · TURKEY

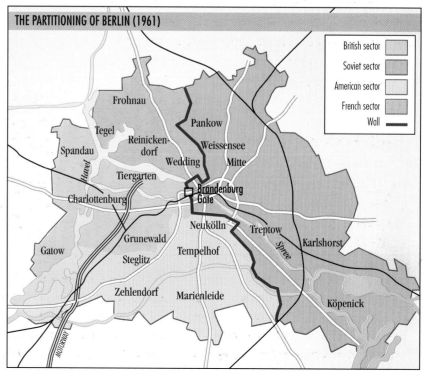

THE PARTITIONING OF BERLIN (1961)

- British sector
- Soviet sector
- American sector
- French sector
- Wall

Frohnau · Tegel · Pankow · Reinickendorf · Weissensee · Spandau · Wedding · Mitte · Havel · Tiergarten · Charlottenburg · Brandenburg Gate · Neukölln · Treptow · Karlshorst · Grunewald · Spree · Gatow · Tempelhof · Steglitz · Zehlendorf · Marienleide · Köpenick · MOTORWAY

(Left:) **STALIN'S DANCE.** *In this French right-wing cartoon, Stalin is depicted as a dancing Cossack. He is about to stab France, having done the same for the eastern European nations.*

(Far left:) **LET'S ROLL UP OUR SLEEVES.** *With the support of the Left, de Gaulle laid the foundations for the economic recovery of France.*

which was situated in the centre of the Russian zone, was partitioned into four sectors with a road and rail link to the rest of Germany. Until 1949, the country was governed by an Allied Control Council made up of representatives from the four military High Commands.

THE TWO BLOCS AND RECONSTRUCTION

The roles of many powers – both winners and losers – had been sharply redefined by a conflict that saw the emergence of two major world players: the United States and the Soviet Union. Although hopes were expressed about a new era of cooperation, they represented two opposing ideological and social models – the Americans were liberal and capitalist, the Soviets were communist and oriented to state control. Advocates of geopolitical interests that were hard to reconcile, the Americans and Russians did succeed in creating the United Nations' World Health Organization to coordinate a peaceful and cooperative international system, but on many issues (international reconstruction, the degree of independence of countries occupied by the Red Army, the possibility of regulating nuclear weapons) mutual suspicion soon gave way to outright hostility. Divisions in Europe and other areas of the world solidified and the antagonistic eastern and western blocs that resulted from this were incompatible from economic, ideological and geopolitical points of view.

The emergence of a Soviet-controlled bloc prompted Churchill to denounce the 'Iron Curtain' dividing Europe, while American conservatives, who had a majority in Congress, urged an anti-Soviet stance in foreign policy. To counterbalance the presence of communist parties in western Europe and to stabilize the democracies there, the

THE TOKYO TRIALS

At the beginning of 1946, General MacArthur, Supreme Commander of Allied Forces, announced the setting up of an international military tribunal for the Far East. This convened in Tokyo to try 25 Japanese military and political leaders and other functionaries accused of having conducted a war of aggression and of having committed and ordered war crimes, atrocities and crimes against peace. The proceedings of the court, which were based on the earlier Nuremberg Trials, began on 3 May 1946 and ended on 21 November 1948. All the defendants were found guilty. General Hideki Tojo and Koki Hirota, the Foreign Minister from 1933 to 1936, were amongst seven people sentenced to death by hanging. Various tribunals set up in other Asian nations tried a further 5,000 Japanese, over 900 of whom were sentenced to death for serious war crimes and for offences against humanity. The people who had been condemned to life imprisonment by the international tribunal in Tokyo were released in 1958. Because Japan had accepted the rulings of the military tribunal, it was exempted from the obligation to pursue war criminals.

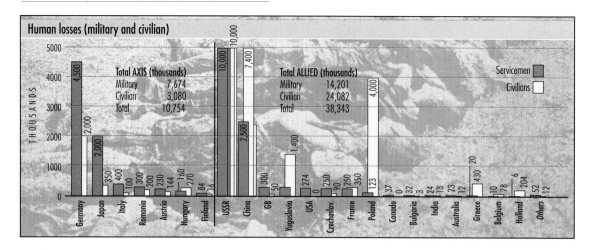

Human losses (military and civilian)

Total AXIS (thousands)		Total ALLIED (thousands)	
Military	7,674	Military	14,201
Civilian	3,080	Civilian	24,082
Total	10,754	Total	38,343

Servicemen / Civilians (in thousands):

Country	Servicemen	Civilians
Germany	4,500	2,000
Japan	2,000	350
Italy	400	100
Romania	300	200
Austria	230	144
Hungary	160	270
Finland	84	6
USSR	10,000	10,000
China	2,500	7,400
GB	300	50
Yugoslavia		1,400
USA	274	0
Czechoslov.	250	90
France	250	350
Poland	123	4,000
Canada	37	0
Bulgaria	32	3
India	24	13
Australia	23	12
Greece	20	430
Belgium	10	78
Holland	6	204
Others	52	12

Americans played a big role in economic reconstruction and there was a massive expansion in the market economy. The Soviets, on the other hand, set up the Cominform (Communist Information Bureau) in 1947, which the principal European communist parties joined. The establishment of this coordinating body signalled the birth of two opposing camps. In the context of this polarization of the international balance of power, nuclear antagonism threw a sinister and apocalyptic shadow over the future of the world, and turned the Cold War – the long period in 20th-century history that ended with the fall of the Berlin Wall in 1989 – into an age of tension between two opposing power blocs. Once again Europe became the scene of a conflict where world peace was at stake. The Soviet blockade of Berlin (June 1948 to May 1949) made the issue of Germany's future more urgent and hastened the establishment of a new Western military alliance. The North Atlantic Treaty Organization (NATO) was formally established on 4 April 1949, and the Federal Republic of Germany came into being on 23 May.

DECOLONIALIZATION AND THE THIRD WORLD

In the decade that followed Japan's surrender, the European empires in Asia crumbled. A non-violent revolt in India forced Great Britain, which had been exhausted by the war,

THE BLOCKADE OF BERLIN. *Supplies arrive at the airport in West Berlin. On 24 June 1948 the Russians blockaded all the entrances to the Western sector of the city, sparking the first crisis of the Cold War. However, Truman did not bow to Soviet aggression, and American and British planes airlifted supplies to the former capital of Germany until May 1949. The incident was depicted by Western propaganda as a symbol of the communist threat to freedom.*

(Left:) **DAVID BEN GURION.**
On 14 May 1948 Ben Gurion proclaimed the birth of the state of Israel. He became the head of the provisional government and the Minister of Defence.

(Far left:) **THE FLAG OF THE NEW JEWISH STATE.**

to withdraw from the country. However, the partitioning of India left a long trail of political and religious violence in its wake. On midnight of 14 August 1947, two distinct and independent dominions, India and Pakistan, came into being. Four years after the Japanese capitulation, in 1949, the communists came to power in China, Asia's largest nation, following a war in which they defeated the Kuomintang nationalists. Mao's Communist Party began ruling the newly founded People's Republic of China, while Chiang Kai-shek took refuge on Formosa. On the strength of a disciplined organization and the restoration of the nation's territorial integrity, the Chinese communists set about disseminating Marxist–Leninist principles throughout the country.

Indonesia gained independence from the Dutch in 1949, following a long armed struggle. Decolonialization also took place in other Asian countries: Korea (1945), the Philippines (1946), Burma (1948), Vietnam, Cambodia and Laos (1954). In the Middle East a UN vote in favour of a Jewish state, and the end of the British mandate in Palestine, led to the birth of the state of Israel in 1948, which was followed by the outbreak of the first Arab–Israeli war and the flight of a million Palestinians. The following year Jordan became a sovereign state. For other Asian and African nations the dream of decolonialization was realized in the 1950s.

BICYCLE RIDE IN JAPAN.
An American seaman cycles through the streets of an occupied city, holding a Japanese umbrella for shade.

Chronological tables
Index of names

1936-39

CHRONOLOGY OF EVENTS

ATLANTIC

NORTHERN AND WESTERN EUROPE

7 March 1936 Germany occupies the Rhineland.

17 July 1936 Beginning of the Spanish Civil War.

25 November 1936 Germany and Japan sign an anti-Comintern Pact.

28 May 1937 Neville Chamberlain becomes British Prime Minister.

1 August 1937 The concentration camp at Buchenwald becomes operational.

11 March 1938 Annexation of Austria to Germany.

29 September 1938 Munich Agreement.

9 November 1938 'Night of Broken Glass': Jews and their property are targeted and attacked in Germany.

31 March 1939 Chamberlain announces that France and Great Britain will guarantee Poland's territorial borders.

1 April 1939 End of the Spanish Civil War.

26 April 1939 Compulsory conscription introduced in Great Britain.

22 May 1939 Italy and Germany sign the 'Pact of Steel'.

3 September 1939 France and Great Britain declare war on Germany.

CENTRAL AND EASTERN EUROPE

5 October 1938 German occupation of the Sudetenland in Czechoslovakian territory.

14 March 1939 Dismemberment of Czechoslovakia following Slovakia's declaration of independence; German occupation of Bohemia and Moravia.

23 August 1939 Signing of the German–Russian pact.

1 September 1939 Germany invades Poland.

17 September 1939 Russia invades Poland.

27 September 1939 Fall of Warsaw.

28 September 1939 Germany and the USSR sign a treaty of friendship and cooperation, and establish territorial demarcation lines.

30 November 1939 Beginning of the war between Finland and the USSR.

14 December 1939 Expulsion of the USSR from the League of Nations.

BALKANS ● MEDITERRANEAN ● ITALY

MIDDLE EAST ● AFRICA

5 May 1936 Italian troops enter Addis Ababa.

9 May 1936 Italy annexes Abyssinia.

11 December 1937 Withdrawal of Italy from the League of Nations.

7 April 1939 Italy invades Albania.

NORTH AMERICA AND SOUTH AMERICA

3 November 1936 Roosevelt reelected President of the United States.

4 November 1939 US neutrality act approved ('cash and carry').

17 December 1939 Sinking of the *Graf Spee* in the Rio de la Plata.

PACIFIC ● FAR EAST

AUSTRALASIA

25 November 1939 Japan signs an anti-Comintern pact with Germany.

13 December 1937 Nanking captured by the Japanese, who massacre the inhabitants.

1 September 1939 Battle of Nomonhan between Russia and Japan.

1940

CHRONOLOGY OF EVENTS

ATLANTIC

NORTHERN AND WESTERN EUROPE

9 April Germany invades Denmark and Norway.

14 April The Allies land their forces in Norway.

10 May Germany invades the Netherlands, Belgium and France. Churchill becomes British Prime Minister.

26 May Beginning of the British retreat from Dunkirk.

28 May Surrender of the Belgian army.

2 June The Allies withdraw from Norway.

4 June Retreat from Dunkirk completed.

14 June Germans enter Paris.

22 June France signs an armistice with Germany.

24 June France signs an armistice with Italy.

28 June Great Britain recognizes de Gaulle as the head of the 'Free French'.

10 July Beginning of the Battle of Britain.

27 September Germany, Japan and Italy sign the Tripartite Pact.

14 November German air raid on Coventry.

CENTRAL AND EASTERN EUROPE

12 March End of the Finnish–Soviet war.

28 June The USSR occupies Bessarabia and northern Bukovina.

14 July Baltic countries annexed to the USSR.

BALKANS ● MEDITERRANEAN ● ITALY
MIDDLE EAST ● AFRICA

10 June Italy declares war on France and Great Britain.

21 June Italy attacks France.

3 July British Royal Navy attacks the French fleet at Mers-el-Kèbir.

4 July Italian troops from Abyssinia occupy frontier positions in Sudan.

4 August Italian troops invade British Somaliland.

12 September Italian invasion of Egypt.

28 October Italy attacks Greece.

11 November British air attack on the Italian fleet in the port of Taranto.

22 November Romania joins the Axis powers.

NORTH AMERICA AND SOUTH AMERICA

26 September America imposes an embargo on the sale of scrap iron and steel to Japan.

5 November Roosevelt re-elected President for a third term.

29 December Roosevelt announces that the USA will be the 'arsenal of democracy'.

PACIFIC ● FAR EAST
AUSTRALASIA

30 March Puppet state headed by Wang Ching-wei is established in Nanking.

1941

C H R O N O L O G Y   O F   E V E N T S

NORTHERN AND WESTERN EUROPE

27 May The British Royal Navy sinks the *Bismarck*.

22 June Italy declares war on the USSR.

23 September De Gaulle establishes the Comité National Français.

6 December Great Britain declares war on Finland, Hungary and Romania.

11 December Germany declares war on the USA.

CENTRAL AND EASTERN EUROPE

13 April The USSR and Japan sign a pact of non-aggression.

22 June Germany invades Russia.

27 June Hungary declares war on the USSR.

21 July First German air raid on Moscow.

19 September Kiev falls to the German Army.

2 October Start of the German offensive to take Moscow.

24 October The Germans capture Kharkov.

3 November The Germans take Kursk.

28 November The 4th Panzer Group is 20km from Moscow.

6 December Beginning of the Russian counter-offensive in front of Moscow.

18 December Brauchitsch asks to be relieved of his command. Hitler appoints himself Commander-in-Chief of the German Army.

BALKANS ● MEDITERRANEAN ● ITALY
MIDDLE EAST ● AFRICA

19 January The British launch an offensive in East Africa.

6 February The British capture Benghazi.

11 February Rommel arrives in Libya.

1 March Bulgaria joins the Axis.

28 March Naval Battle of Cape Matapan.

6–8 April Bulgarian, German and Italian troops invade Yugoslavia and Greece.

17 April Surrender of Yugoslavia.

24 April Beginning of the British evacuation from Greece.

16 May Italians surrender at Amba Alagi.

20 May German parachutists land in Crete.

15 June Croatia joins the Axis.

22 June Romania declares war on the USSR.

28 September The 'Free French' declare the independence of Syria and Lebanon.

11 December Italy and Germany declare war on the USA.

NORTH AMERICA AND SOUTH AMERICA

11 March The 'Lend-Lease' Act becomes law.

8 December The USA and Great Britain declare war on Japan.

PACIFIC ● FAR EAST
AUSTRALASIA

27 July Japanese begin to occupy French Indo-China.

18 October General Tojo becomes Prime Minister of Japan.

7 December Japanese attack on Pearl Harbor.

8 December The Japanese invade Malaya and Thailand.

10 December The *Prince of Wales* and the *Repulse* are sunk off Malaya. Japanese troops land in the Philippines.

11 December Japan invades Burma.

20 December The Japanese attack the Dutch East Indies.

25 December Hong Kong surrenders to the Japanese.

1942

CHRONOLOGY OF EVENTS

ATLANTIC

NORTHERN AND WESTERN EUROPE

30 May British air raid on Cologne.

11 November Germans and Italians occupy French Vichy.

CENTRAL AND EASTERN EUROPE

9 June Massacre of Lidice, carried out by the Germans in retaliation for the killing of Heydrich in Prague.

28 June Germany launches a summer offensive against the Caucasus.

1 July Germans capture Sebastopol.

12–15 August Summit between Stalin and Churchill in Moscow to discuss the opening of the second front in Europe.

13 September Beginning of the Battle of Stalingrad.

BALKANS ● MEDITERRANEAN ● ITALY
MIDDLE EAST ● AFRICA

21 June Rommel captures Tobruk.

1 July Beginning of the First Battle of El Alamein.

24 October Beginning of the Second Battle of El Alamein

8 November Allied troops land in Africa.

11 November Germans occupy Vichy France.

NORTH AMERICA AND SOUTH AMERICA

1 January China, Great Britain, the USA and the USSR sign the declaration by the United Nations.

PACIFIC ● FAR EAST

AUSTRALASIA

15 February The Japanese capture Singapore.

19 February Japanese air raid on Port Darwin (northern Australia).

20 February The Japanese occupy Timor in the Dutch East Indies.

27–29 February Battle of the Java Sea.

28 February The Japanese invade Java.

8 March The Japanese land in New Guinea.

17 March MacArthur is appointed Commander-in-Chief, South-West Pacific.

5 April The Japanese fleet ventures into the Indian Ocean and bombs Ceylon.

9 April Surrender of the American troops on the Bataan Peninsula.

18 April American air raid on Tokyo.

6 May Surrender of the American garrison at Corregidor.

6–8 May Battle of the Coral Sea.

4 June Beginning of the Battle of Midway.

7 August American landings at Guadalcanal.

9 August Start of a 'civil disobedience' campaign against British rule in India.

21 September Beginning of the American offensive in New Guinea.

1943

CHRONOLOGY OF EVENTS

ATLANTIC

NORTHERN AND WESTERN EUROPE

24 May The U-boats withdraw from the North Atlantic.

24 July RAF raid on Hamburg.

24 December Eisenhower is appointed Supreme Commander of the Normandy landings (Operation 'Overlord').

CENTRAL AND EASTERN EUROPE

2 February The Germans surrender at Stalingrad.

8 February The Red Army captures Kursk.

19 April Start of the first insurrection in Warsaw.

5 July Beginning of the Battle of Kursk.

23 August The Russians capture Kharkov.

23 September The Red Army takes Smolensk.

6 November The Soviets recapture Kiev.

BALKANS ● MEDITERRANEAN ● ITALY
MIDDLE EAST ● AFRICA

14–24 January Casablanca Conference.

23 January The British enter Tripoli.

3 May The Allies capture Tunis.

13 May Surrender of the Axis forces in North Africa.

10 July Allied landings in Sicily.

25 July Mussolini is overthrown and arrested. A new government is formed under Marshal Badoglio.

17 August Axis resistance in Sicily ceases.

3 September The Allies land on the Italian peninsula.

8 September Announcement of Italy's surrender to the Allies.

9 September Allied landings at Salerno.

10 September The Germans occupy Rome and much of Italy.

12 September The Germans free Mussolini.

13 September The Germans massacre the Italian troops on the island of Cephalonia.

23 September Foundation of the Italian Social Republic.

13 October Italy declares war on Germany.

28 November–1 December Teheran Conference, attended by Roosevelt, Churchill and Stalin.

NORTH AMERICA AND SOUTH AMERICA

11–25 May Washington Conference.

PACIFIC ● FAR EAST
AUSTRALASIA

13 February First Chindit operation in Burma.

2 March Battle of the Bismarck Sea.

18 April Death of Admiral Yamamoto.

11 May The Americans land on the Aleutian Islands.

29 June American landings in New Guinea.

5–6 November East Asia Conference in Tokyo.

20 November The Americans land on Tarawa.

22–26 November Cairo Conference, during which Roosevelt, Churchill and Chiang Kai-shek agree to insist upon the unconditional surrender of Japan.

1944

CHRONOLOGY OF EVENTS

ATLANTIC

NORTHERN AND WESTERN EUROPE

20 February Start of the British and American bombing offensive against Germany.

6 June Allied landings in Normandy.

13 June Germany starts bombing England with V-1 rockets.

20 July An attempt to assassinate Hitler fails.

19 August Insurrection in Paris.

25 August The Germans surrender in Paris.

8 September First V-2 rocket hits England.

23 October The USA and Great Britain recognize de Gaulle as the head of the provisional French government.

16 December German offensive in the Ardennes.

CENTRAL AND EASTERN EUROPE

44 January The Red Army crosses the pre-war frontiers of Poland.

27 January Lifting of the siege of Leningrad.

9 May The Red Army liberates Sebastopol.

3 July The Soviets capture Minsk.

1 August Second insurrection in Warsaw.

5 October The Red Army enters Hungary.

BALKANS ● MEDITERRANEAN ● ITALY
MIDDLE EAST ● AFRICA

22 January Allied landings at Anzio.

1 February Start of the battle at Monte Cassino.

13 May The Allies take Monte Cassino.

4 June The Allies enter Rome.

15 August Allied landings on the Côte d'Azur in France.

20 August The Red Army attacks Romania.

28 August The French 1st Army captures Toulon.

8 September The Russians enter Bulgaria.

7 October German withdrawal from Greece.

15 October The British enter Athens.

20 October The Russians and the Yugoslav partisans capture Belgrade.

NORTH AMERICA AND SOUTH AMERICA

1 July Beginning of the Bretton Woods conference.

12–16 September Quebec conference.

21 September Beginning of the conference of Dumbarton Oaks.

6 November Roosevelt is re-elected for a fourth term of office.

PACIFIC ● FAR EAST
AUSTRALASIA

31 January The Americans land in the Marshall Islands.

15 February Beginning of the Japanese offensive on the border between India and Burma.

22 April MacArthur's troops land in New Guinea.

15 June American landings on Saipan.

19 June Beginning of the Battle of the Philippine Sea.

18 July Tojo is replaced by General Koiso as the head of the Japanese government.

20 October American landings at Leyte (Philippines).

24 October Beginning of the Battle of Leyte Gulf.

1945

CHRONOLOGY OF EVENTS

ATLANTICO

NORTHERN AND WESTERN EUROPE

13 February Allied bombing raid on Dresden.

26 February The American 9th Army reaches the Rhine.

7 March The American 3rd Army crosses the Rhine at Remagen.

25 April American and Soviet troops meet at Torgau.

30 April Hitler commits suicide.

4 May German forces in The Netherlands, northern Germany and Denmark surrender to Montgomery.

5 May The Germans surrender in Norway.

7 May Jodl signs a document of unconditional German surrender at Reims (2.41pm).

8 May V-E day. Keitel ratifies the Reims surrender document in a further ceremony in Berlin.

26 July Churchill loses the general election in Britain. Attlee becomes Prime Minister.

CENTRAL AND EASTERN EUROPE

14 January The Russians invade East Prussia.

17 January The Russians capture Warsaw.

13 February The Germans surrender at Budapest.

13 April The Red Army captures Vienna.

10 May The Red Army takes Prague.

5 July Great Britain and the USA recognize the provisional Polish government.

17 July–2 August Potsdam Conference.

8 August The USSR declares war on the USSR and invades Manchukuo.

BALKANS ● MEDITERRANEAN ● ITALY
MIDDLE EAST ● AFRICA

19 March Yugoslav partisans launch an offensive against Trieste.

21 April The American 5th Army captures Bologna.

28 April Mussolini is shot by members of the resistance.

2 May Surrender of the German troops in Italy.

NORTH AMERICA AND SOUTH AMERICA

12 April Death of Roosevelt. He is succeeded by Vice President Harry S. Truman.

25 April Start of the United Nations conference in San Francisco.

16 July Experimental testing of the first atomic bomb at Alamogordo (New Mexico).

PACIFIC ● FAR EAST
AUSTRALASIA

9 January American landings at Luzon.

19 February American landings at Iwo Jima.

20 March The British capture Mandalay.

1 April American landings at Okinawa.

3 May The British capture Rangoon.

6 August Atomic bomb dropped on Hiroshima.

9 August A second atomic bomb is dropped on Nagasaki.

14 August Emperor Hirohito announces the unconditional surrender of the Japanese armed forces.

29 August Lord Mountbatten receives the surrender of Japanese forces in South-East Asia.

2 September The Japanese sign the surrender document on board the American battleship *Missouri*, anchored in Tokyo Bay.

Index of names

Photographic credits